FOUNDATIONS OF MODERN POLITICAL SCIENCE SERIES

Robert A. Dahl, Editor

The Analysis

of

International

Relations

FOUNDATIONS OF MODERN POLITICAL SCIENCE SERIES

ENGLEWOOD CLIFFS, NEW JERSEY   Prentice-Hall, Inc.

K A R L   W .   D E U T S C H

Harvard University

To Ruth, my wife, who has widened and deepened
my awareness in more ways than I can tell.

Current printing (last digit):

12   11   10   9

FOUNDATIONS OF MODERN POLITICAL SCIENCE SERIES

Robert A. Dahl, Editor

Preface

An introduction to the study of international relations
in our time is an introduction to the art and science of the survival of mankind.
If civilization is killed within the next thirty years, it will not be killed
by famine or plague, but by foreign policy and international relations.
We can cope with hunger and pestilence, but we cannot yet deal
with the power of our own weapons and with our behavior as nation-states.
    Possessing unprecedented instruments for national action
in the forms of ideologies and weapons, the nation-states have become
ever more dangerous vehicles of international conflict, carrying the potential
for its escalation to mutual destruction and ultimate annihilation.
The nation-state holds the power to control most events within its borders, but
few events—or even its own actions—beyond them.
    International relations is that area of human action where inescapable
interdependence meets with inadequate control. We can neither escape from
world affairs nor wholly shape them to our will. We can only try to adjust the
world while adjusting to it. Within this limited scope, we must retain and,
where possible, enhance our most deeply held values.
    As the practice of international relations has become more difficult
and decisive, its study has moved to keep pace. The dramatic
advances in the field over the last three decades include changes in basic
concepts and theories, changes stimulated by a meeting of the newer
behavioral sciences of psychology, sociology, and anthropology with the longer
established disciplines of political science, history, and economics. These changes
in theory have been accompanied by the development of new methods of research,

the employment of statistical procedures for analysis, and the growing availability of testable empirical data. Throughout this book, I have tried to introduce the reader to these more recent types of research and analysis. All these changes have made the study of international relations more professional than heretofore, making much—though by no means all—of the older literature obsolete.

But international relations and foreign policy are too important to be left to the specialists. Many young men have thought that world affairs need not concern them, until their draft boards told them otherwise. If our lives are so deeply affected by, and our responses so essential to international affairs, then we must increase our capacity to understand, to decide, and to act.

Knowledge is different from values. Values motivate the search for knowledge and make some of its results more salient to us than others. Knowledge tells us which of our values may conflict, and where and when our means begin to injure and destroy our ends instead of serving them.

My own values are made plain throughout the book. You may share or reject them, or select from among them. I have tried to support all judgments and not to let my preferences deceive me. You may decide for yourself to what extent I have failed or succeeded in this search for realism and reality. You may verify the facts presented here and add others that you might find relevant. It is important that you should try to do this, for we are all bound up in the same enterprise—in the search for a tolerable pathway toward peace and freedom everywhere. It will be a difficult search, but we cannot escape it.

In writing this small book, people have aided me in many ways. Colleagues from whose views I have benefited at various times include Hayward R. Alker, Jr., Gabriel Almond, Kenneth E. Boulding, Richard C. Chadwick, Robert Dahl, Alexander Eckstein, Rupert Emerson, Lewis J. Edinger, Carl J. Friedrich, Harold Guetzkow, Ernst B. Haas, Stanley Hoffmann, Michael Hudson, Samuel Huntington, Alex Inkeles, Irving Janis, Herbert C. Kelman, Henry Kissinger, U. W. Kitzinger, Hans Kohn, Harold Lasswell, Daniel Lerner, Seymour Martin Lipset, Roy C. Macridis, Robert Marjolin, Richard L. Merritt, James Grier Miller, Joseph Nye, Talcott Parsons, John Plamenatz, Ithiel Pool, Donald J. Puchala, Lucian Pye, Anatol Rapoport, Rudolph Rummel, Bruce M. Russett, Dankwart Rustow, Burton Sapin, I. Richard Savage, Thomas C. Schelling, Erwin Scheuch, J. David Singer, Richard C. Snyder, Harold Sprout, Raymond Tanter, Robert Triffin, Sidney Verba, Hermann Weilenmann, and the late, unforgotten Norbert Wiener. None of these, of course, bears any responsibility for my views or my mistakes.

For assistance in research, computing, and other matters, I am indebted to Irvin C. Bupp, James Chapman, Gordon Fowler, Linda Groff, Peter Natchez, and Brigitte Rosenbusch, and for valuable secretarial aid to Helen D. Alsen and Lucille McKenna.

The first draft of several chapters was written in the ideal scholarly setting of the Villa Serbelloni of the Rockefeller Foundation at Bellagio, Italy. Research utilized in this book was supported in part by the Carnegie Corporation, by Harvard and Yale Universities, and by the Mental Health Research Institute of the University of Michigan.

Karl W. Deutsch

Harvard University

vi

Preface

Contents

Contents

Contents

x

Contents

Introduction

As Americans see it, most of the world is inhabited
by "foreigners." That is, of the world's 3.2 billion people,
fewer than 200 million—less than one in 16—are Americans. We are
a minority of mankind, not only in numbers but also in land area,
property, knowledge, and (presumably) power. Large as our
country is, we inhabit less than half our continent,
which is but one of five. In terms of economics, even
by a highly favorable method of counting, we have
less than one-third of the gross national product

of the world, and our share of the world's steel production and energy output is still smaller. The same holds for the production of knowledge: only a handful of Nobel Prize winners, and a minority of the world's great inventors and discoverers, have been American. All these facts suggest that much less than half the world's potential for political and military power is under our direct national control.

But much the same problem is faced by all other nations: each of them, too, is a minority among mankind. For instance, numerous as they are, the Chinese are less than one-fourth of humanity, and all the East Indians (all counted as a single people) still add up to less than one-sixth. And, large as the industrial might of the Soviet Union has grown in recent years, its population is less than one-fifteenth of mankind, and its income is still only about half that of the United States, or less than one-sixth of the world total. Every other nation in the world is much smaller still, and hence still much more a minority on earth.

No matter how large or small, however, every nation in the world, including our own, must take very much into account what "foreigners" are doing, and, if it wishes to accomplish more than it can with its own limited resources, it must gain their cooperation. But this is easier said than done, for foreigners can be quite different—starting with such obvious characteristics as appearance. More than two-thirds of mankind are nonwhite,[1] for example, and by the end of this century that proportion is likely to rise to three-quarters. Furthermore, more than two-thirds of mankind are non-Christian. But if Christians are a minority in the world, so are Muslims, Jews, Buddhists, Hindus, Communists, Aristotelians, Logical Positivists, and the adherents of any other single organized religion, philosophy, or ideology. They are all minorities among mankind, and indeed, as far as we know, always have been.

Mankind has very much in common in human nature, human needs, and human hopes; but so far it has been incurably diverse in its languages, cultures, religions, philosophies, ideologies, and (most of all) governments. So far, it never has been effectively controlled or managed by a single ruler, a single organization, or a single creed—although in the course of history, as well as in our time, many rulers, organizations, and creeds have tried or claimed to do just that.

Although men are incurably diverse, they are also inescapably interdependent; and in some respects this interdependence has increased in this day of the shrinking world. After all, even the most widely separated people in the world can live at most only half the world apart—roughly 12,500 miles, or about as far as New York City is from Saigon in South Vietnam. Most other places on earth are much less far away: Pearl Harbor on Hawaii; Tokyo and Hiroshima in Japan; Omaha and Utah Beach on the Normandy Peninsula of France; Berlin divided between East and West in Germany; Taipei on the island of Taiwan; Seoul in South Korea; Port Said on the Suez Canal in Egypt; Budapest in Hungary; Beirut in Lebanon; Havana on the island of Cuba. The spectacular events that happened at each of these places at some

[1] "Nonwhite" includes the black, brown, red, and yellow-skinned peoples—all minority groups themselves within the total of mankind.

Introduction

time during the lifetime of the present generation of adults have made a significant difference to the lives of the American people. Those events have influenced their business and personal opportunities as well as their taxes, and have lengthened the roll call of servicemen killed in open or undeclared warfare on foreign soil.

This interdependence has been increasing fastest in terms of military matters. Every place on earth today is less than two days' flight by jet plane from the farthest other place. By guided missile the distance is approximately 40 minutes. And nearly-instant worldwide communication, long relegated to wireless and pictureless apparatus, now comes in the form of sound plus color images via television relayed by globe-girdling communications satellites. (Satellites with powerful cameras have allowed spying to reach new heights, both of altitude and sophistication.)

There are other, perhaps subtler, signs of growing interdependence. The income-tax rate in the United States, it has been said, is set in Moscow, since our government and our voters have felt that we must at least match and balance the military strength and expenditure of Russia. By the same reasoning, additional elements of our income-tax rate have been set in Peking and Hanoi. The governments in Moscow and Peking, however, have claimed that they must at least match and balance that part of our power that could be brought to bear against them; and thus it may be said that part of their military expenditures—and hence of the sacrifices of Russian and Chinese housewives—have been determined by political decisions made in Washington, D.C. And what is true of the largest and strongest nations in the world is no less true of the smaller ones. All nations are interdependent in terms of politics and strategy. No nation, no matter how small, can in splendid isolation be master of its fate, master of its blood and treasure; but no nation, no matter how large, can compel all others to do its bidding, nor convert them quickly to its own beliefs.

We are, however, interdependent with the rest of the world in far more ways than simply in regard to politics and power. Everybody knows vaguely that science, technology, and medicine are "international," but few of us have stopped to think just what this means. It means, in sober fact, that no people and no country in the world could have reached its present level of technology, prosperity, and health—nor could it maintain its present rate of progress—without the decisive aid of foreign discoveries and foreign contributions. A great leader of American science, the physicist Karl T. Compton, once reminded his countrymen that only three of the 12 basic discoveries that permitted the release of atomic energy were made by Americans. That one-quarter of this world-changing discovery was contributed by one-sixteenth of mankind (which is, as we recall, the share of the American people) may well be reason for national pride, but that we depended upon foreigners for three-quarters of this crucial knowledge may well help us to see ourselves in better perspective.

No country could keep many of its own people alive without the help of foreigners. In our hospitals and doctors' offices, thousands of lives are saved daily by the application of discoveries and medicines developed by scientists in other countries. In the last half-century, penicillin was discovered in England, sulfa drugs in Germany, radioactive isotopes in France, insulin in Canada. If

3

all our packages of medicines were brightly labeled with the names and countries of their discoverers, we would get a course in world citizenship at every prescription counter; and if tomorrow all remedies developed by foreigners should lose their power, the number of dead in our streets would be appalling.

But there is another side to the coin: while the countries of the world are becoming more interdependent in regard to strategy and science, and perhaps to foreign policy, they are becoming somewhat less interdependent in regard to language, education, economics, and perhaps domestic politics. Later in this study, we shall survey some evidence that suggests that the relative importance of the old two "world languages," French and English, has been somewhat declining, and that in many regions of the world, a plurality of national—and sometimes regional—languages have taken at least part of their place. In most countries, economic and cultural advancement is accompanied by a rise in the use of their own national language, and also by a decline of the share of students (and hence, later, of leaders) who have been educated abroad. Among American college students, those studying outside the United States in the early 1960's amounted to about 0.5 per cent of the total, and this small proportion was still somewhat reduced after 1965 by the impact of the draft. Likewise, with economic progress and rising populations, the proportion of foreign trade to the gross national product is declining. Modern technology is a technology of substitutes: much of what had to be imported in the past, such as wool or silk, now can be replaced by something made at home, such as orlon or nylon. At the same time, a growing part of the national income is coming to consist of services which are produced in the main within the country, such as housing, schools, health care, and the like. As a result, the exporters and importers, and all the interest groups concerned with foreign trade, now tend to command a declining proportion of the wealth and manpower in each country, and hence a declining share of the potential resources for exercising influence in politics.

It is hard but necessary to sum up the overall results of this first look at facts and trends. Every people, every race, and every creed is only a minority in a world of foreigners which is both inescapable and unmanageable. It is in many ways unmanageable because it is so pluralistic and diverse; and it is inescapable because our interdependence with other countries and peoples is very great and very real. In some respects this interdependence has been growing in recent decades, while in other respects it has been declining. In almost every country in the world, therefore, both foreign policy and domestic politics often are being pushed and pulled in several contradictory directions at once, and the safety and prosperity of each country, and even the survival of mankind, may depend on the outcome of these multiple contests.

International relations are too important to be ignored, but they also are too complex to be understood at a glance. We must try to do better. In a medical emergency, all those who have had medical training have an obligation to render first aid and otherwise help their fellowmen as needed. In medicine we know that the individual is a victim of illness but also often a major agent in his own recovery. Something similar holds for the citizen: he can be the victim of politics, but he can also do much to improve them and to improve his own fate and that of his country. We who have the opportunity

4

Introduction

and privilege of a higher education owe to our fellowmen the best help that we can give them as informed, competent, and responsible citizens of our countries and of the world; we must do our best to look to the heart of matters and try to help one and all to cope with the recurrent international political crises and emergencies of our time.

But competence here is as necessary as compassion. In medicine, a well-meaning ignoramus is not a doctor but a quack. In an emergency, he may endanger the life of the patient. In politics, an aroused and zealous but misinformed citizen is a menace. He and his fellows may endanger the liberties and lives of millions, including their own. In our own time, the ruins of Hamburg and Berlin, of Hiroshima and Tokyo, have stood as monuments to the high cost of ignorance in international politics. We must study international relations, therefore, as deeply, as carefully, and as responsibly as our limited time and resources permit. No other subject is as likely to have a direct bearing on what the American statesman Bernard Baruch once called "a choice between the quick and the dead."

This brief book can offer only a first introduction to this study. It will do so in five sections. The first of these will deal with what we *want* to know: the substance of international relations. The second section will ask *how* we can come to know about our subject; it will deal with methods of research and analysis, of observation, and sometimes even of experimentation. The third section will sum up a few of the things that have been found. The fourth section will explore various implications of these findings. And the fifth and last section will discuss some of the next steps that can be taken in our search for verifiable and usable knowledge, and for helpful and effective action.

5

Part One

WHAT WE WANT TO KNOW:

THE SUBSTANCE OF INTERNATIONAL RELATIONS

Much of what we want to know about international relations can be grouped under the headings of 10 fundamental questions. In one form or another, these questions have been asked for many centuries by political scientists, as well as by political leaders and by ordinary citizens. To many of them, there are traditional answers of some kind, usually several; but as in most fields of knowledge, these traditional answers must be looked at with caution. It is harder to get more precise answers to these questions, and hardest to acquire even a little knowledge about them that can be impersonally tested, reproduced, and verified, or else disproved, so that it can be called in some sense scientific. Yet we must try to get such knowledge, and in searching for it, our 10 fundamental questions may help us to keep our search relevant to what we want and need to know.

Ten Fundamental Questions

The 10 fundamental questions with which we shall
concern ourselves are these:

1. *Nation and World*: What are the relations of a nation
to the world around it? When, how, and how quickly are a people, a state,
and a nation likely to arise, and when, how, and how quickly are they
apt to disappear? While they last, how do they relate to other peoples,
states, and nations? How do they deal with smaller groups within
them, and with individuals, and how do they relate to international
organizations and to the international political system?

2. *War and Peace:* What are the determinants of war and peace among nations? When, how, and why do wars start, proceed, and stop? How did these processes work in the past, how are they working now, and how are they likely to work in the future? How much and what kinds of fighting are people likely to support? When, for what purposes, and under what conditions?

3. *Power and Weakness:* What is the nature of the power or weakness of a government, or of a nation, in international politics? What are the sources and conditions of such power? What are its limits? When, how, and why does power change?

4. *International Politics and International Society:* What is political in international relations, and what is not? What is the relation of international politics to the life of the society of nations?

5. *Prosperity and Poverty:* How great is the inequality in the distribution of wealth and income among the nations of the world? How great is the inequality in regard to other but related values, such as life expectancy or education? Are economic differences among nations greater or smaller than within them, such as among ethnic or racial groups, or among regions or classes? Are any of these inequalities growing or declining? How fast and by how much? What determines the nature of these distributions and the size and direction of these changes? What could be done to bring about such changes deliberately? How quickly, and by how much?

6. *Freedom and Oppression:* How much do people care about independence from other peoples or countries, and how much do they care about freedom within their own country and nation? What, if anything, are they likely to do about it? When, and under what conditions? What do people perceive as "freedom"—a wide range of choices with tolerance for minorities and for individual nonconformity, or mass submission to majority rule, to tradition, to some trusted leader, or to some congenial and familiar tyranny? To what extent do they perceive freedom as a value in itself, and to what extent do they see it mainly as an instrument to attain other values which to them are more important? What conditions influence or change such perceptions and such choices? How quickly and to what extent? How great are the differences between the kinds and amounts of freedom which people want in different nations, and in different groups within a nation? How great are the differences in the kinds and amounts of freedom which they get? How far and how fast do these distributions change? When, and under what conditions?

7. *Perception and Illusion:* How do leaders and members of nations perceive their own nations, and how do they perceive other nations and their actions? How realistic or illusory are these perceptions? When, in what regard, and under what conditions? Under what conditions are governments and electorates perceptive, and in regard to what matters are they obtuse or blind? To what extent do national governments function as sources of mass deception, myth, and self-deception? What effect does all this have on the ability of governments and nation-states to control their own behavior and to foresee the consequences of their actions? What is the "error average" of statesmen? How often do they make some major decision about war or peace

Ten Fundamental Questions

on the basis of some major error on a point of fact? What could be done, if anything, to make errors more rare and perceptions more realistic?

8. *Activity and Apathy:* What part, and what groups, of the population take an active interest in politics? What part, and what groups, do so in regard to international affairs? What conditions tend to enlarge or diminish these proportions of active participants? How quickly, and in what respects? What broader strata of the population must be considered relevant for politics at some given place and time? What conditions are likely to change the extent of these politically relevant strata? What are the effects of such changes in the amount of actual and potential political participation on the processes of politics and on their outcomes? Particularly, what are the effects of changes in the degree of mass participation in politics upon the conduct and the outcome of international affairs? What kinds of politics and world affairs are likely to exist among populations who are largely limited to subsistence economics and are apathetic about politics? And what kind of national and international politics are likely to develop with a sharp increase in the use of money and in mass communications, literacy, social mobility, and political participation? Obviously, this is a serious problem in developing countries, but it is also a problem for large and advanced countries, such as the United States, France, and the Soviet Union.

9. *Revolution and Stability:* Under what conditions are governments likely to be overthrown? When, under what conditions, and to what extent are entire ruling elites or privileged classes likely to lose all or part of their power and position? What permanent or irreversible changes, if any, are produced by revolutions? When and how are entire systems of law, economics, and society, or entire major patterns of culture, discarded wholly or in part and replaced eventually by other such systems and patterns? How quickly do these large processes of change occur, and at what cost in material damage and human suffering? Upon what groups in the population do these costs fall, for a short time or for long? What benefits, if any, short-run or long-run, do such changes bring, and to whom do they accrue? How long does it take for political and social stability to be established after a period of revolution? How, with what results, and at what costs to whom? And what are the effects of such processes of revolution, counter-revolution, and eventual stabilization of an old or new political or social order upon the course of international politics? How, in short, can domestic revolutions affect international affairs, and how can foreign influences and international events affect the stability or revolutionary upheaval of the domestic regimes and political systems of particular countries? What, if anything, can governments, statesmen, and electorates do about these processes? To what extent can they be influenced or controlled by deliberate action? When, at what cost, and in what direction?

10. *Identity and Transformation:* How, throughout all changes, do individuals, groups, peoples, and nations preserve their identity? What does this identity consist of, insofar as any elements or aspects of their inner structure are concerned, and what difference does it make to their observable behavior? To what extent does an identity of one's own constitute a real need of persons and of groups, and what happens if this need is not fulfilled? To what extent is such an identity of one's own a value in itself, and to what

Ten Fundamental Questions

extent is it a condition or an instrument for attaining other values? How is a sense of identity—and how is the reality of identity—acquired, and how is it lost? How thoroughly, how quickly, and under what conditions? To what extent are persons, classes, elites, governments, peoples, and nations all like leopards, who cannot change their spots, and to what extent are they capable of transformation and self-transformation? To restate now our first question in this paragraph: To what extent can they change their behavior, their goals, their inner structure, and their character, and to what extent can they still, throughout these changes, preserve their own identity? What are the effects of the transformation of personalities and groups upon a nation, and of the transformation of a nation upon personalities and groups? Particularly, what are the effects of international changes on national transformation and national identity, and what are the effects of the transformation of one nation, or of some social groups or classes within it, upon other nations and upon the international system?

Clearly it is easier to ask such questions than to answer them. About each of our 10 fundamental questions, many books and articles have been written in the past. A few of these are listed in the reading suggestions. Many more are likely to be written in the future. Yet, if we wish to be introduced to any more thorough study of international politics, we must at least begin to think about these 10 basic fundamental questions so as to become acquainted with the problems each of them implies.

Moreover, the 10 questions are interdependent. Whatever answers, or parts of answers, we might find to any one of them will make a difference to our answers to some or all of the others. Each of our 10 questions is a good starting-point but, much as several town gates all lead toward the heart of the same city, so our 10 questions all will lead us deeper into the complexities of our single problem: How so many different nations, while coming into existence and passing from the scene, can live together in a mixture of limited independence and interdependence in a world about which they cannot quite agree but which none of them singly can control, and upon which all of them depend for their peace, their freedom, their happiness, and their survival.

Tools for Thinking: A Few Basic Concepts

In order to make our 10 fundamental questions more manageable, both singly and in their interplay, we must use concepts as tools for cutting into them. Since a concept is a symbol, and a symbol is, so to speak, a command to be mindful of those things to which it refers, it follows that a concept is a kind of command to remember a collection of things or memories. The word "concept" comes from a Latin verb meaning "to grasp together," and describes any theme, idea, or label which we may use to group many different items of knowledge.

In tying items of knowledge together we make a set, or what the logicians call a "class," of them. The concept helps us to unify them so that we can remember them more easily and use them more effectively. But an efficient concept also must exclude some things; it should have some clear rule concerning what pertains to it and what does not. Not until we can specify a standardized *operation* (a procedure which other people can repeat with identical results) for testing whether a fact or event belongs under the heading of a particular concept can we call the concept "operational."

In the social sciences, as in all other sciences, concepts are used much as headings are used in filing systems: as tools for organizing information. Concepts in the context of larger conceptual schemes or theories serve not only to organize more clearly the information which we have, but also to help us ask new questions. They may provide, so to speak, some new file-folders for information that we do not yet have but that we need, and that we now can start to look for. A concept is therefore an order to select and collect certain facts, *if* they should happen to exist; it is a command to search, but it is no guarantee that we shall find. Medieval zoologists had a fairly clear concept of the unicorn: it was a graceful, horse-like animal with a thin, straight, yard-long horn growing from the middle of its forehead. But no such animal was ever found, and so the concept or set or class of unicorns remained empty. Political theorists could imagine a group or party of "racist pacifists," but so far as we know there are no such people. The fact is that persons who believe in race discrimination usually also believe in violence as an instrument of politics. (It is also a fact, of course, that not all people who accept violence as a political instrument believe in race discrimination). To find out which concepts are full of cases from reality, and which ones are empty, sometimes may be a search worth attempting.

The test of every concept, and of every organized collection of concepts, or "conceptual scheme," is the same as that for every filing system: its usefulness in practice. As the proof of a pudding is in the eating, so the "proof" of a concept is in remembering, recalling, comparing, inferring, thinking, and discovering what work we can carry out with it. The concepts used in each field of social science have been selected according to two tests: (1) their continuing convenience or usefulness in dealing with problems familiar from the past; and (2) their promise in facilitating new questions, new insights, and new intellectual operations on problems that are becoming salient for the present and the future. For our inquiry, we shall use about two dozen such concepts, organized into four groups.

The first group includes a half-dozen concepts for the general analysis of social systems, and another half-dozen concepts referring more specifically to basic aspects and processes of politics. The second group deals with political aggregates and units relevant to national and international action. The third group of concepts consists of specific conditions and processes which limit the size of government and influence the shift of loyalties and power from one unit or level of government or political community to another. The fourth and last group deals with the transactions and processes—the various acts of cooperation or conflict—that occur among different governments and nations. With the aid of all these concepts, we shall then be able to ask much more precisely just what has been learned thus far from the study of international relations and what is challenging us right now to be investigated or discovered.

Some Concepts about Social Systems

The four concepts we shall start with were proposed by sociologist Talcott Parsons. He derived them from the idea that there are certain fundamental things that must be done in every social system, large or small (that is, in every group, every organization, every country) if it is to endure. First, there is *pattern maintenance:* the system must be preserved in its essential patterns —that is, these patterns must be reproduced time and again so as to preserve them over a succession of persons, groups, or generations. In most societies the main function of pattern maintenance is served by households and families; in every society it is also served by many other institutions and agencies, though to a lesser degree.

Second, there is *adaptation:* every organization and every society must adapt itself to its environment, derive its sustenance from it, and adjust to its changes. In every country the chief task of adaptation is performed, according to Parsons, by the economic sector of life and its institutions and activities, including those of technology and science. Adaptation is thus primarily served by the factories, farms, mines, and research laboratories of each country, whether they are under private or public ownership. Men adapt to oceans by fishing, to plains by growing wheat on them, and to rivers by building power-stations—and such a social adaptation changes the environment as well as the society, for if it changes a hunter into a farmer, it also changes a plain into a field.

Third, there is *goal attainment:* every organization and society has one or several goals which it is trying to approach or attain, or which its members wish to attain, and in terms of which its behavior is being modified beyond the simple requirements of pattern maintenance and adaptation. In every country, Parsons suggests, most of the function of goal attainment is served by the government, and more generally by the political sector, with its processes and institutions. It is through government and politics that most often the human and material resources of a country are gathered and reallocated to the pursuit of whatever goals, peaceful or warlike (ranging from attaining general literacy to conquering a coveted frontier province), that the leaders or the people of the society have accepted.

These three functions—pattern maintenance, adaptation to the natural and human environment, and the pursuit of goals—are not easy to carry on at one and the same time if resources are limited, as they usually are. Yet none of the three can be sacrificed. Every country, every society, and every complex organization, Parsons points out, therefore always faces a continuing and basic fourth task—the task of *integration.* Integration consists in making these different activities compatible and keeping them so, and in making and keeping the expectations and motivations of people compatible with the roles they have to play. The function of integration in most countries is served primarily by their cultural, educational, and religious practices and institutions, but many other elements of society are participating in this task, even though usually to a somewhat lesser degree.

Tools for Thinking: A Few Basic Concepts

Within each organization or group—that is, within every smaller or larger system—the same four functions are being served. In the U.S. State Department, pattern maintenance may be thought of as being carried out largely by the accounting and auditing services, the personnel bureau, and the security office, while much of the routine work of its consulates and embassies, as well as of its offices of congressional liaison and of public relations (or "public affairs"), may be considered to be serving the tasks of adaptation to various parts of its environment. The task of goal attainment is pursued through the more "political" efforts of our diplomats abroad, through the statements and press releases of departmental spokesmen, through the drafting of international treaties or national legislation proposed by the department, and through the policy-making efforts of its top-ranking officers. The latter, from the Secretary of State on down, also face the unending task of integration—that is, of trying to coordinate and to keep mutually compatible, or if possible even mutually supportive, all the department's numerous activities, bureaus, agencies, and officials, and their efforts.

For the United States at large, goal attainment must be served mainly by the President and Congress, and to a lesser but increasingly significant degree by the Supreme Court. All three branches of the government, however, also have important tasks in regard to pattern maintenance, integration, and adaptation.

At a still higher level, the United Nations is attempting to attain its goals mainly through the work of its Assembly, its Secretary General, and its Security Council. Much of its work of adaptation is carried out through its Economic and Social Council (ECOSOC), and major efforts to serve its integrative function are made through the United Nations Educational and Scientific Council (UNESCO). The task of pattern maintenance largely appears to be left to its member governments and nations.

As these examples show, the four basic functions, to some minimal degree at least, exist in every social system. But they are not always neatly separated in practice, nor are all of them always developed to the same extent. Every stable and identifiable system must have pattern maintenance if it is to survive in at least one unchanging environment. Those systems which are capable of surviving in environments that are varied or changing must develop the function of adaptation. Only systems of some complexity have external goals, and thus the task of attaining them; and only systems of similar or greater complexity may require the most elaborate facilities and processes of integration.

Two further basic functions become important only in regard to still more highly developed systems. One of these is _goal setting_. While simple goal-seeking systems have built into them once and for all the propensity to approach one goal, or at most very few equivalent or alternative goals, a more advanced system has the ability to set goals for itself in the sense of making changes in the pursuit of a larger repertory of existing goals, and of creating for itself new goals which it had never sought before. Originally "isolationist" countries, for example, can acquire large military establishments and extensive military goals or "security interests" in distant parts of the world, as England did from the sixteenth to the mid-twentieth century, and as the United States has done gradually since the 1890's, and more rapidly since

15

Tools for Thinking: A Few Basic Concepts

1945 and 1965. Conversely, countries may drop, gradually or quickly, some goals which formerly seemed paramount to them. The rulers of England in the sixteenth century dropped their three-centuries-old ambition to rule part of the continental territory that today is France. In the end, they abandoned Calais and began to pursue instead the goals of seapower and of power in regard to some of the lands of the New World. The partial shift of Russian and American attention since the late 1950's, away from competing mainly for influence and bases on this crowded planet and toward the array of goals implicit in the conquest of space (and eventually of the planets), may yet develop into another example of a change in national goals.

There may even be a change in the quality of goals and "vital interests" pursued by a nation. The Swiss in the sixteenth century dropped the pursuit of power over Lombardy; the Swedes in the eighteenth century dropped the pursuit of empire in the Baltic; the British between 1945 and 1965 gave up an empire that would contain by now about 700 million people. Each of these nations, once they did drop the pursuit and preservation of dominion over foreign populations, then shifted to an entirely different set of goals: the cultivation of their domestic affairs, of economic prosperity, and eventually of science, education, and the pleasures and problems of the welfare state.

If a system changes its goals repeatedly and successfully, then it is becoming in one sense potentially greater than the goals which it happens to pursue at any moment, for it may be capable of choosing, pursuing, and attaining greater or more worthwhile goals in the future. This may remind us in a sense of the warning of some philosophers and theologians against "idolatry"—that is, against the worship of passing and transitory things, of small tin gods, as if they were infinite and eternal. In world politics, too, any nation could be tempted toward the idolatry of some partial and transitory goals and interests, and toward forgetting that, if the nation survives, many of its goals will in all likelihood change.

The ability to set goals and to change them is likely to require material and human resources within the system. The greater the range of choice among old and new goals, the larger is likely to be the proportion of resources within the system that may have to be employed in making these choices and setting these new goals, and that may have to be reallocated for implementing their attainment. The latter (the proportion of resources within the system that are available for reallocation to new patterns of behavior) form an important element in the *learning capacity* of the system—that is, in its capacity to "learn" how to behave, and to respond to events in its environment in new ways, or at least in different and more rewarding ways.

Some governments, some elite groups, and some peoples in particular historic periods have shown a markedly greater or lesser capacity to learn in this sense than have others. Of the Bourbon monarchs of France, it was said early in the nineteenth century that they had forgotten nothing and learned nothing, even after the social earthquake of the French Revolution; and they were soon thereafter eliminated from French politics. By contrast, the learning capacity of the American government and people in the Great Depression of the 1930's, again during World War II, and once more during the "sputnik" crisis of the late 1950's, turned out to be unusually high. A decade later, by early 1968, the military crisis of Vietnam, the monetary crisis of the gold

Tools for Thinking: A Few Basic Concepts

value of the dollar, and the crisis of American cities, civil rights and race relations suggested once again that the repetition of past policies might not suffice, and that in the coming decade the political learning capacity of the American government and people might face another period of testing.

If a very large or crucially important part of the resources of a system is reallocated to a new structural pattern of the system, and simultaneously to a new set or range of goals and patterns of behavior, we may say that the system has become *transformed*. If this transformation has occurred mainly through initiatives and resources from within the system itself, we may speak of a self-transforming system. This function of *self-transformation* is the sixth, and in a sense the highest, of our basic functions of a social system. Any organization or nation that has it, together with the ability of sufficient partial pattern maintenance to preserve also a significant degree of continuity and identity, is more likely to survive, to grow, and to develop, than any that lacks it. Many of the great religious and secular organizations of the world are examples of such self-transformation. The Catholic Church of the Crusaders and their militant Popes of the twelfth and thirteenth centuries was very different from the small communities of early Christians who met in the catacombs, and from the state-supervised church of the days of the Emperor Constantine, and again from the present-day Roman Catholic Church that proclaimed at the Second Vatican Council the principle of religious liberty within the state. Yet a great deal of continuity of spirit within it has endured. The same is true of many nations: France, Russia, Japan, and the United States all are now very different from what they were in 1770 or 1780, yet a significant amount of identity and continuity has been preserved in each.

Some Concepts about Politics

Among the vast number of different human relations, just which ones are *political?* What does politics do that is not being done by other human activities or institutions?

Politics consists in the more or less incomplete control of human behavior through voluntary habits of *compliance* in combination with threats of probable *enforcement*. In its essence, politics is based on the interplay of habits of cooperation as modified by threats.

The *habits* of behaving, cooperating, obeying the law or the government, or respecting some decision as binding, tend to be voluntary for most people. After all, that is what habits are: they become "habitual" for us—that is, part of our nature and of the way we more or less automatically act. Without these habits of the many, there could be no law and no government as we know them. Only because most drivers stick to the right-hand side of the road and stop at red lights can the traffic code be enforced at tolerable cost. Only because most people do not steal cars can the police protect our streets and parking lots against the relatively few who do. If a law is not obeyed voluntarily and habitually by say at least 90 per cent of the people, it becomes either a dead letter or very expensive to enforce, or perhaps, like Prohibition in the 1920's, a noble but unreliable experiment. The voluntary or habitual com-

17

Tools for Thinking: A Few Basic Concepts

pliance of the mass of the population is the invisible but very real basis of the power of every government.

But although this compliance is in large part voluntary, it is not wholly so. If it were entirely voluntary, we should be dealing not with politics but with the realm of folkways, custom, and morality. In the area of politics, the compliance habits of the many are preserved and reinforced by the credible *probability of enforcement* against the few who may transgress the law or disobey the government.

Enforcement consists in the threat or the application of positive or negative sanctions—that is, in rewards or punishments. In practice, punishments are used more often than rewards. They are usually cheaper; some people enjoy applying them under any ideological pretext such as Communism or anti-Communism; and many people like to think that punishments are more reliable. Clearly, where most people are in the habit of obeying law or a government anyhow, it would seem costly and needless to offer them rewards for it; it seems cheaper and more efficient to threaten penalties for the few who deviate from the obedience or compliance of their fellows. Punishments may deter some of the few transgressors from repeating their offense, but it is more important that the fate of those few may deter some others from following their example.

Enforcement usually is not certain; most often it is only probable. But ordinarily the threat it poses is quite enough, together with the compliance habits of most of the population, to keep the proportion of serious transgressions down to a tolerable level. If nine out of 10 murderers are convicted and punished, this may be enough to deter many of that fraction of would-be murderers who contemplate murder as a calculated method to attain some gain. And if only one-fourth of automobile thefts were followed by convictions, this might suffice, together with the law-abiding habits of most people, to keep most automobiles unstolen and their theft insurance rates tolerably low. But even the most certain or the most cruel punishments, of course, do not deter that fraction of would-be murderers who are too thoughtless, too confident, or too passionately excited to care or think realistically about the chance of getting caught. Here is one of the several limits to the effectiveness of deterrence against murder in the lives of individuals, as well as against war in the lives of nations.

What decides the effectiveness of enforcement are thus much the same conditions that decide the frequency of compliance (that is, of obedient or law-abiding behavior). First of all, this is to a very large extent the strength of the compliance habits of the bulk of the people, and their willingness to give active support to the government in upholding its commands, or in upholding the law. In the second place, there are all the other conditions which influence the relative probabilities of the law-abiding versus the law-breaking behavior to which the threat of enforcement is being applied. If there is hunger among the poor, more people are likely to steal bread. Only in the third place come the size and efficiency of the enforcement apparatus: the skill and zeal of the officers and soldiers and of the judges and policemen, and the quality of their weapons and equipment. And only in the last place comes the changing of rules, the passing of new laws, or the threatening of more severe punishments.

18

Tools for Thinking: A Few Basic Concepts

Mass habits of compliance, and general social conditions, however, which have the most powerful long-run effects on the behavior of the population, are most difficult to manipulate. Even the size, training, equipment, and morale of the enforcement personnel—the armed forces, the police, the judiciary, and to some extent the civil service—can be changed only slowly and at great cost. The weakest lever of control remains attractive, therefore, because it is the cheapest to move. Passing another law, or threatening a more severe penalty, or being less careful about evidence and about not punishing some innocent people, are much cheaper and quicker, and hence, despite their relatively slight effectiveness, they seem often more inviting than the longer and harder task of bringing about more fundamental changes in the situation.

Politics, then, is the interplay of enforcement threats, which can be changed relatively quickly, with the existing loyalties and compliance habits of the population, which are more powerful but which most often can only be changed much more slowly. Through this interplay of habitual compliance and probable enforcement, societies protect and modify their institutions, the allocation and reallocation of their resources, the distribution of the values, incentives, and rewards among their population, and the patterns of teamwork in which people cooperate in the production and reproduction of their goods, services, and lives.

Once we keep our concept of politics clearly in mind, we can readily understand the two related political concepts of rule or dominion, and of power. By the *rule* or *dominion* of a leader, the German sociologist Max Weber meant the chance (that is, the probability) of his being obeyed. Of two leaders or governments, according to Weber's reasoning, the one more likely to be obeyed by a given population has more dominion over them than does the other.

If we carry this reasoning somewhat further, we recognize what T. W. Adorno once called "the implicit mathematics in Max Weber's thought."[1] A probability, strictly speaking, is a number: it denotes the frequency, usually expressed as the percentage, with which events of a certain type (here, acts of obedience to the commands of the ruler) occur within a larger ensemble of events (here, the general behavior of the population). Rule, as defined by Weber, can therefore be expressed as a number; in principle at least it can be measured in quantitative terms.

At the same time, we can see on the one hand the close relation between Max Weber's idea of the chance or frequency of acts of obedience to the commands of a government, and on the other our own concept, discussed earlier as the rate of compliance (that is, the frequency of acts of compliance). The latter (the rate of compliance) is somewhat broader in that it includes also acts of passive submission, tolerance, or apathy, in addition to the more positive acts of obedience emphasized by Max Weber, wherever such

[1] T. W. Adorno, *Oral Communication*, Fifteenth German Congress of Sociology (Max Weber Centenary), Heidelberg, May, 1964.

Tools for Thinking: A Few Basic Concepts

more passively compliant behavior plays a significant part in determining the outcome of the political process.

Our concept of *habitual* compliance, however, is somewhat narrower than Max Weber's "chance of being obeyed," for our concept excludes mere acts of submission to the immediate threat of naked force. People obey a gunman in a holdup, or a foreign army of occupation, as long as the intruder has a gun pointed at them. These are still cases of Max Weber's "rule" or "dominion," but they are processes of force, not of politics. They become political only insofar as this obedient behavior continues after the gunman's, or the invader's, back is turned. Then only, in the interplay of remembered fear and continuing compliance, are we dealing once again with politics.

When we say that politics is that field of human affairs whereupon domination and habitual compliance overlap, we are already implying that politics, owing to its double nature, is apt to be an area of recurrent tension between centralization and decentralization. For domination or rule usually can be exercised more easily by centralized organizations, and threats of enforcement, too, can be manipulated more effectively from a single center. But the dependable habits of large numbers of people can be created rarely, if ever, through a single center of command alone, and they cannot be created quickly. Habits more often grow from a multitude of different experiences, repeated over time in many ways. The centralized use of threats or force rarely creates, therefore, a durable community of politically relevant habits; it is much more often such a community of habits that provides the possibilities for the exercise of centralized power.

In a later part of our discussion we shall pursue these matters further, in the context of the processes that determine the size of nations, states, and other political units, and of the migration of power among the various levels of local, national, and supranational government. Here it is only worth noting that these processes, with their vast consequences, have their roots in this double nature of politics itself.

Tools for Thinking: A Few Basic Concepts

Power
and the
Nation-State

Recognizing the dual nature of politics also helps us to realize
the limits of the concept of political power. Some brilliant writers
have tried to develop a theory of politics, and particularly
of the relations among states, largely or entirely based
upon the notion of power—among them Niccolò Machiavelli
and Thomas Hobbes, and in our own time Hans Morgenthau and Frederick
L. Schuman. At the same time, the notion of power as the basis
of international politics still is widespread in the popular
press, and even in the foreign services

and defense establishments of many countries. What then, we ask, is the element of truth contained in this notion, and what are its limits?

In our discussion we shall be concerned not only with the power of nations and of international organizations in the world, but also with the power of governments, of interest groups, of elites, and of individuals, insofar as any of these seems likely to affect significantly some outcome of international politics.

Power, put most crudely and simply, is the ability to prevail in conflict and to overcome obstacles. In this sense Lenin, before the Russian Revolution, posed to his followers as a key problem of politics the two-word questions, "Who whom?" It meant: Who is to be the subject and master of actions and events, and who their object and victim? During the 1932 depression, a German protest song called up a related image: "We want to be hammers, not anvils," it announced. Who is stronger and who is weaker? Who will get his way and who will have to give in?

Such questions as these, when asked about many possible or actual encounters among a limited number of competitors, lead to rank lists—such as the rankings of players in tennis or chess tournaments, of baseball clubs in the world series, of chickens in the peck order of the chicken yard, and of great powers in world politics. The fewer the recent actual encounters that have occurred, of course, the larger the extent to which such rank lists must be built up from hypotheses based upon the past performances and present or expected resources of the contestants.

The Basis of Power

POWER POTENTIAL AS INFERRED FROM RESOURCES

An example of the relative power potential of two coalitions of nations is given in Table 1. Here, power of the Allied and the Axis countries in World War II is measured, or at least indicated, by the percentage of total munitions which each side produced during each year.

The table reveals that the Axis powers produced far more munitions than the Allied countries in 1938, 1939, 1940, and 1941, but that their lead diminished in 1940 and was lost decisively in 1941 and 1942. After this turning point, the Axis powers fell ever further behind until their total collapse in 1945.

An example of a hypothetical ranking of the power of the major nations for the period 1960–1963 and 1980 respectively can be given from recent calculations (Table 2) of a West German physicist.

The projections to 1980 in Table 2 are based on figures of the expected growth of per-capita steel and energy production, and of total population, in each country. For China of 1980, a population of about 1,100,000,000 and an annual (per-capita) steel output of about 400 pounds, or roughly half the 1963 level of the U.S.S.R. and of Japan, are projected. Whether these projections will turn out to be realistic for 1980, or even for any later time, no one, of course, can yet be sure—particularly after setbacks to the Chinese economic growth in the early 1960's. In any case it seems noteworthy

Power and the Nation-State

Table 1 PERCENTAGE OF TOTAL COMBAT MUNITIONS OUTPUT
OF THE MAIN BELLIGERENTS, 1938–1943*

Country	1938	1939	1940	1941	1942	1943
United States	6	4	7	14	30	40
Canada	0	0	0	1	2	2
Britain	6	10	18	19	15	13
U.S.S.R.	27	31	23	24	17	15
Total: Allied countries	39	45	48	58	64	70
Germany†	46	43	40	31	27	22
Italy	6	4	5	4	3	1
Japan	9	8	7	7	6	7
Total: Axis countries	61	55	52	42	36	30
Grand Total:	100	100	100	100	100	100

* Includes aircraft, army ground ordnance and signal equipment, naval vessels, and related equipment.

† Includes occupied territories.

Source: Klaus E. Knorr, *The War Potential of Nations* (Princeton: Princeton University Press, 1956), p. 34.

Table 2 SOME HYPOTHETICAL RANK ORDERINGS OF THE POTENTIAL POWER
OF MAJOR COUNTRIES, 1960–1963 AND 1980*

Actual Figures for 1960–1963			Projections for 1980		
1. U.S.	100		1. China		250
2. U.S.S.R.	67		2. U.S.		160
3. China	41		3. U.S.S.R.		120
4. German Federal Republic	15		4. Japan		39
5. Japan	14		5. German Federal Republic		25
6. Britain	12		6. Britain		19
7. France	7		7. France		11
Sub-total: 1–7		256			624
8. India	6.8		8.		
9. Poland	4.3		9.		
10. Italy	3.7		10. No data		
11. Canada	3.1		11.		
12. Czechoslovakia	2.6		12.		

* Based on energy production, steel output, and cube root of population; from data in Wilhelm Fuchs, *Formeln zur Macht: Prognosen über Vökler, Wirtschaft, Potentiale* (Stuttgart: Deutsche Verlagsanstalt, 1965), Figs. 37–38, pp. 129–131.

that in the projections, too, the power of the strongest single country, in 1960–1963 as well as in 1980, is rated at well below half the total power of the first seven countries. Thus, in both periods, the strongest single country will still represent only a minority in terms of world power.

The aggregate power resources of a nation are sometimes called its "power base," since they can be thought of as the basis upon which potential power can be converted to a greater or lesser extent into actuality. A related

Power and the Nation-State

but somewhat different notion is the concept of a "base value," as defined by Harold D. Lasswell and Abraham Kaplan. According to this reasoning, a power base for actor *A* (where *A* could be a person or a country) is an amount of some value for actor *B*, which is under *A*'s control. Actor *A*, that is to say, controls some possible increase or decrease in *B*'s wealth, well-being, or enjoyment of respect. Since *B* desires more of this value which *A* controls, *B* must try to please *A*, in order to induce *A* to let him have more of this value. Thus if a developing country needs and wants economic aid to improve its technology, or if a hungry country needs wheat in order to stave off famine, and if the United States or the Soviet Union controls some of the available supplies, then the United States (or the Soviet Union) will have a *power base* for exercising influence over these more needy countries.

It is, of course, another question how effectively the United States government, or the Soviet government, will use this power base or "base value" so as to acquire actual influence and power over the behavior of some or all of those countries in regard to some "scope value"—such as a favorable vote in the United Nations—which the poorer countries control and the richer countries want. *A*'s power in all such cases is based on three things: first, on *B*'s relative poverty and want in regard to some base value of which *A* controls a relevant supply; second, on *B*'s control of a relevant supply of some scope value which *A* desires and which *A* is trying to get by using its power over *B*; and finally, *A*'s skill and effectiveness in converting the potential of its power base into actual power over *B*'s behavior.[1]

THE WEIGHT OF POWER AS INFERRED FROM RESULTS

Power potential is a rough estimate of the material and human resources for power. Indirectly, it can be used to infer how many and how great successes in a power contest a country ought to have, if it uses its resources to advantage. It is possible, however, to reverse this calculation. We can ask: How successful has this actor (this leader, this government, or this nation) been in changing some outcome in the outside world? And we can then infer the "weight" of his power from the amount of his success. (The four chief dimensions or aspects of power are its weight, domain, range, and scope; of these, weight is closest to the intuitive notion which most of us have when we think of power.)

The weight of the power or influence of an actor over some process is the extent to which he can change the probability of its outcome. This can be measured most easily wherever we are dealing with a repetitive class of similar outcomes, such as votes in the United Nations Assembly. If it should turn out, as a hypothetical example, that in that Assembly those motions supported by the United States have been passing on the average three times out of four, or with a probability of 75 per cent, while those motions not supported

[1] For more extended discussions see H. D. Lasswell and A. Kaplan, *Power and Society* (New Haven: Yale University Press, 1950), and K. W. Deutsch, "Some Quantitative Constraints on Value Allocation in Society and Politics," *Behavioral Science*, Vol. 11, No. 4 (July, 1966), pp. 245–252.

Power and the Nation-State

by the United States have been passed only 25 per cent of the time, then we might say that the support of the United States can shift the chances for the success of a motion in the United Nations Assembly on the average from 25 to 75 per cent—that is, by 50 percentage points. These 50 percentage points then would be a rough measure of the average weight of the power of the United States in the Assembly during the period under study. (The measure is a rough one, and it may understate the real influence of the United States, since many potential motions opposed by the United States might seem so hopeless to their would-be sponsors that they might not even be proposed, and thus might not enter our statistic.)

The calculation or estimate of the weight of power is more difficult when we are dealing with a single event. What was the power of the atom bombs dropped on Hiroshima on August 6, 1945 (or of the one which cremated Nagasaki three days later), in speeding up the surrender of Japan and in shortening the Second World War? An outstanding expert on Japan, Professor Edwin O. Reischauer, who in 1961–1967 was United States Ambassador to Japan, concludes that the bomb shortened the war by only a few days.[2] In order to make any such judgment, it is necessary to imagine that the event—the dropping of the bomb at a time when Japan already was largely defeated and exhausted, and her government was seeking for a way to surrender—occurred many times. One then would have to try to imagine what would have happened on the average in all those imagined cases in which such a bomb *would* have been dropped, as against the average result in all those imagined cases in which this had *not* been done.

This seems far-fetched, but it is not. Indeed, it is not very different from the reasoning of an engineer as to what caused the breakdown of a particular bridge, or the reasoning of a physician as to what caused the death, or the recovery of a particular patient. In all these cases, in order to estimate the effect of what *was* done—and perhaps to estimate what *ought* to have been done in terms of "good practice"—we convert the unique event into a member of a repetitive class of hypothetical events quite similar to it. We then try to estimate the extent and probability of alternative outcomes in the presence and in the absence, respectively, of the action or condition the power of which we wish to gauge; and we then infer the power of the actor in the situation from the power of the act or the condition he controls.

Power considered in this way is much the same thing as causality; and the weight of the power of an actor is the same as the weight of those among the causes of an outcome which are under his control.[3]

Modern governments, compared to those of past centuries, have greatly increased the weight of their power over their own populations. Taxes are collected, soldiers drafted, laws enforced, and lawbreakers arrested, all with a much higher probability than most medieval rulers could have dreamed of. By the same token, the weight of the power of governments of industrially advanced countries usually is much greater than is the case in contemporary

[2] E. O. Reischauer, *The United States and Japan*, rev. ed. (New York: Viking Press, 1962), p. 240.
[3] Cf. Robert A. Dahl, unpublished paper at the annual meeting of the New England Political Science Assn., Northhampton, Mass., April 25, 1966.

Power and the Nation-State

countries which are in the early stages of industrial development. Also, among governments of the latter, the weight of domestic power varies widely.

In world politics, on the contrary, the weight of the power of most governments, and particularly of the great powers, has been declining ever since 1945. No government today has as much control over the probable outcome of world affairs as had Great Britain, say, between 1870 and 1935. At present, Britain cannot control its former colonies; the United States cannot control France or Cuba; the Soviet Union cannot control Yugoslavia or China; and China cannot control its neighbors. The attempt by the Soviets to control the politics of Czechoslovakia through a military occupation in August, 1968 seemed to provide no lasting guarantee of success. The reasons for this decline in the weight of power of most of the large countries will occupy us later, but the fact seems worth noting now.

On closer inspection, the weight of power may turn out to include two different concepts. The first deals with the ability to *reduce* the probability of an outcome *not* desired by an actor. In domestic politics we sometimes speak of "veto groups" who can prevent or make unlikely the passage of some piece of legislation they dislike. In international politics we find a very considerable veto power formally accorded the five permanent members of the United Nations Security Council by the United Nations Charter. Less formally, we may speak of the power of a nation to deny some territory, or region of influence, to some other government or ideology. Thus the United States in the 1950's successfully denied South Korea to its North Korean attackers, and it denied in the early 1960's much of South Vietnam to the Viet Cong.

It should be easy to see why this is so. The specific result which we may wish to prevent may not be very probable in the first place. Suppose that a Communist guerrilla campaign in an Asian or African country had roughly one chance in three, or 33 per cent, of establishing there eventually a stable Communist regime. In that case, an anti-Communist intervention by a foreign power, carried out with limited power—say with a weight of about 28 per cent—could reduce these chances of success for the guerrillas from 33 per cent to only 5 per cent, and create a 95 per cent, or 19:1, probability of their failure. The outcome, which is already moderately improbable, thus can be made highly improbable by the application of even a relatively limited amount of power. In such situations, the change in the probabilities of this particular outcome will seem to us quite drastic, and this limited amount of power will seem to us to have changed considerable uncertainty into near-certainty, and thus to have produced spectacular results.

The same degree of power produces far less impressive results, however, when it is applied to promoting an outcome which is fairly improbable in the first place. If we wish to produce a stable constitutional and democratic regime in our imaginary strife-torn Asian or African country, then we might have to remember that only about one out of every 20 of the very poor countries in the world has a stable democratic and law-abiding form of government. India has been one of these rare examples during the last two decades, but there are not very many others. Rather, the great range of alternatives to democracy—such as dictatorships, military juntas, corrupt oligarchies behind constitutional façades, foreign occupation or colonial administration, civilian one-party regimes, successions of *coups d'etat* or civil wars, or combinations and

Power and the Nation-State

successions of all these—have been much more frequent. But if the chance of democracy in a recently emerged country is only 5 per cent, then the application of power of a weight of 28 per cent would still produce only a 33 per cent probability for the successful establishment of a democratic regime in that country, and would leave us with a 2:1 chance for its failure.

In fact, even this calculation is far too optimistic, for it has assumed without justification that power to promote one outcome can be transformed without loss into the same amount of power to produce another. We all know very well that this is simply not true. The power to knock down a man does not give us the power to teach him to play the piano or to do calculus or figure-skating. The power to bomb and burn a village cannot be completely or easily transformed into the power to win the sympathies of the inhabitants, or to govern it with their consent, and even less can it be transformed into the power to produce among them the many skills, values, and freely given loyalties which are essential for democratic government.

The more highly specific a positive outcome is, the more are the alternatives excluded by it. Hence it usually is more improbable, and thus more difficult to make it highly probable by the application of limited power. Limited power is most effective, therefore, when used negatively as veto power, or as power of denial against some highly specific outcome, because then it is being used (in effect) to increase the already considerable probability of the entire range of possible alternatives to it, with much less or no regard as to which particular alternative will materialize.

The power to increase the probability of a specific positive outcome is the power both of *goal attainment* and of *control* over one's environment. Like all goal attainment and all control, it necessarily implies a high degree of self-control on the part of the actor. A charging elephant can smash down a large obstacle, but he cannot thread a needle. Indeed, he cannot make a right-angle turn within a three-foot radius. The greater the brute power, mass, speed, and momentum of the elephant, the harder it is for him to control his own motions, and the less precise his control becomes. Most of us know something similar from driving: the bigger, heavier, faster, and more powerful our car becomes, the harder it is to steer. An attempt to measure its power in terms of its performance would give us, therefore, at least two different numbers or ratings—a high one for its power to accelerate, but a low one for its power to stop or to turn.

Does something similar hold for the power of governments and nations? The larger the country, the more numerous its population, and the larger the proportions of its population and resources which have been mobilized for the pursuit of some policy (and, we may add, the more intense and unreserved their emotional commitment to that policy), the greater is likely to be the power of that country and its government to overcome any obstacles or resistance in its path. But national policies usually require more than merely overcoming resistance; often they aim at specific positive results. They often require, therefore, the pursuit of some constant goal through a sequence of changing tactics, or even the enhancement of some basic value through a succession of changing goals. The more people and resources have been committed to the *earlier* tactics, policies, or goals, however, and the more intensely and unreservedly so, the greater is the wealth of the interests, careers, reputations, and emotions thus dedicated, and the harder it is for any member of the government, or even for the entire government, to propose a change. Unless substantial and timely precautions have been taken, therefore, governments may become prisoners of their past policies, and their power may blindly push them into a logjam or a trap.

These dangers tend to grow with the amount of national power and with the intensity of efforts to increase it. Ordinarily these dangers of partial loss of self-control are greater for large nations than for smaller ones, for dictatorships than for democracies, and for times of war and near-war than for times of peace. If these dangers are not guarded against, the weight of power in the long run may in part become self-defeating, or self-destructive.

Some Other Dimensions of Power

DOMAIN, RANGE, AND SCOPE

Over whom is power exercised? The answer to this question consists in the *domain* of power—the set of persons whose probable behavior is significantly changed by its application. The domain of the power of a village chief consists roughly in the inhabitants of his village; the domain of the government of Sweden is largely limited to Sweden but also includes Swedish ships and Swedish citizens abroad. The domains of the government of the United States and of the Soviet Union are limited in many ways to their respective countries—and to their ships, troops, bases, and citizens abroad—but in other and important ways they affect, at least indirectly, each other's behavior, and the fate of most of mankind.

Some powers may have domains that cut across national boundaries in other ways. Insofar as Roman Catholics follow the pronouncements of their church in matters of political importance, or in matters where politics and religious doctrine overlap (such as in regard to public policy about population growth and the teaching of birth-control methods), the political power or influence of the Pope reaches into many countries. The same is true for many other religions, since all great world religions teach, explicitly or by implication, that there is a higher moral law and a higher moral authority than the changing policies of any nation-state. Every such religion, in interpreting this moral law, creates opportunities for the exercise of moral leadership, influence, and quite possibly power across the boundaries of nations.

Something similar holds, of course, for some secular philosophies. The degree to which Communists in many countries used to follow the directions and policies of Moscow through every change of course has been notorious. Since the emergence of several variations of Communist doctrine—such as the Chinese, Yugoslav, and Russian versions, each of which is backed by an established government—the degree of compliance of Communist movements abroad with the commands of any single center of direction has lessened perceptibly, but thus far has by no means disappeared. (The Czechs, too, tried to establish a more liberal version of their own, until the Soviets in August, 1968 occupied their country.) To a lesser degree, adherents of other philosophies or ideologies, such as conservatives, monarchists, liberals, social-

Power and the Nation-State

ists, existentialists, and adherents of free private enterprise, all sometimes try to exercise some influence or power over congenial or susceptible groups in other countries, and thus to extend the domain of their power.

Essentially, the domain of political power always is the collection of people that are subject and obedient to it. It is more loosely referred to as the geographic area in which power is exercised over most of the population. It is important to be clear which usage is intended. The first (and preferable) meaning of the domain of the power of a government includes only those persons in a territory who obey the government's commands, or at least passively comply with them; while the second, a geographic definition of the domain of a government, would include even the guerrillas on its territory fighting against its rule—at least so long as these guerrillas do not succeed in converting some districts into a stable domain of their own.

A third possible meaning of the domain of power might include not only the persons subject or obedient to it, but also those amounts of land, capital goods, and general resources controlled by them. To have power over a hundred paupers, by this reasoning, is less than to have power over a hundred well-equipped men with ample resources at their disposal. This third view of the domain of power comes close to our earlier notion of power defined in terms of a collection of resources.

All three notions of the domain of power have been used if we neglect,

Table 3   THE DOMAIN OF NATIONAL POWER IN TERMS OF POPULATION, 1962

Rank	Population in Millions	Percentage of World Total
1. China (mainland)	700	22
2. India	449	14
Subtotal: 1–2	1,149	36
3. U.S.S.R.	221	7
4. U.S.	187	6
Subtotal: 3–4	408	13
5. Indonesia	98	3
6. Pakistan	97	3
7. Japan	95	3
8. Brazil	75	2
9. West Germany	54	2
10. United Kingdom	53	2
11. Italy	50	2
12. France	47	2
Subtotal: 5–12	569	19
13. Mexico	37	1
14. Nigeria	36	1
15. Spain	31	1
16. Poland	30	1
Subtotal: 13–16	134	4
Grand total:	2,260	72

Source: Data in K. W. Deutsch, *Nationalism and Social Communication,* rev. ed. (Cambridge: M.I.T. Press, 1966), p. 65.

Power and the Nation-State

for the moment, the possibility of disaffected and rebellious populations and districts in a country; for then we can measure the direct domain of its government in the first sense of the concept by its population; in the second sense by its area; and in the third sense, at least roughly, by its gross national product.

A comparison of the domains of the power of some of the main countries of the world in terms of the first concept of domain (*i.e.*, population) is given in Table 3. This neglects, of course, the populations outside the political boundaries of each country which may yet be subject to its power, but it is still a first approximation worth considering.

We obtain a somewhat different rank list from the geographic concept of domain, as shown in Table 4.

Table 4   THE DOMAIN OF NATIONAL POWER IN TERMS OF AREA, 1962*

Rank	Area in Million Square Kilometers	Percentage of World Total	
1. U.S.S.R.	22.5	17	
2. Canada	10.0	8	
3. China (mainland)	10.0	8	
4. U.S.	9.5	7	
5. Brazil	8.5	7	
6. Australia	7.5	6	
Subtotal: 1–6	68.0		53
7. India	3.5	3	
8. Argentina	3.0	2	
9. Sudan	2.5	2	
10. Algeria	2.5	2	
11. Congo (Leopoldville)	2.5	2	
12. Mexico	2.0	1.5	
13. Libya	2.0	1.5	
14. Iran	1.5	1.5	
15. Saudi Arabia	1.5	1	
16. Mongolian People's Republic	1.5	1	
17. Peru	1.5	1	
Subtotal: 7–17	24.0		18.5
Grand total:	92.0		71.5

*The percentage of world total uses a total land area of 130,351,734 sq.km. (rounded to 130.4), the sum of the land areas of the 113 countries listed in the *World Handbook* and in the *U.N. Statistical Yearbooks*. Data for each country's total land area include inland waters and uninhabited land lying within the boundaries. Wholly uninhabited areas (polar regions and a few small islands) are usually excluded. *World Geographic Atlas: A Composite of Man's Environment*, designed and edited by Herbert Bayer, Chicago, printed privately for Container Corp. of America, 1953; pp. 24–25, cites an aggregate figure of 145,616,303.49 sq.km. (rounded to 145.6) for total land area of the world (including Antarctica but opposed to total water area of the world). If one were to use this second figure, the changes in percentage share of the various countries are unimportant. All figures and totals are subject to rounding errors.

Source: Data in B. M. Russett, *et al.*, *World Handbook of Political and Social Indicators* (New Haven: Yale University Press, 1964), p. 139.

Power and the Nation-State

The third rank list of domains of national power, and perhaps in some ways the most realistic one, is in terms of gross national product, as shown in Table 5.

Table 5   THE DOMAIN OF NATIONAL POWER IN TERMS OF GROSS NATIONAL PRODUCT, 1962

Rank	GNP (in billions)		Percentage of World Total	
1. U.S.	556		33	
2. U.S.S.R.	256		15	
Subtotal: 1–2		812		48
3. West Germany	89		5	
4. United Kingdom	89		5	
5. France	79		4	
6. China (mainland)	60		4	
7. Japan	56		3	
8. Italy	53		3	
Subtotal: 3–8		426		24
9. Canada	39		2	
10. India	33		2	
11. Poland	21		1	
12. Australia	19		1	
13. East Germany	17		1	
14. Netherlands	16		1	
15. Sweden	16		1	
16. Mexico	15*		1	
17. Brazil	15		1	
Subtotal: 9–17		186		11
Grand Total:		1,424		83

* Estimated from gross domestic product.
Source: Data in K. W. Deutsch, *Nationalism and Social Communication,* rev. ed., p. 67.

The concept of domain could be extended to include the domains of knowledge, technology, and weapons systems. How large a share of the world's scientists at the Ph.D. level or its equivalent are in the domain of this or that government? The United States, with over 100,000 scientists at this level, may have more than one-quarter of the scientists in the world. The share of the Soviet Union may well be of the same order of magnitude. Together, the governments of these two giant countries may have under their sway well above half the scientists on this planet—a larger share than their respective proportions of world income. A similar calculation could be carried out in regard to the average annual share of each country in the scientific papers published in the world. The results of this calculation presumably would yield more similar national rank orders and percentage shares than would the counts of scientists, but they could serve as cross-checks and supplements for missing data.

31

Another extension of the concept of domain would apply it to weapons systems. Here again, the concept of domain overlaps the concept of resources. Which governments control what sizes of armies, navies, air forces, rocket forces, and nuclear weapons systems? What are the shares of a particular government in the respective world totals for each of these? Some extremely rough and tentative estimates for nuclear weapons are presented in Table 6.

This table shows how, under its assumptions, the rank order of nuclear powers seems to remain constant until a power reaches the assumed saturation level of more than 10,000 nuclear warheads. However, it also shows, under the same assumptions, five countries already having a nuclear "veto power" by 1967—each of them having by then, that is to say, the ability to deter an attack upon itself by threatening to inflict unacceptable damage upon its attackers. The fact is, even a dozen nuclear warheads are enough to threaten credibly the destruction of the capital city and much of the central government and metropolitan elite of the enemy country—a degree of damage which most sane governments could not consider an acceptable price for the pursuit of any external or distant objective. But at the same time, not even a threat with 10,000 warheads may suffice to force a country into complete capitulation in its central area and thus into the surrender of its dominant values, habit patterns, institutions, and elites. In other words, atomic black-mail has its limits. If during the next decade nuclear weapons spread to another half-dozen countries or more, this will make the world that much harder for anyone to control, as well as more dangerous; and "the bomb" will no longer be of much help to any country attempting to gain any significant positive political objectives.

Nuclear weapons also raise the problem of the *range* of power. This range (as we shall use the term) is the difference between the highest reward (or "indulgence") and the worst punishment (or "deprivation") which a power-holder can bestow (or inflict) upon some person in his domain. Though a ruler could have many men in his domain, the range of his power over some of them might be much smaller than over others. Over those who wanted nothing and feared nothing, who were indifferent to pain or gain, his power would be small indeed.

In the course of recent centuries, the range of the power of governments in domestic politics has tended to become smaller. Extravagant rewards (such as to be given one's weight in gold, or to get the king's daughter in marriage) and extravagant punishments (such as being drawn and quartered, or burned at the stake, or otherwise publicly tortured to death) have disappeared in most countries, and they have become disreputable almost everywhere. Insofar as modern states rely on power, they normally govern not through the range of their power but rather through its weight—that is, through the high probability of the enforcement of their orders. Tyrants who rely mainly for their domestic power on the range of their staggering rewards and cruel punishments are not likely to last very long under present-day conditions.

In recent years, matters sometimes have seemed to trend in a different direction in international politics. Here, governments seem to have increased the range both of rewards they offer and of punishments they threaten, in their efforts to control the behavior of other countries and their governments. Certainly, foreign subsidies and loans are being offered more freely than they

Power and the Nation-State

Rank	1945	1949	1952	1955	1958	1961	1964	1967	1970	1973	1976
1. U.S.	2	32	128	512	2,048	8,192	10,000+	———			
2. U.S.S.R.	—	2	16	64	256	1,024	4,096	10,000+	———		
3. Britain (2 in 1951)	—	—	4	24	98	396	1,584	6,336	10,000+	———	
4. France (2 in 1957)	—	—	—	—	4	24	98	396	1,584	6,336	10,000+
5. China	—	—	—	—	—	—	2	16	64	256	1,024
6. Country 1	—	—	—	—	—	—	—	2	16	64	256
7. Country 2	—	—	—	—	—	—	—	—	2	16	64
8. Country 3	—	—	—	—	—	—	—	—	2	16	64
9. Country 4	—	—	—	—	—	—	—	—	2	16	64
10. Country 5	—	—	—	—	—	—	—	—	—	2	16
11. Country 6	—	—	—	—	—	—	—	—	—	2	16
12. Country 7	—	—	—	—	—	—	—	—	—	2	16

* Assuming annual doubling of output for first 3 years, and doubling every 18 months thereafter until approach to saturation level of more than 10,000 warheads. The actual development of nuclear weapons may have been faster in some years and slower in others. It seems plausible, however, that the growth of nuclear stocks in each country starts slowly, then accelerates, and finally slows down near some saturation level.

Source: Adapted from estimates in K. W. Deutsch's multigraph, "A Note on Nuclear Weapons and the Balance of Power, 1945–1965" (New Haven: Yale University, 1966).

were at the beginning of this century, and the threat and practice of aerial bombardment, with its attendant slaughter of civilians, including women and children, has been used by some governments in the mid-1960's on a much larger scale than would have been thought compatible with civilized standards 60 years ago, when the international Hague Conventions about the rules of warfare were written and accepted. The threat of wholesale nuclear massacre has further expanded the range of threats now available to the great powers and their rulers, and indeed such threats of nuclear warfare were actually employed, in disguised but unmistakable language, by both the United States and the Soviet Union in the Cuba crisis of 1962.

In fact, however, this temporary expansion of the range of power in internatonal politics has had quite limited effects. The practice of controlling foreign governments through gifts and loans has by now become notorious. Since rival powers are willing to continue at least part of the same subsidies, the governments of most of the third countries have less to gain or lose from switching benefactors, or from calling on two or more of them at the same time. Similarly, any dire threat can be weakened or limited by calling upon the protection of a rival power, or else, given at least minimal deterrent strength of one's own, by threatening retaliation. As a result, the recent expansion of the range of power in international politics has made any active and ambitious foreign policy much more expensive, without making its fruits more ample or more dependable.

Another dimension of political power that has expanded in recent decades is its *scope*, an expansion which has had momentous consequences, **33**

Power and the Nation-State

and is still having them. By the scope of power we mean the set or collection of all the particular kinds or classes of behavior relations and affairs that are effectively subjected to it. The scope of the power of parents over young children is very large in one sense, for it includes almost all the child's activities. It is limited, however, in another sense, for even though the parents could control almost all the activities of the child, there are not, after all, very many things a young child can do. The scope of power thus increases with the capabilities of the persons included in the domain of power, in respect to the kinds of behavior subject to it. Political power expands in scope, therefore, whenever additional subject matter or additional kinds of behavior are put under its control. How much weight or effectiveness this control will have is, of course, another question of fact, as was pointed out in an earlier section.

During the past 100 years, and particularly during the last 50, the scope of politics has undergone a vast expansion. Many different activities are now being regulated by governments and laws, and hence by politics, which in the past were left to custom or to individual decision, or which did not exist at all. No medieval king or oriental sultan would have thought to make all children in his realm between the ages of six and 14 years get up on every working day before 8 A.M. and go to public buildings and remain there for several hours. Yet the modern state, with its compulsory education, school systems, and truancy laws, undertakes to do just that; and such is the weight of its power, based on the compliance and active consent of most of the population, that in all the advanced countries of the world this control is almost entirely effective: almost all children go to school and nearly all adults are literate. In many developing countries, on the other hand, this expansion of the scope of public power and of public services is just now under way; it is part of the great process of transformation which these countries (and with them the majority of mankind) are now undergoing.

Many other responsibilities and services have been added in recent decades to the scope of government, such as public health and a growing array of medical services; old-age pensions and other forms of social security; public works, including roads, harbors, airports, flood control, and power dams; the regulation and support of farm prices; the regulation of the purity and quality of food and drugs; the development and financing of research and of whole new industries, including nuclear energy, supersonic air travel, rocketry, and space transportation; greatly expanding educational services, from publicly financed kindergartens all the way through the great state universities and their graduate schools; and the vastly expanded burdens of defense.

Each new responsibility of the government, such as a new road system, or public education, or a publicly organized medical service, shifts the distribution of a few additional percentages of the gross national product into the public sector. It raises the stakes of politics. It widens the circle of persons who stand to gain or lose directly from the results of political decisions. It increases the potential and actual politicization of society. And it strengthens the conditions which favor eventually in every country the increasing participation of larger masses of people in politics.

The size and speed of these changes can be seen in the history of such countries as France, Britain, and Prussia-Germany during the last 150 years. Though their statistics are difficult to compare because of national differences

Power and the Nation-State

in record-keeping, as well as of inaccuracies and gaps, so that at some points one must use estimates, the general outline of the picture is quite clear. In the mid-nineteenth century, the per-capita gross national product in these countries was no more than perhaps $350 in today's money, or about one-fifth of what it is today. On the Continent, rural and small-town people formed the large majority. Only roughly one-fourth of the population of France—somewhat more in Germany and much more in Britain—lived in cities of over 20,000 inhabitants. More than half of all adults, however, already were literate, and in both France and Prussia at any time about 1 per cent of the population—or about 1.7 per cent of the population of working age—served in the peacetime standing army. Politics, however, still was a matter for the few. The total expenditures of the central government in each of the three countries averaged below 10 per cent of the gross national product, and even the addition of provincial and local government spending did not bring the proportion much higher. If the stakes of politics were relatively small, so was participation. Usually less than one-third of the adult population had the right to vote, and less than one-fourth (that is, less than half of the men) actually voted.

By 1910–1913, on the eve of World War I, per-capita gross national product had risen to perhaps $700, or nearly half of what it is today. Urbanization was higher, and literacy was close to 98 per cent. The central governments now spent about 13 per cent of the gross national product; and perhaps 40 per cent of the adult population, or about 80 per cent of the men, actually voted. Military participation in peacetime was substantially unchanged, but the war of 1914–1918 was to mobilize every involved population to its depths.

By 1928, the war damage had been more than repaired and the per-capita gross national product was near $1,000 or better, in present-day money. Now, however, general governmental expenditures had risen to about 24 per cent of the gross national product, and voting participation, including the enfranchised women, was close to 75 per cent of all adults. The Great Depression of 1929–1933 enhanced this trend. Per-capita income stagnated or fell, but expenditures rose as more government services were needed. By 1938, total governmental spending in Britain and France was close to 30 per cent of gross national product, and it was about 42 per cent in Nazi Germany, where it included a frantic rearmament campaign.

After World War II, a new plateau was reached. Once the war damage was repaired, per-capita gross national product rose to about $1,700 in the late 1960's; and now it included a greatly expanded social service sector. Total governmental spending in the major countries of Western Europe now averages about 37 per cent of gross national product. Military participation in peacetime has declined slightly, to about 1.5 per cent or less of the population of working age (15–64), but voting participation continues high, at 80 per cent or above.

The figures are presented in Table 7. Together, they show how relatively slowly the world was changing between 1815 and 1914; how rapidly and radically it changed between 1914 and 1950; and how much may depend on the speed and direction of change between 1950 and 1975. This much, though, has become clear already. For good or ill, foreign policy, like all

35

Power and the Nation-State

Year	Total Population[1] (in millions)				GNP per Capita[2] (in 1000 U.S. 1965 $)				Urbanization[3] (% of pop. in cities of 20,000 and over)				Literacy[4] (% of literates over 10 or 14 yrs., or among recruits or newlyweds)				Adults Voting[5] (as % of total pop.)			
	U.S.	U.K.	FR.	G.F.R.	U.S.	U.K.	FR.	G.F.R.	U.S.	U.K.	FR.	G.F.R.	U.S.	U.K.	FR.	G.F.R.	U.S.	U.K.	FR.	G.F.R.
PERIOD I																				
1830	12.9	23.8	32.4	29.4	—	—	—	—	4.1	32.5	7.9	—	—	56.0	—	—	9.1*	—	.4 (1831)	—
1850	23.3	27.5	35.6	35.3	—	—	—	—	8.9	38.3	10.1	8.6	—	62.0	—	—	12.8*	—	.6 (1846)	—
1870	39.9	31.3	37.3*	40.8	.5	—	—	.3	14.6	42.0	15.6	12.5	80.0	77.0	≃	96.5	15.2*	4.5 (1874)	[31.1] 20.0 (1876)	9.9 (1871)
1890	63.1	37.5	38.4	49.2	.9	.8	.4	.5	22.2	56.6	19.3	21.9	86.7	91.0	85.0	99.5	18.6*	11.4 (1892)	[28.8 1881] 20.7 (1889)	15.5
PERIOD II																				
1913	97.2	45.6	39.8	67.0	1.3	1.0	.7	.7	32.2	62.1	26.3	35.8	92.8	over 96.0 (1912)	88.8	over 99.9	15.8 (1912)	11.7 (1910)	25.9 (1914)	33.5*
1928	120.5	45.6	41.1	64.4	1.7	1.0	.9	.8	39.8	64.4	30.0	41.3	95.4	↓	—	↓	[51.7] 30.5	[70.1 1931] 49.6 (1929)	22.3	49.9
1938	129.8	47.5	42.0	68.6	1.7	1.2	.8	1.0	39.9	65.5	32.2	43.8	97.0	—	96.1	—	[57.3]* 36.7	[34.6] 46.9 (1935)	23.7 (1936)	65.6
PERIOD III																				
1955	164.3	50.9	43.3	52.4	2.9	1.5	1.4	1.5	42.7	66.5*	33.3	45.5	97.6	over 97.0	—	—	[59.1] 37.0 (1956)	[80.0 1951] 52.5	[74.0] 50.7 (1956)	56.7*
1965	193.8	54.4	48.7	58.3 (1964)	3.5	1.9	2.1	2.2	45.4*	67.2	38.9	49.5	97.7	↓	—	↓	[61.4*] 36.9 (1964)	[74.2] 51.2 (1964)	[60.9] 40.8 (1962)	56.6

* Data for this table were collected by Linda Groff and Marguerite Kramer, during the 1966–1967 academic year, as part of a larger data collection and analysis project under the direction of Professor Karl W. Deutsch and sponsored by the Yale Political Data Program. All the figures in this table are the actual data for the years indicated, unless no data were available, in which case the figures are either for the next closest year (indicated in parentheses), or are estimates (indicated by an asterisk), interpolated from the trend of the data for adjacent years.

1 Population figures are mid-year estimates by official government sources in each country of the de facto or legal population habitually residing in that country, as defined by the territory of the period in question. In the case of the United Kingdom, population figures are for England and Wales, Scotland, plus Ireland up through 1913, while only Northern Ireland is included in the 1928 and later data. In the case of Germany, these figures are for the 1913 Reich plus Alsace-Lorraine through 1913. From 1928 through 1938, the figures apply to the 1935 Reich plus the Saar. Finally, the population figures for the years 1955 and 1965 refer to the German Federated Republic and West Berlin.

2 The conversion into 1965 U.S. dollars of this per capita Gross National Product data for all countries (except France, where National Income data were used up through 1949) was accomplished by a method devised by Professors Gerald and Marguerite Kramer, which did not use official exchange rates, but rather aimed at reflecting—more accurately than do exchange rates—the real purchasing power of the various currencies in question, vis-à-vis the U.S. dollar.

3 Urbanization is defined as the percentage of the population living in cities of 20,000 and over for the United Kingdom, France, and Germany, and in cities of 25,000 and over for the United States, due to the nature of the data available for each country.

4 Literacy is defined (1) for the United States and France, and for the United Kingdom after 1913, as the percentage of literates in the population aged ten or fourteen years and over; (2) for Germany, as the percentage of literates—who can read and/or write—among the army recruits or conscripts each year; and (3) for the United Kingdom before 1913, as the percentage of literates—who could sign the marriage register—among the newlyweds each year.

Power and the Nation-State

Military Personnel[6] (as % of working-aged pop., 15–64 years)				Defense Expenditure[7] (as % of GNP)				General Government[8] Expenditure (as % of GNP)				Foreign Trade[9] (as a % of GNP)			
U.S.	U.K.	FR.	G.F.R.	U.S.	U.K.	FR.	G.F.R.	U.S.	U.K.	FR.	G.F.R.	U.S.	U.K.	FR.	G.F.R.
–	1.1	–	–	–	3.4	–	–	–	15.6	12.4	–	–	21.5	10.7	–
.16	.5	–	–	–	2.8	–	–	–	12.1	15.2	↑	–	32.0	19.2	–
.2	1.0	.2	–	–	1.9	2.4	2.1	↑	9.4	12.7	under 10.0 (1881)	12.1	44.5	22.7	32.0 (1880)
.1	.9	2.2	1.7	1.1 (1900)	2.1	3.1	2.1	under 6.9 (1902)	8.9	13.1	13.2	12.1	44.9	32.8	32.3
.2	1.4	2.3	2.1	.7	3.0	4.7	–	8.0	12.4	13.1	17.7	10.5	49.2	39.6	38.1
.3	.9	1.8	.3	.7	2.8	3.2	–	11.7	24.2	15.8	29.4	9.3	42.4	37.4	50.4
.4	1.2	.3*	.3 (1934)	1.2	8.9	2:1	–	20.7	30.0	18.4	42.4	5.9	26.3	17.2	18.1
2.8	2.2	–	.3 (1958)	10.2	9.5	6.3	4.1	30.4	36.6	38.0	39.0	6.7	40.0	19.8	27.8
2.3	1.2	2.4	1.0	7.4	7.5 (1961)	5.5 (1961)	4.3	30.5	39.1	40.0 (1964)	46.9*	6.8	33.9	21.8	31.7

5 Adults voting is defined as votes cast in national legislative elections, for the United Kingdom, France, and Germany, and votes cast for the President (not for Representatives) in U.S. national elections, all taken as a percentage of the total population in each country. A more desirable indicator of political participation would be votes cast as a percentage of adult population aged twenty or twenty-one years and over, which when available has been indicated in brackets. A third possible indicator of voting behavior— votes cast as a percentage of legal-registered voters—was rejected because of its failure to reflect those persons who do not vote because they are denied legal voting status.

6 Military personnel includes all Army, Navy Air Force, and Marine Personnel on active duty, and is taken as a percentage of the working-aged population (15–64, or 14–64 years) in each country. Note that the 1938 figure for Germany is based on 1934 data, and thus may under-represent the actual figure for that year.

7 National defense expenditure is taken as a percentage of Gross National Product for all countries, except France, where Net National Product or National Income figures were used before 1938. Of all the data in this table, this data should be used with the greatest caution, since defense expenditure data can vary significantly from one source to another, and even within one source, it can fluctuate considerably from one year to the next.

8 General Government expenditure includes budgetary expenditures on the Central (or Federal), the State (or District), and the Local Government levels, for the United States, the United Kingdom, and Germany. These calculations are based on the assumption that for France, where the entire budget is administered at the Central Government level, General Government expenditure is the same as Central Government expenditure. As before, all government expenditure data are taken as a percentage of Gross National Product for all countries except France, where National Income or Product is used instead.

9 All foreign trade data, for all countries, come from official national government sources or estimates. In the case of the United States, the United Kingdom, and Germany, foreign trade includes imports and exports of merchandise only, while for France, foreign trade includes imports and exports of merchandise and gold. Trade data for all countries are taken as a percentage of Gross National Product, except France before 1938, when National Income or Product is used instead.

politics, can no longer be made wholly by the few. It must take into account the votes and wishes of the many. The same political evolution, in its great outlines, can be traced in the history of the United States, and indeed in the history of all non-Communist countries that have reached a high level of economic development.

The testimony of this lengthwise cut through the history of a few countries is generally confirmed by the evidence of a cross-sectional study as shown in Table 8, which compares many countries at or near a single point in

Table 8 **AVERAGE LEVELS OF DEVELOPMENT AND THE RISING STAKES OF POLITICS: A CROSS-SECTIONAL STUDY OF 107 COUNTRIES AT THE START OF THE 1960'S**

1 Number of Countries (averaged)	2 Development (estimated level)	3 Population in Millions (averaged)[1]	4 GNP (1957) per capita ($)	5 Cities over 20,000 (%)	6 Literate Adults (%)
11	I	105 (10)	56	6	13
15	II	1,359 (91)	87	13	24
31	III	342 (11)	173	21	42
36	IV	733 (20)	445	34	77
14	V	410 (29)	1330	45	98

7 Newspaper (radio) Audience (%)[2]	8 Central Government Expenditure (% GNP)	9 General Government Expenditure (% GNP)	10 Military Participation (% population 15–64)	11 Voting (% population, adults)	12 Foreign Trade (% GNP)[3]
(5)	19	25	0.8	30	43 (35)
(8)	17	23	0.8	49	34 (35)
(23)	26	35	1.7	41	40 (35)
(63)	28	37	1.4	69	36 (27)
(100+)	30	40	1.5	78	39 (43)

[1] Figures in parentheses are average for all countries, regardless of size.
[2] Estimated at 3 per copy and 4 per set.
[3] Figures in parentheses are average for middle-sized countries only (5.3 to 37.0 million population).
Source: From data in Bruce M. Russett, *et al., World Handbook of Political and Social Indicators,* pp. 294–298. The rough method of estimating general government expenditures (*i.e.,* the total of central, provincial, and local government spending, but excluding transfers from one level of government to another) as one-third more than central government expenditures probably understates general government spending somewhat at higher levels of development, and generally in the case of federal systems. When more reliable data become available these rough estimates will be corrected.

time. Together, the long-term trends and the cross-sectional data show that developed non-Communist countries tend to put between 30 and 40 per cent of their gross national product through the governmental sector, and that between two-thirds and three-fourths of this (between 20 and 30 per cent of gross national product) tends to be controlled directly by the central government of each developed country. The data also show how the modern world has changed from the patterns of nineteenth-century Western Europe. There, and in those days, the rise in urbanization, literacy, and income preceded the

38

Power and the Nation-State

rise in voting and in the relative size of the governmental sector. This suggests that in the leading Western countries the productive capacity to satisfy many basic human needs and wants, such as food, shelter, health, education, and a rising living standard, increased before the rise in domestic popular demands and competitive international pressures, as represented by increasing voting participation and rising governmental expenditures. In the developing countries of the second half of the twentieth century, the opposite has happened. The social changes through the initial and partial monetization, industrialization, and urbanization of many Asian, African, and Latin-American countries have combined with the demonstratable effects of modern transport and mass communication to stir many peoples to their depths, long before they have acquired the full educational and productive capabilities of modern life. Accordingly, voting participation, military participation, and the share of governmental spending all are rising now at a much lower level of literacy, income, and urbanization, and thus at a much earlier stage of social and economic development, than they did in the Europe of a hundred years ago. The stakes, the hopes, and the frustrations of political power all are now rising faster, and in more countries, than they ever did before.

In three-quarters of the countries of the world, insofar as we have data, the nation-state today is spending or reallocating at least one-fourth of the national product, and in the remainder—the world's poorest countries—all are moving in the same direction. This contrasts with the roughly 1 per cent of the world's gross national product which is now being spent by all international organizations together. In spending power alone, nation-states outweigh international organizations by a ratio of more than 25 to one. Today, and for one or more decades to come, the nation-states are and will be the world's main centers of power. They will remain such centers as long as the nation-state remains man's foremost practical instrument for getting things done.

Power and the Nation-State

The Limits
of Power:
Symbol
and Reality

By now it should be clear that power is not one thing
but many. Or rather, "power" is one single label or symbol
which we use to refer to many different things, resources, relationships,
and probabilities. All these, as we have seen,
have to do with our ability to change at least somewhat
the outcome of events. Beyond this, however, they are diversified
indeed, and this diversity is only poorly hidden by the symbol
"power" which we are using as their common label.

Like every other *symbol*, the word "power" is a sort of message ordering us to recall something from memory for further consideration or association in our thoughts and feelings. This is in contrast to a *sign*, which is an order, so to speak, to expect something to be present or to happen in the near future.[1] When we define sharply the collection of memories that are to be recalled with the help of a symbol, the symbol will function as a concept, in the sense in which we have discussed concepts earlier in this book.[2] Conversely, when a concept comes to be used in a broader and less sharply defined sense, evoking many different and only partly overlapping memories among different people, it will serve them as a symbol. Concepts and symbols thus are not sharply separated from each other; rather, they can be thought of as located at opposite ends of a continuous spectrum on which many of the key words and ideas of politics are located somewhere in the middle. The sharper such a word is then defined in its denotations, the more nearly or more often it will serve as a concept, but the broader, deeper, and more ill-defined are its connotations—that is, the images, the memories, and the emotions of which it reminds us—the more nearly or more often will it be used as a symbol.

Power is such a symbol of the ability to change the distribution of results, and particularly the results of people's behavior. In this respect, power can be compared in some ways to money, which is our usual standardized symbol of purchasing power—that is, of our ability to change the distribution of goods and services. As such a symbol, money then functions as the currency of our economic life. It is the medium of exchange that makes easy the exchange of labor services for goods and other services, and the reverse exchange of goods and services for labor. A worker usually receives money as his wage or salary. He and the members of his household then spend this money for the goods and services which they take from the national economy. The basic exchange is a single one—work for goods—but the form in which this exchange occurs is, so to speak, double: an exchange of work for money, and then a second exchange of money for goods. This more complex arrangement permits wider and more flexible cooperation, accountability, and division of labor.

Power as a Currency

Just as money is the currency of economic life, so power can be thought of as the currency of politics. Here, power is the currency or medium that makes easy the exchange of more-or-less enforceable decisions for more-or-less dependable support. When a decision is very likely to be enforced by some kind

[1] When a doorman announces "The President!" we take it as a sign and expect the Chief Executive to enter; but when a lecturer on government says "the President," we usually take it as a symbol and recall that there is such a person and office, and perhaps various details associated with these. See Susan K. Langer, *Philosophy in a New Key*, 2nd ed. (New York: New York American Library, 1951), p. 37.

[2] See above, pages 12–19.

The Limits of Power: Symbol and Reality

of penalty or sanction, physical or psychic, we think of the decision as "binding"; once it has been made, we say it can be "made to stick." If this decision is one which some people wanted very much, they are likely to support the decision-maker—the government or leader—who made it, and in many cases they are likely to help and support him in enforcing this decision they favor.

The basic exchange process of politics from this point of view, as Talcott Parsons has pointed out, is the exchange of binding decisions for support. But in a more developed political system this exchange process, too, occurs in two stages. The leader, ruler, or government assumes general responsibility for making and enforcing many decisions of all kinds; in the extreme case, the government assumes general responsibility for making and enforcing any and all important decisions that might need enforcement. When a prince, a ruler, a party, or a group of revolutionists assumes this general role, we say that they "take power," or "take over," even though it may sometimes turn out later that they lacked the resources, or the capacities, or the concentration of purpose, necessary to hold on to it. If, however, the group or government that is "in power" (in the sense of being in a generalized role of maker of most or all of the more-or-less enforceable decisions) also succeeds in making decisions to the satisfaction of many of those people who count in politics, then these people in turn are likely to give to this government their generalized loyalty. That is, they generally support its decisions, not necessarily because they approve of each particular decision in itself, but because each is the decision of the government—"the law of the land," the decision of "legitimate authority."

Here, power is a symbolic role taken by the government, and ascribed to it by the people, and made credible by an initial minimum of readiness, resources, and capabilities to govern. And this symbolic role of power, together with this real or reputed capability, serves as a currency which mediates the exchange of the many diverse needs and wishes—the "interest"—of the many for the single, legitimate, and widely supported role of decision-makers of the few.

To be sure, the similarities between power and money should not be overstressed. As a rule, money is easily divided into standardized accounting units such as dollars, rubles, or grams of gold. Power is not so easily countable and divisible. Votes can be used as counting units in some cases, whether in a popular election or in a close vote in the Senate or in one of its committees, or in the General Assembly or the Security Council of the United Nations. In other cases, power has been counted in units of armed force, such as warships, bombing planes, tanks, soldiers, or divisions.[3] All such counting, however, is far more uncertain, inaccurate, and dependent on particular situations and contingencies than is the relatively smooth and accurate accounting in terms of money, which has facilitated in many fields the development of a more scientific style of economics. No precise parallel for this can be hoped for in politics.

[3] "How many divisions does he have?" the late Soviet premier Joseph Stalin is supposed to have asked once ironically about the Pope—apparently not realizing that, for all its imperfections, the reputation of the Papacy was to prove more durable than that of many secular rulers.

The Limits of Power: Symbol and Reality

Political science cannot and will not become simply the "economics of power," but it can benefit from the limited similarities between money and power by using them as guides to the deeper similarities and differences behind them. For these similarities, though limited, are by no means trivial. In economics, money represents a man's power to buy, and his credit represents his reputed power to do so. And what holds here for men also holds largely true for governments. They, too, need money or credit to buy in the world's markets. Similarly, in politics, prestige is to power as credit is to cash. This, too, applies not only in domestic politics but also in international affairs. Again, in economic life, people may lose their trust in the notes issued by a bank, or in the paper money issued by a government. When they thus stop believing what a writer on economics has called "the promises men live by," they usually must be shown the power to purchase in its most tangible form: they must be shown gold. Indeed, in international affairs, where trust among governments is somewhat rarer, and its misplacement could be more costly, gold is used more extensively in settling many of the balances of international payments. As gold is to ordinary bank deposits or cash in paper money, so force is to the ordinary forms of influence and power. Much as a show of trucks bearing gold may restore the faltering credit of a bank, so a show of force, such as tanks appearing in the streets of a nation's capital, may restore, at least for a while, the shaky prestige of a government. And so may a demonstration of warships or airplanes near some disputed border, coast, or small third country bolster the strained political position of a great power that has committed itself in an international dispute too closely to the limits of its credibility.

Overcommitment of Prestige and the "Row of Dominoes" Image

The parallel is quite imperfect but it has some sobering policy implications: governments that must continually prove their will and capacity to fight probably do not have quite enough prestige for the policies they are engaged in, much as banks that must constantly supply spectacular proof of their capacity to pay probably do not have quite enough credit for the scale and style of all the business activities they are trying to conduct. An insufficiency of prestige, like a lack of credit, is no trifling matter.

A government is similar to a bank also in that the sum of its commitments is much larger than the sum of its resources. A bank lends out more money than it takes in as deposits—in the United States about 7 times as much—because its managers can be fairly sure that not all its depositors will ask for their money back on exactly the same day. If all or even very many depositors *do* want their money back at once—perhaps because they no longer trust the bank—they generate a run on the bank that may break it and force it into bankruptcy. Similarly, every government promises to enforce more laws and to guard more objects and persons than it has policemen, soldiers, and resources so to do. When in domestic politics too many people at the same time disobey the government in too many serious matters, the result is something like a run on the government, which we call unrest or revolution.

Something similar can happen in foreign policy, too. Even an awesomely mighty and wealthy nation's government may enter into so many commit-

The Limits of Power: Symbol and Reality

ments to defend, develop, or control so many different colonies, satellite countries, or weaker allies, that it simply may not have the wherewithal to do so if its power in more than a few of them should be challenged simultaneously by local uprisings, outside attacks, infiltration, or combinations of all these. Here again a government and nation may find themselves overcommitted, vulnerable to any really serious crisis in their prestige that might precipitate a run by their client countries on all their commitments and promises. To some of the rulers of that great power, their allies and clients may then come to take on the aspect of a row of dominoes: if any one of these smaller countries or regimes should fall because it lacks trust in its great protector, they fear, all the others will fall with it. In this way, the "row of dominoes" image often has its roots in a preceding overextension and overcommitment of resources and prestige on the part of some metropolitan power.

Despite this slim link to reality, however, the "row of dominoes" image most often is a fantasy. In most countries and at most times, the stability of domestic regimes and the orientation of foreign policy, foreign trade, foreign credits, and needs for military equipment and spare parts all are determined by many and diverse conditions which usually do not change quickly, nor simultaneously, nor all in the same direction. A marginal change in the military prestige of a great power usually is not enough to change the balance of domestic conditions in each allied country which produced its foreign-policy alignment in the first place, and which continues to maintain it. This large, autonomous ingredient in the foreign-policy alignment of most countries may perhaps explain why France kept so much of her influence in the new successor states of French Africa, even after the French evacuation of Algeria, and why Britain retained so much of her trade and influence in India, in Pakistan, and in many other parts of Asia, even after the end of her imperial rule there in 1947 and after her final loss of control of the Suez Canal in the crises of 1954 and 1956. Similarly, the establishment of a Communist regime in Cuba in 1959–1960 was not followed by any stampede to establish similar regimes elsewhere in the Caribbean. In none of these situations of local setbacks in prestige—the French, the British, and the American, respectively—did any substantial "row of dominoes" effect prevail.

Power as a Means and as an End

THE POLITICS OF POWER AND THE POLITICS OF GROWTH

Power can be thought of as a means of getting other things that men value. In this sense, the concept of power seems almost self-implied or tautological. To desire any value—wealth, wellbeing, respect, affection, or any other—necessarily implies desiring the power to get it, somewhat as in much of economic life to desire any good or service is to desire the ability to buy it. As men spend money in economic life to buy what they want, so in politics men spend their power to get what they desire.

But if men only *spend* their money, they end up penniless, and if politicians only *spend* their power, they end up powerless. The thrifty

The Limits of Power: Symbol and Reality

businessman is an *investor*. He spends his money on those goods and services (such as valued commodities or capital goods) which eventually will bring him more money than he spent on them. For instance, an investor may buy a factory to produce goods which he will then sell for more money than he had to spend on getting them produced. Thus, to *invest* is to *spend* money to *get more* money, in cycle after cycle, again and again.

In politics some men invest in power. They spend their power on other values in such a manner that these values in turn will bring more power back to them. They are driven, as Thomas Hobbes suggested more than 300 years ago, by "a thirst for power after power which only ceases in death."[4] In order to invest thus, they must use the political support which they have at one time, so as to make more-or-less enforceable decisions of such a kind as to get more support; and then they must use this increased support for new decisions that will produce still more support for further decisions, in an expanding feedback cycle, as far as they can carry it.

In essence it was this that Machiavelli urged his prince to do. A prince who did not wish to lose his realm, he suggested, always had to think and act in terms of power. He had to hoard and increase his resources, not dissipate them; to strive to enhance his own power and prestige and to diminish those of his competitors; to keep the common people passive and content, but willing to fight loyally at his command; to rule by force and fraud, being admired and feared but not hated; and to keep or break his word in quick accordance with whether loyalty or perfidy at any moment would more enhance his power. A prudent prince, Machiavelli thought, should never be neutral in a war among his neighbors, for if he let his weaker neighbor be defeated by some other prince, the strengthened victor would then turn on him. If he helped his weaker neighbor, however, they might jointly defeat the stronger neighbor who was the greater threat to both of them. Or thus allied, even if defeated, the two weaker princes might at least be allies in misfortune. Generally, however, today's ally was tomorrow's enemy, and one's strongest ally was one's greatest threat, for a prince promoting another's power, Machiavelli said, ruins his own.

In theory, this calculus of power politics was impersonal and inexorable. Every prince and would-be prince—that is, every political actor—had to act out of necessity, since every other prince would do the same harsh things to him; and those who failed to do so would soon cease to be princes and would lose all their domains. Much as businessmen eventually will be pushed out of the market if they cannot meet their expenses and make their capital grow at least as fast as the prevailing rate of interest, so governments and rulers eventually will be eliminated from the political arena if they cannot make their power grow at least as fast as that of their competitors. Power politics, in short, appeared to Machiavelli as the characteristic of the large political system which in turn determined the characteristics of all competitors surviving in it.

Clearly, Machiavelli's model of an extremely competitive system is one of the great achievements of the human mind. His political man is an intellec-

---

[4] Thomas Hobbes, *Leviathan*; cf. H. D. Lasswell and A. Kaplan, *Power and Society* (New Haven: Yale University Press, 1950).

The Limits of Power: Symbol and Reality

tual ancestor (or at least a close relative) of the equally competitive "economic man" of Adam Smith and his followers, and of the almost no less competitive animals and plants produced by Charles Darwin's process of "natural selection."

Yet all these models, fruitful as they were in their own day, are only partly true at best. In politics, Machiavelli's model in important aspects is quite false. It is inadequate in a way similar to that in which a mere model of extreme competition would miss the essential core of economics. It is true in economics that buying power for the individual means his power to appropriate goods and services for himself, usually in competition against sellers and against other buyers. But for society as a whole the heart of economics, as Adam Smith already had made clear, is not the power of individuals to appropriate, but the ability of a country or nation to produce goods and services, and in particular the enhancement of this productive capacity through the division of labor, increased and speeded through the ability to exchange such goods and services with the aid of money.

Something similar holds for political power. For the individual, it means his ability to command and be obeyed, in competition with rival commands by other contenders, and in competition with the autonomous desires of his audience. For society as a whole, however, politics in any country—and among any group of countries—means the ability of the whole political community to coordinate the efforts of its members, to mobilize their support, and to redirect their patterns of cooperation; and, in particular, to do all this more quickly, more widely, and more accurately through the manipulation of power in the interplay of the probabilities of enforcement, compliance, and support.

If this is true, we can already now foresee a coming change in much of our political thinking. Economics has shifted from a "bullion theory" that identified wealth with gold, to more sophisticated theories of capital investment and the division of labor, and to theories of economic growth and industrial development. Somewhat similarly, our political theory in time may come to shift from a theory of power to a theory of the interplay of spontaneity and sanctions in the steering and coordination of men's efforts, and in the processes of autonomy and social learning—that is, toward a theory of the politics of growth. Such a theory of political growth and development will be needed for every level of human organization, from the politics of small groups and of local communities all the way to the politics of nations at all levels of economic advancement, and even to the politics of all mankind. Such a theory will necessarily direct our attention to the limits of power. It will make us look to the limits of the scope of power—the things power can and cannot do—and to the limits of its domain, the boundaries where power cannot be relied on to prevail and where the breakdown of political control explodes into war.

THE LIMITS OF POWER AND THE RISKS OF WAR

At the limits of its domain, as well as at the limits of its scope and range, power declines sharply, and it no longer brings about control. If such control is still needed, its failure causes damage to some or all of the actors involved in

The Limits of Power: Symbol and Reality

the situation, and at least some of them are apt to resort either to force, or else to withdrawal, as the most likely forms of damage control.

In a political system, power is used for all basic system functions—pattern maintenance, adaptation, goal attainment, and integration. Where power fails, any and all of these functions may be endangered. Often, therefore, where compliance and persuasion fail, power is invoked; where power fails, force is called in; where force fails, withdrawal is attempted. Where even withdrawal fails, or is impractical, tensions and frustrations rise within the system, and its functions of adaptation must be improved correspondingly; or else, where adaptation and integration fail, pattern maintenance is endangered and the breakdown of the system becomes imminent.

These are the situations that breed war. Full-fledged war is the organized application of the most intensive and greatest force of which a society is capable. To abolish war, therefore would be to abolish this "last resort of kings" and one of the ultimate damage-controls of society. Yet just this must be done, and it must be done substantially within the rest of this century, if all-out nuclear war is not to abolish the whole vulnerable civilization of cities and factories on which our lives depend. We must therefore ask when, where, and how nations get into wars and out of them; and we must ask which sources and forms of wars perhaps can be abolished soon, and in fact which ones even now may be in the process of being abolished or of withering away. Before we can ask these questions, however, we must ask who are the actors—the nations, governments, and influential groups—acting in international politics and liable to get into warlike conflicts.

The Limits of Power: Symbol and Reality

Part Two

THE ACTORS IN INTERNATIONAL POLITICS

International politics generally involves groups and states. In all politics, individuals usually act effectively through groups, through other groups on whom they may exert some influence from the outside, or through influencing some government. And many actions of governments can best be understood in terms of the interplay of the interests and efforts of some of the groups behind them.

Groups
and Interests

What makes a "group" and what constitutes an "interest"?
A *group,* for the purposes of our analysis, is a collection of persons
who are linked by two things: they share some relevant common
characteristic, and they fulfill some (at least one pair of) interlocking
roles. In other words, in some respect they resemble one another
sufficiently to be recognizable as members of a group, and in some
other respect they act in sufficiently different but interlocking ways
so as to be able to cooperate and act in concert "as a group."

An *interest* in an individual, as well as in a group, is again defined by two things: it means both a distribution of attention and an expectation of reward. If something "arouses our interest," it attracts our attention, and it does so either by giving us at once some rewarding experience, actual or symbolic, or else by arousing in us expectation of such a reward.

To get a reward is to get more of something we value, or else to avoid an otherwise imminent loss of some of it. The substance of such a reward, actual or expected, can consist therefore in any one or several of the eight kinds of basic values which men desire: wealth, power, respect (or status), rectitude (or righteousness), wellbeing (or sense of gratification), enlightenment (or knowledge), skill, and affection (including friendship as well as love). Or the reward could consist in the expectation of enjoying any one of these values in a particular desired manner—for instance, safely, and for a long time, which we call "security"; or else enjoying it spontaneously and with a wide range of opportunities for meaningful choice, which we call "freedom"; or enjoying it in a manner preserving our "integrity"—that is, our ability to learn autonomously and to govern our own behavior; or preserving our "dignity"—that is, our opportunity to act, learn, and change only at a speed slow enough to preserve our autonomous control of our own behavior.

Finally, most men wish to enjoy any desired value "legitimately"—that is, without having to expect that its pursuit or enjoyment will lead them into an intolerable conflict with some other basic values that are relevant to them. Thus most men wish to gain wealth, but not at the price of ruining their health or well-being; they seek rectitude but usually will not bankrupt themselves for it; they wish for affection but not at the price of losing all power; nor do most of them wish for either wealth or power at the price of losing all rectitude or all affection. *Legitimacy* is the expectation of freedom from such intolerable value conflict. Legitimacy, therefore, is the expectation of the compatibility of values, or of the consonance of values. Most people feel a need for it; and they also feel a need, conscious or unconscious, for the compatibility or consonance of their knowledge.

Men want "cognitive consonance" in what they know, as well as in what they want. They wish their world to make sense, to add up to some meaningful and manageable, or at least tolerable, whole. In this desire for cognitive consonance they suppress or reject items of information that do not fit into their image of the world; or they may seek, consciously or unconsciously, for some simplified image of the world that will seem clear, understandable, and consonant to them, and that will relieve their feelings of disorientation, frustration, alienation, and anxiety. An *ideology* is just such an image of the world, or a set of such images, which reduces the disquieting and often painful cognitive dissonance in the minds of the people who hold it. All of us have in our minds such simplifying and possibly more-or-less unrealistic pictures of the world. These pictures most often are partly realistic and partly quite fanciful, but in any case they reassure us through their greater consistency and tidyness. Usually we take them so much for granted that we are not even aware of them. We are sure of our own realism, but we are appalled at the ideological blinkers of other people—or other nations—who disagree with us. The less conscious we are of our own ideology, of our own set of helpful but simplifying pictures of the world, the more apt we are to value and defend them as parts of our own identity and personality. In politics, national and international, many men have preferred losing power, wealth, or life to losing their illusions.

There is a much longer (indeed, perhaps infinite) list, of course, of things which men value enough to make a difference to their politics. For most practical purposes, however, the eight substantive values (power, wealth, respect, rectitude, wellbeing, enlightenment, skill, and affection) and the six modal or instrumental values (security, freedom, integrity, dignity, legitimacy, and cognitive consonance) are likely to be at the heart of most of the interests and interest-based politics that matter in international affairs.

Most such rewards are very real to the individuals and groups who seek them. Their judgments of the probability of any such reward following from some particular policy or action, however, are fallible indeed, and their attention to matters and events which they think are relevant may be appallingly misplaced. When a hungry cat concentrates his attention on a mousehole, there usually is a mouse in it; but when the government of some great country has concentrated its attention and efforts on some particular foreign-policy objective, the outcome remarkably often has been unrewarding. Granting that their problems are vastly more complex, it still seems that in judging their own interests, nations and their governments often have done much less well than cats.

This is no joke. During the half century from 1914 to 1964, the decisions of major powers to go to war or to expand a war, and their judgments of the relevant intentions and capabilities of other nations, seem to have involved major errors of fact perhaps in more than 50 per cent of all cases. Each of these errors cost thousands of lives; some of them cost millions. The frequency of such errors seems to hold for monarchies and republics, democracies and dictatorships, non-Communist as well as Communist regimes. It would be interesting to look for evidence whether present-day governments are any more or less prone to error in perceiving what they suppose to be their interests.

Special-Interest Groups

An *interest group* is a collection of persons who expect a parallel or joint reward from some possible course of events, and who are therefore likely, though not certain, to act in some ways in common in regard to what they perceive to be their common chances. This definition enables us to recall the twofold nature of interest, which involves both actual attention and a probable reward, and hence the ever-present risk of misplacing attention and misjudging the probabilities of outcomes and their consequences.

Some of the probable rewards, of course, are fairly obvious. When people buy more milk and cheese, and milk prices go up, most dairy farmers benefit. They receive parallel rewards from the rising prices for their product, and the breeders of dairy cattle and the manufacturers of cream separators, milk trucks, and milk cans also may all gain some share of the joint rewards from the increasing demand for the products of all the industries that cooperate directly in milk production. Accordingly, the dairy industry has long been organized, and has long made known its interests—such as more

Groups and Interests

milk consumption and a higher milk price—to both Congress and the public. As a result, legislators from midwestern dairying states have not been unmindful of their needs.

In the pursuit of this interest, however, the dairy industry has met opponents whose interests conflict with theirs. Within the United States there are groups, such as the cotton growers and the manufacturers of cottonseed oil and margarine, who would benefit if butter were replaced more widely by "the low-priced spread." This viewpoint is vigorously promoted by their own interest organizations, and it is well understood by many legislators from the cotton-growing states. And not to be sniffed at is the menace of competition from cheesemakers of Denmark, Finland, Switzerland, Italy, and other foreign countries—competition promoted by governments trying to promote their national exports. Many of our own patriotic cheese manufacturers may clamor for protection, but if we put a high tariff on, say, Swiss cheese, this might make the Swiss retaliate by raising their tariff on American automobiles. And a foreign tariff increase on our cars would hurt the interests of the automobile industry in Detroit, all the way from its executives to the automobile workers' union, and many of the voters for the Senators and the Governor of Michigan. When a major revision of tariffs is to be negotiated (such as the so-called "Kennedy Round" of mutual tariff concessions between the United States and the six countries of the European Common Market), a very large number of interest groups on both sides of the ocean is involved.

Some of these interest groups may in fact extend across more than one country. American and Canadian farmers both stood to gain from a foreign policy under which some of their wheat went to Western Europe under the Marshall Plan in 1948–1952; and more recently they stood to gain from a foreign policy that permitted them to sell substantial amounts of grain to the Soviet Union and other Communist countries. Both American and British oil companies are interested in maintaining good political relations with the Arab countries where now many of their oil fields and pipelines are located; but Jewish groups in the United States, as well as in Britain, are more interested in economic and political support for the State of Israel in its protracted conflict with its Arab neighbors.

Interest, as this last example reminds us, need not be economic but can cluster around religion, ideology, or any other value men desire. Most individuals have many diverse interests, some of which may be in conflict. A Catholic tobacco farmer in Connecticut might stand to gain somewhat from increased American tobacco exports to Poland, which might follow from a friendlier United States policy toward that Communist-ruled country; but he might also believe that greater United States pressure on Poland might procure there somewhat more freedom for his church. As a taxpayer he might gain from a cut in defense spending, but as the owner of some land near a defense factory he might gain from increased spending for preparedness. As father of a son well employed in a watch factory, he may wish for a tariff to protect it, while as a consumer he would gain somewhat from a low-tariff policy.

When a person's interests are widely scattered, or when he is immobilized by the "cross-pressures" of conflicting interests, he is unlikely to do much to promote any one of them. He will give little active support to any interest

Groups and Interests

group, and he will have little influence on politics. Those individuals, by contrast, for whom one particular interest is much more salient than most others, are likely to push those interests through their pressure groups, and they are more likely to get at least part of what they want. Carried to the extreme, however, such a pursuit of a special interest would give its practitioner at best more and more influence over less and less of the politics of his country and the world.

More General-Interest Groups and Social Classes

Some interests, however, are less narrowly specialized than others. If they still can be pursued effectively and if a large enough array of influence or of numbers of people can be held together in their support, such a diffuse interest will permit to those who share it a considerable amount of influence over a much wider range of situations. It may indeed often produce power of both greater weight and wider scope than a more narrowly specialized interest group could command.

In the non-Communist countries the largest banks, investment houses, and private business corporations, with their relatively well-concentrated top management, their command of high-level talent, their widely diversified holdings, and the high-powered law firms associated with them, usually all are among the most effective interest groups of this broader kind. A list of the United States Secretaries of State and of Defense, together with many of the men at the Undersecretary and Assistant Secretary level, say, since 1947, would read like a roll call of the major groups of this kind; and much the same would hold for many other countries.

Another general-purpose interest group in many countries is the military, either as a single group or somewhat divided into several services. The military usually favors more defense spending and the acquisition of more powerful weapons. In many countries it favors the acquisition of nuclear armaments, the proliferation of which United States policy has in the past aimed at retarding. The military in many countries favors a more authoritarian posture in domestic politics, and a more vigorous pressing of national territorial or ethnic claims against various neighbors. In non-Communist countries they usually stress their anti-Communism, even though experience shows that many such military interest groups or regimes are eager to accept armaments from Communist countries. In addition, their readiness to use violence in territorial disputes sometimes endangers or disrupts the unity and stability of the non-Communist world, as occurred in the 1960's in the near-war between two NATO members, Greece and Turkey, over Cyprus, and more tragically between India and Pakistan over Kashmir.

Still another important group with common but relatively broad interests is the higher bureaucracy, which counts for much in such countries as France, Germany, India, and also, discreetly but effectively, in Britain.

The most general of these occupational-interest groups are the mass media and the professional politicians. The mass media include mainly newspapers, books and periodicals, radio, television, motion pictures, and to some extent the advertising industry. The attitudes of the media toward politics, and particularly to foreign-policy questions, reflects a combination of the views of their owners, their advertisers, their readers, and their personnel—in proportions that vary from medium to medium, from paper to paper or network to network, and from case to case. In critical cases, owning a paper is still a great help in making your views prevail in it. Even the owner, however, must be mindful of the trend of preferences among his readers and his advertisers, and of the limited supply of first-rate talent for his staff: in the last two decades, several newspapers in Britain and in the United States, with strong-willed owners who were in some ways out of tune with their times and environment, kept losing money until they ceased publication or were absorbed by competitors, while other periodicals and their more skillful owners flourished.

The politicians are still more general in the interests they represent, but even so their interests, attitudes, and attention patterns differ in many ways from those of the businessmen and financiers, or of the military or the civil service. They are often specialists in generality. As has often been said, they must act as brokers among the interests of different groups and regions; and they must produce somehow enough agreement on a "national" interest to attract sufficiently broad support to permit carrying on the government of the country in its domestic and foreign affairs. In trying to accomplish this, politicians often find that it is easier to win broad agreement on foreign rather than on domestic matters. For one thing, most voters know much less and care much less about foreign affairs, whereas they more often have a fairly shrewd idea of their domestic interest and of the probable impact of some proposed domestic policy upon them. Moreover, politics, like all decision-making, requires choices which often cannot please everyone, and in such cases it is safer to displease foreigners who cannot vote, and who often cannot retaliate immediately and directly, as an offended domestic-interest group would be apt to do.

Professional diplomats, who must be concerned about the slower but no less real responses of foreign nations, are often worried, therefore, at the ease with which political appointees to the top levels of our State Department, and domestic politicians generally, often produce a national consensus on nationalistic policies that misjudges or disregards the expectable international responses to it. This tendency increases with the size and power of the country, and it is a characteristic weakness of the largest and most powerful nations. The smaller a country, on the contrary, the more skillful usually are the more experienced among its politicians in taking into account the probable international repercussions of their actions.

In recent years, a new and relatively general interest group has been emerging in many developing countries, as well as in some of the most advanced ones, and it may well have come to stay. This new group consists of the universities with their students, faculties, research staffs, and administrations, together with the growing scientific and research institutions and "think industries" outside the universities—such as computer and biological and medical research industries. All of this expanding activity is required by the demands either of a growing technology or of a more complex social and economic organization, as well as of a growing governmental and public-service sector. The resulting growth of the universities and their offshoots is

Groups and Interests

therefore not likely to be reversed, nor even to be appreciably slowed down in the near future.

In the United States, the universities now represent one of the country's larger industries, and together with the rest of education, which they greatly influence, they represent one of the largest and fastest-growing ones. With more than 5 million undergraduates in 1966, about 1 million graduate students, half a million faculty and academic staff, and at least another half million other employees, the universities are becoming a political factor to be reckoned with, even though only one factor among several. In the view of a university professor and former United States Ambassador to India, John Kenneth Galbraith, the failure of President Johnson in 1965 to win the support of a large part of the university community of the United States for his policy of escalating the war in Vietnam may have marked a significant change in the foreign-policy process in this country for the next decade.

In the developing countries, to be sure, the proportion of university students, faculties, and resources is much smaller, but their political potential often is enhanced by the absence or weakness of most other educated groups, and by the concentration of much of the young, educated leadership talent of the country in the student body of the universities. Although student activities and student politics tend to fluctuate, the political relevance of universities and students in many countries is likely to remain higher than it has been in the past.

Other interest groups with some degree of generality are labor unions, farm groups, and churches. Each of these groups has some primary special interest or group of interests, such as wages, employment, and welfare benefits in the case of organized labor; farm prices and rural services for the farmers; and matters of church support, schools, and public morality for the churches. Beyond this, however, labor is interested in the growth of the economy, the cost of living, the availability of housing, the status of the workingman in the community, and the educational opportunities open to his children. Farmers must care about the costs of credit and of transport, and the supply of educational and medical services in the countryside. Churches concern themselves with the entire quality of modern life, including the ethics of the young— which often are a response of sorts to the observed behavior of their elders— and they are concerning themselves inevitably with the relations among the races, which are putting so many of their teachings to the test. To some extent, all these groups represent fairly broad ranges of interests, and many of these impinge more or less directly on foreign policy, and on the political climate increasing the likelihood of war or peace.

All the interest groups named so far are concrete, defined by specific occupations or relationships which leave relatively little uncertainty as to whether a person belongs to a particular group of this kind or not. There is another set of interest groups which is still broader but which is much less sharply defined, leaving far more for uncertainty, vagueness, or controversy in its definitions. This is the set of social classes, or in any case, the set of concepts of "social classes." In some countries, such as the United States, some aspects of the class concept (though not all of them) appear somewhat unreal, while in some other countries class looks like an obvious reality. In all countries, however, a good deal of talking and thinking about politics at one

Groups and Interests

time or another has been in terms of class, or has touched upon notions of class, and in the Communist-ruled countries, class has remained one of the central concepts of politics. For these reasons, classes and the concept of class are definitely relevant to our discussion.

When the people speak of social class, they are often referring more-or-less simultaneously to many different relationships. Six of these relationships implied in the common usage of the word "class" are particularly relevant for political analysis.

First of all, "class" often refers to a *general economic interest* which may link a large number of people who occupy parallel positions in the economic process. Thus, all or most landowners are likely to gain if rents and real-estate prices rise and real-estate taxes are kept constant or decline. The "landed interest" appears as a particularly clear example of such a class interest in the writings of Edmund Burke, Adam Smith, and David Ricardo. Similarly, if prices fall and interest-rates rise, all or most creditors are likely to gain, while debtors stand to lose. This common interest of creditors was well known to Alexander Hamilton; indeed he used it deliberately to strengthen the young federation of the United States. It seems obvious that most employers would gain if labor at all levels of skill were plentiful, working hours were long, and wages were low, while employees and workers would gain if labor were scarcer, hours shorter, and wages higher. Indeed, many employers and many labor unionists incline toward these views.

There is, of course, an opposite "high wage" or "purchasing power" argument to the effect that many employers could make higher profits by selling more goods to better-paid workers; and there is a "labor productivity" argument that many workers would gain if their employers made higher profits which these employers would then invest, according to this argument, in more efficient and productive machines whose more abundant output need not cause unemployment but could lead to greater prosperity for everybody. These arguments, in short, stress not antagonism, but at least partial harmony of interests, among employers and employed.

Just when, under what conditions, and to what extent any of these arguments of "class harmony" or "class conflict" are realistic is still a matter for debate among economists, and the evidence is likely to vary for different periods and countries. In many times and places, however, the clashes of such interests have seemed pervasive and persistent. Noble and serf, landlord and tenant, creditor and debtor, employer and employee, management and labor, property owner and the propertyless, capitalist and proletarian, often have been described as members of opposing classes, and often—but by no means always—have so identified themselves.

Class, however, often does not refer primarily to economic interest. Rather, it often refers to social *status*—that is, to the easier or more difficult access of individuals to the attention, consideration, and respect of other members of the society, and to greater or lesser influence over thir actions. The social status of an individual is his degree of access to deference or respect in his society. It is the level of preference or priority which is accorded to his messages in the network and flow of communications in the society in which he lives. Depending on local custom, persons of high status are given precedence in entering rooms and passing through doors; they sit at or near **57**

Groups and Interests

the head of the table, or next to their hosts; they are listened to with more attention and less overt dissent. Further, their letters are read and answered first, their telephone calls are put through to the head of the corporation or agency, and their wishes and suggestions are at least somewhat more likely to be heeded. As a socially accepted claim to deference, status includes a secondary ingredient of power; as an accepted claim to respect, it implies a secondary element of righteousness.

As populations grow, peoples are mobilized and communications equipment becomes plentiful; the pressure of a growing number of messages upon the limited amount of available time becomes more severe. Communication channels become overloaded, and decision-makers overburdened. The worse the overload, the greater is the need for priorities for those messages that are still to go through, and for those individuals who still are to have access to the powerful or prominent. This process is worldwide, and it tends to increase the potential or actual importance of bureaucracy, hierarchy, and social status.

Social classes are often seen as status groups by their own members as well as by some social scientists. Sociologist Lloyd Warner distinguished six social classes in the United States. He called them the Upper Upper (the old family in the big house in the best part of town), the Lower Upper (the high executive, or professional man, who made his own fortune), the Upper Middle (the local doctors, lawyers, executives, and the like), the Lower Middle (the small businessmen, officials, and white-collar employees), the Upper Lower (the skilled workers), and the Lower Lower (the semiskilled and unskilled workers and rural laborers). He then developed techniques that permitted him to predict with fairly good success into which one of these six groups any individual or family in a small town, or in any local community, would be consigned by their neighbors.

Status is closely related to many kinds of *communication*. Members of the same social stratum or status group often talk and visit more easily among themselves. They often are a bit self-conscious in meeting those of higher status, and they tend to look down upon—or in any case, to be somehow less accessible to—those who seem below them on the status ladder.[1]

Accordingly, social classes often are also communities of more frequent and more freely shared communication. To communicate within one's own class, social scientist Joseph Schumpeter once observed, is like swimming with the current, but to try to communicate across class boundaries often is like swimming against it.

Thus, social classes often constitute something like *subcultures* in their society. The members of a class may live in a particular area in a town, such as the "right" or the "wrong" side of the railroad tracks. They may frequent the same types of places to eat and drink. They may have similar ways of dressing, which identify their "blue collar" or "white collar" status. They may have similar table manners, courtship habits, and expectations of friendship and of intermarriage.

Out of all these experiences of economic interest, social status, frequency

[1] Despite the great value which Americans put on equality in the 1920's—almost as much as they do today—the status-conscious behavior of Mr. George F. Babbitt has provided some sad and richly comic pages in Sinclair Lewis's famous novel.

Groups and Interests

and ease of mutual communication, and the folkways of a common subculture, there may come a perception of a common economic interest, and the
acceptance of special *organizations* to promote it. Thus, labor unions are often
seen as serving not merely some special interest, but also the general interests
of labor.

The perception of a common class interest may become broadened
further to a general sense of cultural or historical *mission*. Noble landowners
may not only feel that they are defending their interests as owners of large
estates, but they may see themselves as the defenders of all the values of
aristocracy, and even as defenders of an entire way of life in which the mass
of commoners ought to be ruled for their own good by this small class of "the
rich, the wellborn, and the wise." Members of other classes, too, can develop
such a sense of mission. Businessmen often see themselves as the champions of
free private enterprise, which they would like to spread to some as-yet-unen-
lightened nations of Asia and Africa, and even, if possible, to some or all of
the peoples and countries under Communist rule. In many countries, a sense
of historical mission has also become part of the ideology of many industrial
workers and other members of the poorer classes. Many workers in Italy,
France, and other countries have accepted some version of the Marxist theory
according to which it is the historic task of the working class to become the
ruling class of their nation, and to use a transitional period of "proletarian
dictatorship" to transform the economic and social system of their country
from a capitalist into a socialist or Communist pattern. Obviously, each of
these ideologies of historic mission—the conservative aristocrat's, the free-
enterprise businessman's, and the Marxist worker's—pictures the world as a
good deal simpler than it is. But each of these simplifying visions can become
a force in both domestic politics and foreign policy if it takes hold of the
minds of a large enough number of people. Whether any such thing will
happen depends very much upon the particular conditions prevailing in each
country, as well as upon the skill and eloquence of its prophets.

In many countries of the Old World, all six aspects of social class
coincided to a large degree for the same groups of persons. Workers were
much concerned about lower or higher wages, their social ties, and their housing conditions; and their disdainful treatment by employers and government
officials and members of the middle class made them acutely and resentfully
aware of their disadvantaged social status. They lived in crowded working-
class districts. Their hands were rough from manual labor. Their speech, their
manners, and even their cloth caps set them apart. Their unions seemed the
chief or only champions of their bread-and-butter interests, and their Socialist
or Communist parties became to many of them symbols of affection and of
aspiration—symbols of their pride, their hope, and their sense of a great
mission. Where these conditions prevailed, class ideologies and class politics
persisted, sometimes for three or four generations, and indeed increased
where economic development exposed masses of newcomers to industry and
city life to some such long-lasting combination of conditions.

In the United States a very different set of experiences has prevailed.
Birth into a class has meant less to the life chances of many people; they (or at
least their children) often have been able to rise in the social and economic
system. New immigrants from abroad (more recently, from Puerto Rico and

Groups and Interests

from the cotton regions of the South) kept taking over the least-skilled and worst-paid jobs at the bottom of the ladder, and thus improved the career chances of former occupants of the bottom rung, and so in turn of everyone else on the ladder. American workmen, particularly those ambitious enough to acquire a better-paying skill, have been freed by the automobile from the crowding of the tenement districts. Lockers installed in factories have enabled workers to wear their own uniforms only on the job; to and from the job they wear ordinary business or street clothes and cannot be readily identified as belonging to any particular social class or working group. Motion pictures, radio, and television—and the ubiquitous and steadily improving high-school education—have furnished very nearly the same cultural models for all strata of society. Higher wages and shorter hours have offered wider ranges of options, including widespread home ownership, and working on weekends in one's own back yard. Unions, once expected to fight for only the barest economic interests of their members, now are seen most often trying to lay hold of an ever larger share of the profits and benefits of the business enterprises in which their members work. To be sure these conditions until now have held to a much lesser degree for many American Negroes, either in the southern countryside or in the big cities of the North. For the great majority of their white fellow citizens, however, the issues of class ideology and class mission have appeared increasingly irrelevant; and even the Negro protest has found expression most often in terms of a distinct people or a race, rather than in terms of class. By now, so many processes have gone so far that it may require a mental effort for many Americans to realize that the conditions for the salience of class politics in many other countries may be quite different.

In spite of what we have just said, however, class perceptions and class attitudes sometimes do exercise a potent (though subtle) influence on the foreign-policy attitudes, and policies also, of even the most advanced and socially well-integrated countries. Our higher living standards make it easy for us to establish sympathetic contacts with many of the middle and upper classes of the world's poorer countries, but we have even fewer direct human contacts with the poor abroad than we have at home. Whatever we hear from our friends abroad about the politics or economics of their countries, we hear most often from friends who belong to their relatively privileged minorities— and experience in Cuba and elsewhere has proven that their grasp of the situation often has been weak. For instance, preference for upper-class contacts contributed to a bias in the treatment of the different regions of Nigeria in the British-designed constitution of that country. British civil servants in the late 1950's found it easier to trust North Nigerian nobles (the Emirs) than the obstreperous and more vulgar commoners of the south and east. When giving a constitution to the newly independent country, they gave the lion's share of power to aristocratic northerners whom they trusted. Within a few years, this arbitrarily selected regime was overthrown, its Prime Minister was left to die in a ditch, and a period of instability and violence was ushered in that was to claim many thousands of victims. Many American businessmen, and also some diplomats, may be looking upon Latin America through the eyes of their associates in those countries, whose outlook may represent the views of perhaps not more than the top fifth or tenth of their population. And Soviet diplomats, in turn, have at times put more trust in the

Groups and Interests

view of small groups of local Communists than in the available evidence of the actual attitudes of the majority of the general population. Such class biases in perception and in policy can be quite real. However, they need not be irresistible. Governments have to weigh the interests of their own nationals, and of the classes and elites of their own countries, against the perceptions and the interests of the classes and elites of other countries. They must do this even if some of those foreign classes and elites seem very similar to, or nearly identical with, their own most influential elites at home. Attention to possible class bias as a source of distortions of reporting (in diplomacy, business, and military affairs) may be an essential precaution in order to protect the national interest.

Groups and Interests

The Power
of Elites

C H A P T E R   S I X

Social classes, as we have seen, can be much more directly relevant
to the politics of some countries than to those of others.
Elites, by contrast, are relevant in every country.
By an "elite" we mean a very small (usually less than .5 per cent) minority
of people who have very much more of at least one of the basic
values than have the rest of the population—usually at least five to
10 times as much on the average, in the case of values that
can be counted in this way. The members of an economic elite
have much more wealth. Those of a political elite

have much more power. Those of an enlightenment elite, such as top-level scientists, have and command much more knowledge, and the members of a respect elite, such as high-court judges, or the bishops of a church, are more highly respected. (In the United States they probably do not enjoy five to 10 times as much respect as other people, but if we try to measure respect more sensibly on a rank order scale, social elites emerge even here.)

An elite usually is a much smaller group than a class. The more-or-less underprivileged classes in most societies, of course, are very large. Fully 50 per cent of the West German population are wage workers and their families. The middle classes, too, are large. Roughly another 20 per cent of the West Germans are members of the lower middle class of small-salaried employees, and more than another 20 per cent are members of the self-employed lower middle class in town and country, consisting of small businessmen, artisans, and peasants. But even the upper middle class of managers, executives, professional people, and substantial property owners, still amounts to perhaps 4 per cent; and the upper class of those of still greater wealth or higher status is still between perhaps .5 and 1 per cent, or between 50 and 100 persons out of every 10,000 of the population. In the United States, too, the upper middle and upper classes make up an even larger proportion of the population.[1] By contrast, an elite in terms of respect or reputation in the United States, such as the persons listed in *Who's Who in America,* constitutes only about .03 per cent, or about three persons in 10,000. Even if we should include their families, they would amount to less than 1 per cent of the population. The elites of wealth, or power, or of any other basic value, are of similarly small size—1 per cent or less of the population.

As a rough rule-of-thumb, therefore, we may expect even a large elite to be at most about one-third the size of the smallest social class, and usually its size is more likely to be one-tenth or less. Only for the very top classes in an extremely unequal society does this difference begin to blur. In France on the eve of the French Revolution in 1789, the nobility and the clergy each constituted roughly .5 per cent of the French population, so that those classes at that time were almost small enough to be thought of as elites.

In principle, there could be as many different elites as there are different values. In practice, elites overlap, but they do so only more-or-less imperfectly. Scott Fitzgerald and Ernest Hemingway in their dialogue understated the situation when they said: "The very rich are different from you and me . . . they have more money." Many of the very rich also have a good deal of power in politics; many enjoy high status and respect; many are highly educated and rank high in enlightenment and skill. Conversely, top scientists and experts are well-paid and usually well respected, but not powerful. Top-level politicians in non-Communist countries, even if they were poor at the start of their careers, sooner or later are likely to become rich; and nowadays they can do so quite legitimately by drawing on their respect and enlightenment rather than their power: their memoirs and other writings earn high royalties, and their purchases of real-estate or other investments are likely to be soundly judged and well-informed.

[1] See Morris Janowitz, "Social Stratification and Mobility in West Germany," *The American Journal of Sociology,* Vol. 64, No. 1 (July, 1958), pp. 6–24.

The Power of Elites

As a general rule, a person who ranks high on any one of the basic values is quite likely to rank high also on other values. This is called the *agglutination* (clustering) of his values. In many highly traditional countries, this agglutination of values is high. The rich have high status, and the status elite is rich; and this joint elite has most of the power, enlightenment, and skill, is most often respected and admired, enjoys the relatively best health and physical wellbeing, and is considered most often righteous in terms of the official ideology or church doctrine prevailing in the country which they rule. To the extent that these conditions prevail in the United States, they will testify to the existence of what some writers have called a "power elite" or "power structure" in this country. To the extent, however, that values do not agglutinate, or no longer do so, the "power elite" concept is inappropriate or obsolete. In the extreme case, one could imagine a country, or a local community, in which all elites would be completely specific, and no overlap among them would be larger than what could be expected from pure chance. In such a country the powerful would have no significant wealth and the wealthy would have no particular influence in politics; and neither group would enjoy any special amount or degree of well-being, enlightenment, skill, or affection, nor would either group be particularly respected or considered righteous.

Reality in most countries, including the United States, is somewhere between these two poles of complete agglutination and complete nonagglutination of values. Elite status in regard to any one value counts for something in one's chances of getting more of another value, but it does not count for everything. In the United States, there is some impressive evidence that the amount of elite agglutination has somewhat declined. Our elites have become more specialized and more open, some of them to a notable degree, and it seems that the American people is continuing in this process of replacing the old, single, all-purpose elite by a pluralistic array of specialized elites connected by a complex network of communication and bargaining, and more widely accountable to a more highly educated and politically more active population. But this process still has a long way to go.

Indications of similar trends have been observed in other advanced Western countries where a plurality of specialized elites has gained at least somewhat in power at the expense of the older, more narrowly recruited, and more highly integrated elite structure; and something similar may also be happening in the more advanced of the Communist-ruled countries. As a result, there is now in many countries a higher proportion of *marginal* members of the various elites, much as there is now also a larger proportion of marginal members of social classes. That is to say, an even larger percentage of the population, belongs at one and the same time to several different groups, oriented toward different life-situations, experiences, and values. This growing proportion of the population, who are in some sense marginal in many or all groups to which they belong, is less likely to respond to the slogans and alignments of class politics, and somewhat more likely to accept the symbols of national politics and national identification. At the same time, however, the experience of being marginal in one's elite or social group tends to make people more critical of prevailing beliefs and practices, and more inclined to reach out for new ones.

64

The Power of Elites

Elites, too, are being modified by this trend. They become more specialized, more open to newcomers, and less agglutinated in regard to the values and relative privileges which their members enjoy. More among their members are in some sense marginal, vaguely dissatisfied, and sometimes more open to new ideas and to communications from outside their familiar circle of experience. Half a century ago, before and after World War I, many workers in the industrialized countries were class-oriented and somewhat internationalistic in sympathies, while many intellectuals, particularly in Europe, were nationalistic in outlook. Today, however, the working men in most of the advanced countries respond more readily to the symbol "people" than to the symbol "class," and many intellectuals in non-Communist as well as Communist countries feel somewhat more uncomfortable in their nation-states, and more critical of existing institutions and national policies—including more often some national policies in world affairs.

Interest groups, if they are large, usually give rise to particular elites who lead them. Most often, these elites consist of the top personnel of the special-interest organizations. Large labor organizations have given rise to an elite of union officials and labor leaders. Business organizations, farm groups, and churches all have produced their own leadership groups and strata. The members of each of these special elites must be acceptable to the members of their larger interest constituency if they are to remain its leaders for long; but at the same time the members of these diverse elites may develop some similar habits, attitudes, living standards, and culture patterns. They may meet each other more often, professionally and sometimes socially. If this process goes far, common attitudes and interests may emerge to unite these diverse leadership groups, together with the more general political and bureaucratic elites, into a broader and more general elite, "establishment," or leading class.

Individual leaders, in turn, are more likely to be accepted by the elite groups on whom they must rely much of the time for support, if they share and express the salient attitudes and desires of the elite members. In much the same way, elites are more likely to be accepted and supported by larger segments of the population if these elites express the attitudes, and do the jobs, which are important to their followers.

Individual leaders can make a significant difference in the outcome of a chain of events by making a personal decision at some critical juncture. Franklin D. Roosevelt, Winston Churchill, Charles de Gaulle, Joseph Stalin, Harry S Truman, Dwight D. Eisenhower, John F. Kennedy, and Lyndon B. Johnson each in his time has made one or several decisions of this kind. Some leaders have been strained to the breaking-point by the burden of decision (as were perhaps Woodrow Wilson and James V. Forrestal), while other leaders seem to have thrived on pressure. Most of the time, however, leaders can only make decisions which are acceptable to their elite collaborators and allies, and to their followers on the intermediate and mass level. The President of the United States, as Richard Neustadt has pointed out, often must act as a broker or mediator among the demands of different powerful interest-groups. Only on relatively few occasions is he free with a wide range of discretion to make a critical decision alone.

On such occasions, however, a single statesman's decision can be fateful. If it leads to success, he may be acclaimed for his boldness and wisdom. If it is

The Power of Elites

followed by failure, both he and his defenders (the statesman himself usually in his memoirs) are likely to deny that this was a freely-taken decision, insisting that there was no alternative, that no other decision could have been taken under the circumstances of the time. Such simplified versions of environmental or historical determinism have often been a last refuge for unsuccessful politicians.

Leaders sometimes can and do make decisions that change history, but they can do so only within the limits of their resources, their situations, and their minds. Usually, a "strong" leader is not only a man with a firm, decisive personality, but also one with a strong group, or a strong coalition of groups, behind him (and these backers hamper his personal powers and acts of leadership, he sometimes finds, if that suits their interests). A weak leader, on the contrary, often is one whose supporters are few, or else are poorly united by weak and inconsistent bonds of attitude and interest.

But there are also limits to the leader's mind. We have already implied that the success of a leader depends in large part on how well his policies and his doctrines fit the needs of his time and place. But the leader has his own needs as a person. He is most likely to adopt for himself only those views and policies that jibe with his own as judged according to the extent of *his* experience and imagination, *his* cast of mind, and *his* limited time and inclinations to consider more unfamiliar alternatives. Leaders thus often are— and perhaps must be—sparing in their mental efforts. And, not unexpectedly, perhaps, so are (or must be) the groups that follow and trust them because the outlook and beliefs of these leaders seem to resemble so reassuringly the thoughts and feelings of the groups that follow them, as well as of the small elites that often form the leader's immediate environment.

So we see that leaders are often in part the captives of their external resources, or supporters, and also in part the captives of their own habits and of their mental needs for consistency and consonance in their images of the world. More often by mere economic interest, or by cold calculation of strategy and power, leaders have been moved and driven by tenaciously held images of the world which became the basis of their popularity with masses or elites, as well as the basis of their own self-image and self-respect. With momentous decisions to be made on war and peace, and with so little and yet so fateful freedom to make them, the existential condition of national leaders in our time often has been close to the edge of tragedy.

The Power of Elites

All-Purpose

Interest

Groups

If an interest group, such as stamp collectors, rabbit breeders,
and those involved in the oil or the aircraft industries, for instance,
is oriented toward a *single* reward, or a single kind of reward, we say
that it has a "specific" interest. In its unity of interest
this type of group is sure to enjoy a certain amount
of solidarity. If a group is united by *several* kinds of expected rewards,
and hence by several specific interests, its solidarity is likely
to be even stronger. And if the common bonds deal with *very
many* common rewards and values, this solidarity

may become general or "diffuse" among its members; they will now feel united not only in regard to this or that specific interest, but in regard to any and all needs, interests, and values that may come to concern them. And each of them may be willing to help any other just because he is a member of this group rather than because of the merits of his particular case.

The relationships among the smallish interest-group known as the nuclear family—consisting normally of husband, wife, and their children—come close to this latter form of solidarity. On a somewhat larger scale, in many cultures today the extended family of kin group has formed a similar all-purpose interest group. In their great days a still larger group, the ancient Greek city-states, approached this feeling of all-purpose solidarity among their citizens. Under modern conditions, the largest all-purpose group whose members can have such a sense of diffuse solidarity is a people, although some of the noblest visions of politics have dealt with the possibility of extending this general sense of solidarity or brotherhood to all mankind.

A *people* is a group of persons with complementary habits of communication. Their ways of speaking, listening, and understanding fit together as a key fits a lock, or like pieces of a jigsaw puzzle. They usually speak the same language (though the members of the British, the Swiss, the Welsh, the Jews, and some other people have spoken more than one language). Conversely, however, even though they speak the same language, Englishmen, Irishmen, and Americans belong to different peoples, and the same is true of the several French-, German-, and Spanish-speaking peoples of the world.

What is essential for forming a people is that its members have a community of shared meanings in communications, so that they can understand each other effectively over a wide range of different topics. A common language, though not indispensable, is clearly very helpful to this end, and a common culture which provides the common meanings is decisive. Such common meanings are based on common or interlocking memories given in a common culture, and on common habits of communication learned and practiced in real life.

Such cultural memories and practiced communication habits become part of the personality structure of each individual, and thus of his own self. Usually, they are learned most easily in childhood, when so much of our habit structure and personality is formed, but they can be learned even late in life (albeit with greater effort and less perfectly). The American people includes many persons who learned to speak, listen, feel, and act more or less like Americans only late in life, but who have become thoroughly assimilated just the same. (This has been a vivid experience for many recent Americans: to feel not merely harbored but included.) Something similar holds true for many other countries of immigration, if they offer newcomers a genuine opportunity to assimilate, closely linked to a substantial gain in the important values in search of which they came.

It is possible, therefore, for an individual to be in transition from membership in one people to membership in another. But it is also possible for millions of persons to belong to two peoples at the same time, if they can communicate and cooperate in both, just as it is possible (within limits) for anyone to communicate meaningfully with more than one partner. Thus, Scotsmen for over two centuries have been both Scots and British. French

All-Purpose Interest Groups

Canadians are both *habitants* and Canadians. Many Bavarians are both staunchly Bavarian and intensely German. American Negroes may consider themselves members of the Negro people in the United States, and also as Americans. American Jews feel and act as Americans, but many of them also share significant communications and solidarity with other Jews and with the people of Israel. Bengalis and Maharashtrians are members of their respective peoples, and at the same time members of the people of India.

As the world becomes more modern, membership in a people becomes more important. The ability to communicate and to understand one another increases the likelihood of mutual trust. It makes for easier cooperation and organization. It facilitates employment and promotion, the extension of credit, the forming of more frequent ties of friendship and of intermarriage and thus of family ties and of the transmission of property. In all these respects, membership in the same people links all its members through common bonds not only of communication but also of more probable joint rewards, and thus through expectations of common interest which have some basis in reality.

As life becomes more mobile, competitive, and insecure in the course of a country's transition to modernity, individuals can rely less on the old security of family and kin, of neighborhood and village, and are exposed even more to the bewildering and threatening changes in the market for their labor, their produce, and their necessities of life. The greater these changes, the more important it becomes to cling to the remnants of security and predictability offered by a common language and culture and common membership in a people. It now is this common membership in a people that promises to turn strangers into brothers, or at least into friends, and to align them for at least somewhat predictable cooperation and mutual support.

Membership in a people thus coordinates the communications, the expectations, and to some extent the interests of individuals. The more quickly changing and insecure the conditions of their lives, the more salient and urgent will be their needs for such coordination. As in many cases of social coordination, much of it is based on voluntary or habitual compliance, but some of it can be reinforced by some probability of organized enforcement. Once individuals have come to desire the coordination of their behavior through the common culture of a people—and usually through a common language—they are also likely to desire, support, and demand appropriate common organizations for enforcement in order to make this emerging coordination of their behavior more dependable.

In this manner, the interest in a common culture and language becomes a political interest. The desire to belong to a common people leads to the desire to gain control of an existing government and state in order to implement this interest, or to create a suitable new "national" state and administration where none before existed. In this manner, the less than two dozen nation-states in the world of 150 years ago have been replaced by perhaps twice that number on the eve of World War II, and by the late 1960's by more than 140 nation-states and would-be nation-states still in the process of emerging.

All-Purpose Interest Groups

The Modern Nation

A *state* is an organization for the enforcement of decisions or commands, made practicable by the existing habits of compliance among the population. Such organized enforcement is an all-purpose instrument. It can serve to reinforce any decision or any command, as long as most of the population will comply or can be persuaded to do so. The more dependable and general such popular compliance, the greater is the potential power of the state. This is true of all dimensions of its power: its weight, scope, range, and domain all can be increased with greater popular compliance. Such compliance, as we noted earlier, can be passive or active. It can be based on mere indifference and apathy, or it can include voluntary positive support even at the cost of sacrifice. Such active compliance and support can be increased most readily by solidarity and by persuasion, and thus it can be increased most effectively through the human communication network of a people.

A state can be used to reinforce the communication habits, the cooperation, and the solidarity of a people. And a people through its community of communication, compliance, and active solidarity can greatly increase the power of a state. This is one of the reasons why the combinations of a people and a state in the modern nation-state has proved so powerful in politics, and why during the last 150 years the nation-states have dominated the earth.

If a significant proportion of the members of a people are trying to get control of some substantial part of the machinery of enforcement and government—such as city councils, school boards, or provincial legislatures—we call them a *nationality*. If they succeed in getting hold of significant capabilities of enforcement over a large area—that is, usually, if they get control over a state—we call them a *nation,* and ordinarily they will so call themselves.

A nation, then, is a people in control of a state. But people and state need not coincide exactly: some members of the people may live abroad, forming minorities in other states, and members of other peoples may form minorities in this one. In every nation-state proper there is one people more closely identified with the state and with its personnel, and usually also somewhat more favored in regard to political power, respect, and often wealth and other values, than are the other peoples in that state. This favored nationality need not form the numerical majority of the total population of the state, but in its claims to influence, preference, and deference it is apt to act like one. Often it will call itself "the majority," or it will be called so by observers, while the other groups in the state will be called "minorities" regardless of the actual numbers in each group.

In Spain, the speakers of Spanish form a real majority of the population, and the Basques and Catalans are genuine minorities. But in India, the speakers of Hindi are less than half the population, and so are the Urdu-speaking West Pakistanis within the total population of Pakistan. The Austrians and the Hungarians together furnished not much more than one-third of the Austro-Hungarian Empire that broke up in World War I, and the ruling Amharic-speakers are a much smaller minority in Ethiopia. In the

All-Purpose Interest Groups

Soviet Union the speakers of Great Russian still are a majority, but the speakers of other languages may outstrip them before the end of this century. Even in the United States, the "white Anglo-Saxon Protestant" old-stock Americans are not a majority, but only the largest minority among the population.

The status of a "minority" often depends much less on its numbers than on the presence or absence of discrimination, or on its kind and degree. French-speaking Swiss are a minority of the Swiss people, among whom nearly three out of four speak German, but most of the French-speakers are in no way treated as a minority and they willingly identify themselves as Swiss. Where minorities are victims of discrimination in a nation-state, however, they are likely to become alienated from that state, and they often look abroad for friends and protectors, either to help them join with other groups of similar language and culture outside their present state, or else to secede and set up a smaller nation-state of their own. In all such cases, dissatisfied and "unredeemed" minorities can become actors in international politics and contribute significantly to the instability of existing political and social institutions and to pressures for more-or-less drastic change.

If such a minority, or formerly disfavored group, however, succeeds in setting up its own nation-state, dominated by its members, then it may quite easily find some still smaller minority, or even some other less powerful numerical-majority population, to look down on, to oppress, and to discriminate against. The ancient Romans told the story of a slave set free by his master, who was asked what he would do first of all in his new freedom, and who replied: "Why, buy myself a slave, of course!" Something similar can be said of many nationalists. Indignant about any oppression of their own people, they eagerly look for other peoples to oppress. The habits of privilege and oppression have entered their minds as thoroughly as they had entered the mind of that long-dead Roman slave.

Empires and International Organizations

When the favored people is a relatively small minority predominating in a relatively large state over many countries and populations, then we speak of this large composite state as an *empire*. Such an empire usually includes a dominant or imperial people which supports and defends its government. It also usually has a metropolitan region around the imperial capital and a periphery of subject provinces or colonies which must submit to various forms of economic, military, political, and social exploitation. These latter receive the benefits of the imperial peace, law, and administration, but they must bear most of the costs of empire in peacetime and during the recurrent wars to which empires are liable.

Writers from old imperial capital cities, metropolitan regions, or relatively favored nationalities often are impressed with the splendors, advantages, and benefits of empire, while observers from the provinces and colonies and from the disfavored subject peoples more often tend to note the sufferings, indignities, and costs which empire entails.

In the extreme case, a nation could establish an empire over other peoples so successfully that its own members might all rise in the economic and social scale to the point where the ruling nation within the empire would come close

All-Purpose Interest Groups

to becoming its ruling class. To turn a nation into a favored class would be indeed the ultimate triumph of nationalism, and such words as *"Herrenvolk,"* "master race," "ascendancy," "supremacy," and the like, testify to the persistence of the underlying image.

The basis of empires is the political apathy of most of their population. This apathy, it was noted, in turn used to be based upon their backwardness, poverty, and rural isolation and seclusion. All these basic conditions are now disappearing in most countries of the world. As a result, political apathy has been dwindling, and the foundations of empire everywhere have become increasingly shaky. The epoch of the crumbling of empires has arrived, and there is very little likelihood that this process will be reversed in any near future.

During the Middle Ages political organization was a matter of five levels: village, district or barony, province or duchy, kingdom, and empire, corresponding loosely and in part to the ecclesiastic divisions of chapel, parish-church, bishopric, archdiocese, and the empirewide or worldwide jurisdiction of the papacy. Much of modern international politics occurs largely on three levels only: the subnational politics of interest groups, minority peoples, and regions; the nation-states, successors to the medieval kingdoms; and the plurality of empires—such as the British, French, Spanish, Ottoman, Russian, and Chinese—that had been prominent in the nineteenth century, only to decline or be replaced by other patterns in the twentieth.

The old worldwide mission of the medieval empire—to unify mankind at least in symbols and aspirations—has been taken over by a new group, the international organizations. Some of these are highly specific, such as the Universal Postal Union. Others are closer to the character of all-purpose organizations, such as the United Nations, without attaining thus far the general scope, salience, and power of the nation-state. Any and all of them can intervene on occasion in the process of international politics, in ways that will be discussed somewhat later.

The result of the interplay of all these trends and actors is a world of states, buffeted by international competition from without and by competing political pressures and struggles from within. Many of these governments and states are highly armed, all are highly fallible, and almost all are in serious danger of some violent collision. Under these conditions, their survival and that of the international system depends to a crucial extent on the capacities of each state and each government—and generally, of each international actor—for guidance and for self-control.

All-Purpose Interest Groups

Part Three

THE INTERESTS OF ACTORS:

PROCESSES OF CONTROL AND CONFLICT

Individuals, groups, and nations alike all are said to act, in politics, "in accordance with their *interests*"—that is, according to their distribution of attention and their expectations of reward. We know that their interests may be inconsistent and their own perception of them highly fallible. But in order to understand how states can act in pursuit of what their leaders think to be their interests, we must first understand how a state controls its own behavior. In particular, how is foreign policy made and executed? What is the place of the foreign-policy sector in the total network of national decision-making? And when does foreign policy take primacy over domestic politics?

How
a State Controls
Itself

All self-control involves the continuous mixing, blending, analyzing,
and selective use of the contents of three separate streams of information.
One of these is the stream of messages from the outside world;
the second is the stream from the actor's own system and resources
(which tells of their status); the third is the stream of messages recalled
from memory. Any autonomous (self-steering) system, therefore, must
contain within itself three operative information-processing
"structures" (we might say "receptors," "channels," and the like) with which
74   to do the job that combining and balancing these streams requires.

Only when it is thus properly equipped can any self-steering system, or for that matter any higher organism, any personality system, any social organization, or any government, find, gain, and maintain its autonomy, selfhood, and freedom.

Decision-Making: Combining New Information with Old Memories

The vast majority of even the most outstanding memories of individual men are stored only in their heads; the memories of states are stored in many places. Of course, the lesser state memories are stored (more or less as memoirs) in the heads of state rulers and high officials, in the heads of members of state elites, and in the more numerous heads of the members of all the state's politically relevant social strata. But the really important memories are stored in the heads of the entire population, *and* in their culture and language. (These stores of words and images and cultural and moral preferences may imply important biases and predispositions toward certain kinds of responses to certain kinds of events—predispositions of which the individuals concerned often themselves may not be aware until the moment of responding.) They are stored in papers, books, and files; in maps, pictures, monuments, and libraries; in diplomatic reports and policy memoranda; in staff plans for war; in the records of government bureaus and of business organizations; in laws and in treaties. (The government—or the government agency, such as the State Department, or the Central Intelligence Agency—which has the larger files will have the "better" memory, if it can find in them quickly and accurately the information that is relevant to the decisions it must make.)

Let us say that a message comes to the United States government about a sudden political crisis in a foreign country. The responsible officer in the State Department has to recall from his memory the most pertinent facts: where the country is and what are the main political, economic, and military conditions prevailing there; what American interests are involved there in terms of American nationals and investments in the country, as well as in terms of our broader political, economic, and strategic interests; what resources in the way of economic or political influence, as well as in the way of bases, troops, ships, and airplanes the United States may have nearby; and what allies we have in the area. In addition to information about the state of our interests and our armed forces, the officer must remember the state of our domestic political opinion, the views of the President and of Congress, and the known preferences and probable responses of our major domestic-interest groups, of the mass media, and of the national electorate.

To supplement his own memory, this official may draw upon files of earlier reports, on memoranda on current policy, and on other written sources; he may consult other officials in his own and other agencies, civilian and military; and he may refer the matter upward for decision to his bureaucratic superiors or to the President of the United States, whose own memories and remembered images and preferences may then become decisive in the matter. Between them, these men represent the effective memories of the United States government in making this decision.

How a State Controls Itself

On the night of June 25, 1950, the message came to Washington that North Korean troops and tanks had crossed in strength the thirty-eighth parallel into South Korea and that a war had started. During the night, more and more high-ranking officials were called back to the State Department. They remembered—and later repeated—a variety of pertinent bits of information. For instance, they remembered how the Western powers had hesitated overlong in the 1930's to oppose the Japanese aggression against Manchuria in 1931 and against China in 1937, and the German aggression in Central Europe in 1938 and 1939. In pondering the expected effects on world opinion of a Communist triumph, and the political and strategic interests of the United States in not letting South Korea be overrun by Communist armies, they also remembered that their country had for some time been a reluctant participant in a dangerous "cold war" with the Soviet Union. They remembered too the view, widespread at the time, that Stalin's Russia was continually testing the resolve of the United States, and that larger Communist attacks would follow elsewhere if any one should succeed. They recalled the state of American domestic opinion in 1949: the indignation in Congress and among a substantial part of the general public at the Communist victory in the Chinese civil war in that year, and at the limited character of the American aid given to the defeated Chinese Nationalist faction. And they were aware of past reports of the strength of American naval, air, and military power available in the region from United States bases on the island of Okinawa and in Japan.

Not all these memories pointed in the same direction. Secretary of State Dean Acheson some time earlier had described South Korea as outside the perimeter of major American national defense interests; and some respected military leaders had described an American military engagement there as highly undesirable. These memories, however, counted for very little in the decision process when weighed against the preponderance of memories making for United States intervention, and within a short time, substantial American forces were fighting in Korea. Apparently one particularly pertinent set of memories was not recalled by any of these officials during that June night in 1950: the memories of August, 1914, when a local conflict between two secondary powers quickly escalated into a great power conflict which engulfed the world. At least none of these officials is recorded as having brought that incident to the attention of the others.

Incoming information also added to the outcome of the American debate on Korea. There was the plea of the South Korean government for help; and there was the willingness of the then Secretary General of the United Nations, Trygve Lie, to cooperate in obtaining a vote in the United Nations Security Council during the temporary absence of the Soviet representative (who earlier had walked out on the meetings of the Council in the belief that his absence would have the automatic effect of a legal veto on all important Council decisions under the United Nations Charter), so as to empower the United States to take military action in Korea under the flag and in the name of the United Nations. Finally, there was the impact of the memories and the personality of the President of the United States, who had to complete the decision on which his advisers had substantially agreed; and

How a State Controls Itself

Harry Truman was not a man to hesitate before a fight that he thought justified.

The bulk of United States opinion agreed with Truman. There was positive rather than negative feedback from Congress and the press, while protests against American involvement in a land war in Asia remained minor and scattered. Outside the country, there was support from America's allies, albeit on a very limited scale, while Soviet opposition to United States intervention in Korea was violent in words but otherwise remained strictly limited chiefly to economic and logistic aid to North Korea. Moreover, the early experiences with intervention soon grew favorable. In October, 1950, the United States forces won a major victory at Inchon. The United States government thereupon sent its troops into North Korea for the conquest or liberation of that country; and they advanced across most of it toward the Yalu River and the Chinese border in Manchuria. The original United States decision to resist aggression in South Korea had become transformed into a larger and far more risky undertaking.

Freedom and Policy: The Need to Make Consistent Decisions

Particular decisions arrived at by such an interplay of current messages and recalled memories, as well as by the interplay of foreign and domestic messages, are not inevitable. Though some particular outcome of the decision process may be much more likely than another, the process remains combinatorial and probabilistic in its nature. Just this seems characteristic of the autonomy of individuals and groups, and of the sovereignty of states—in short, characteristic of self-governing freedom. From decision to decision, its outcome cannot be predicted with complete certainty, neither by any outside observer nor even from within the acting system itself.

Policy is an explicit set of preferences and plans drawn up in order to make the outcomes of series of future decisions more nearly predictable and consistent. Having a consistent policy protects the decision-maker from undoing on one day what he did the day before; from undoing on odd-numbered days the work done on even-numbered ones. The more decisions a government must make, the greater is its need for policy. Once formulated and accepted, such preferences and plans—for instance, for the United States to support and promote the unification of Western Europe—are assigned a preferred place in the memory system of the government and its relevant personnel; and this policy is then given particular weight in the decision-making process, where it may then outweigh the other memories and current messages which conflict with it. Such policies may have to be changed from time to time to meet changing circumstances, but they must not be changed too often if the consistency and effectiveness of the government's actions is not to be reduced or lost.

Tentative foreign-policy plans for the government may be drawn up by one or a few officials. In British foreign policy, a famous memorandum drawn up by Sir Eyre Crowe in 1907 treated Germany, rather than France or Russia, as the most immediate threat to British interests, and British governments acted accordingly during the years that led to World War I. In the **17**

United States, George Kennan has become known as the author of an article in the magazine *Foreign Affairs* in 1947, signed only by "Mr. X," which urged a long-term United States policy of "containment" of any further expansion of Communist and Soviet influence anywhere in the world. The policy was adopted, and Kennan, then still a member of the Policy Planning Staff of the State Department (subsequently United States Ambassador to the Soviet Union, and later to Yugoslavia), had occasion to take part in the execution of the policy which he once had helped to formulate (and which has undergone some modification in the course of time).

A Plurality of Decision-Makers and Decision Elements

THE PINBALL MACHINE EXAMPLE

Even if clearly formulated, a policy has to be adopted. Just as we can think of the entire United States government as a single decision system with its memory and external and internal intake channels, so we can also think of smaller subsystems within the United States—such as major government agencies like the State Department or the Department of Defense, or the major political parties and congressional groupings—as each forming such a decision system with its own memories and intake channels. Any actual major foreign-policy decision would then be made as the result of the interplay of these several contending domestic actors, and any long-term foreign policy would have to be adopted through a similar pluralistic and competitive process.

The making of foreign policy thus resembles a pinball machine game. Each interest group, each agency, each important official, legislator, or national opinion leader, is in the position of a pin, while the emerging decision resembles the end-point of the path of a steel ball bouncing down the board from pin to pin. Clearly, some pins will be placed more strategically than others, and on the average they will thus have a somewhat greater influence on the outcome of the game. But no one pin will determine the outcome. Only the distribution of all the relevant pins on the board—for some or many pins may be so far out on the periphery as to be negligible—will determine the distribution of outcomes. This distribution often can be predicted with fair confidence for large numbers of runs, but for the single run—as for the single decision—even at best only some probability can be stated. To ask of a government of a large nation who "really" runs it—presumably from behind the scenes—is usually as naïve as asking which pin "really" determines the outcome of the pinball game.

A similar combinatorial process, resembling in some ways our pinball machine game, also may be going on in the mind of any individual political leader or decision-maker. He is likely to receive many different messages from the outside world, all bearing on the decision he must make; and he may recall many different items from his memory—both memories of facts and memories of preferences—which bear on his decision. No outside observer, nor indeed even the decision-maker himself, may be able to say which single outside message, or which single item recalled from memory, decisively

How a State Controls Itself

influenced the way in which he finally made up his mind, and the course of action which he chose.

Though it is difficult to predict the outcome of a single run on a pinball machine, it is not nearly so hard to predict the distribution of a series of such runs. (Similarly, in rolling two true dice, you cannot predict the numerical value of any single throw, but if you keep making throws you can, according to fairly reliable mathematical odds, expect to get the number seven about one-sixth of the time, and the number 12 about one-thirty-sixth of the time.) Knowing the probability distribution of outcomes or payoffs on a gambling device, such as a pinball machine, would be the basis for your rational strategy if you had to gamble. Knowing (even approximately) the probability distribution of the decisions of a political leader, or of a political organization, a government, or a nation, is to know something about what we call their political "character"; and it is the basis of any rational strategy that could be pursued in regard to them in politics.

Political Goals and Goal Images

All that we have said so far about political decisions—the bases for them and the predictability of them—does not mean that governments are unlike other groups and organizations—that they do not have *goals* and do not pursue them. Governments certainly do. And some of the most important of these goals are in the field of foreign relations.

Governments may pursue their goals in either a conscious or a machine-like fashion. A *goal (or goal state)* for any acting system is that state of affairs, particularly in its relationship to the outside world, within which its inner disequilibrium—its drive—has been reduced to a relative minimum. If a state is in some sort of disequilibrium or tension—and most states, like most other acting systems, are in some disequilibrium of this kind—it will tend to change some aspects of its behavior until this disequilibrium is reduced. When the inner disequilibrium is fully enough reduced, the goal has been reached. The goal-seeking state (or any other acting system that seeks goals as we have defined the term) will tend to repeat those patterns of behavior and to persist in those states of affairs in which its inner disequilibrium will be relatively less, and likewise it will tend to avoid or to forsake quickly those states of affairs in which its inner disequilibrium for one reason or another increases. Any system, organization, or state that behaves in this manner will tend to approach its goal states, or goals, and to stick with them. It will exhibit goal-seeking behavior, and it will seem to be following a purpose, even if the persons within the organization or the state (be it one or the other) should not be aware of it.

Thus a great power, whose Department of Defense is under pressure from its armed services to establish strategic naval and air bases in foreign countries, and which is also under other pressures to minimize both financial costs and political problems with the host nations, may end up putting its overseas bases into some of the world's poorest and most backward countries, where unpopular and corrupt or oppressive governments may be willing to offer strategic sites for such bases to a foreign power most cheaply or with the least insistence on any share in their political control. As a result, a great **79**

How a State Controls Itself

democracy such as the United States, without any necessary deliberate intention of its leaders, may find itself allied around the world with a remarkable collection of backward monarchies, authoritarian regimes, and military or civilian dictatorships. The *goal image* held in the minds of many statesmen, writers, and voters—the image of a free world as a grand alliance of free countries—describes only very imperfectly the actual short-term *goal* which the United States government tries to approach in seeking such political necessities as compliant foreign allies and strategic overseas bases on the most favorable short-range terms.

Feedback and Goal-Seeking Behavior

In theory, governments (as with many other acting systems) could seek their goals by simple trial-and-error. They could try out different kinds of behavior toward their environment, and enter into different situations in relation to it; and they could then stay with those types of behavior, and stay in those situations (called, as we have seen, *goal situations* or *goals*) in which their own internal disequilibria or tensions would be smallest. Actually, most governments (like all reasonably effective goal-seeking organizations) can do a great deal better. They can use *feedback* information to guide themselves step-by-step toward their goals.

The feedback process is at the heart of all effective goal-seeking behavior. It consists in feeding back to the acting system a stream of information about the results of its own earlier actions. The system thus gets information about the results of what it has just done, and uses this information to modify its subsequent actions. Feedback works in cycles: from *action* to *echo* (that is, to the return of messages about the results of that action), and then from echo to *reaction* (that is—as the next step—either to a repetition of the original action or to an action at least somewhat different from the original).

If the system is more complex, we can think of it as having specific components and subsystems, called *effectors,* through which it acts on the outside world. Soldiers, policemen, diplomats, and administrators of foreign economic aid, all can act as effectors for a government, carrying out its orders more-or-less precisely and effectively. Here again, a feedback process may inform the government of just what its subordinates have done and what were the results of their actions; and in the light of this information the government may modify the further commands which it gives to them. At the same time, a shorter feedback process may bring back to the effector component itself (such as to the local commander of the nation's military force in the area) just what have been the results of his preceding action, and he may take some corrective steps on his own, without waiting for the next order from his nation's capital. Indeed, much of the art and science of administration in foreign affairs, as in other matters, deals with the problem of how many and what kinds of decisions to allocate to the short-range local feedback circuits of the effector subsystems—the local embassy, the military theater commander, the local economic-aid office—and which kinds to reserve for the larger and often slower feedback channels of the national government, or even of the larger national decision system which may include the legislature, pressure groups, public opinion, and eventually the electorate. (A problem of this kind

How a State Controls Itself

arose, for instance, in President Thomas Jefferson's quick decision in 1803 to back the decision of the United States representatives in Paris to buy the Louisiana Territory and thus much of the North American continent. This decision could not possibly have been made by any lesser official, such as the United States' ambassador in Paris—but even when taken by the President, as it actually was, it was without full constitutional authority and was ratified only subsequently by Congress.)

Feedback signals, we have said, may be used to bring about an increase or a decrease in the intensity and/or frequency of the original behavior that gave rise to them. If the feedback always *increases* the intensity and/or frequency of the original behavior, then it is called *positive* or *amplifying feedback*; and it will drive the original behavior of the system higher and higher until some element in the system or in its environment breaks down, or until some essential resource or supply is exhausted. Somewhat as money at compound interest grows slowly but by ever larger absolute amounts, and as a forest fire grows on what it feeds on, so the actions of the members of a crowd in a panic serve as mutual signals, driving them all to more extreme panic behavior. In politics, as Thucydides had already found in Athens in the fifth century B.C., the speeches of competing politicians may drive them to demand ever more extreme strategies in the foreign affairs of their country. The mutual growls of two dogs at a street corner, the mutual insults of two boys in the school yard, the mutual threats or arms appropriations of two competing great powers—all these may escalate a conflict to ever more intense levels of hostility. Escalation and all other forms of positive feedbacks are characteristic of incipient runaway situations. If persisted in, they are soon apt to get out of control, regardless of the moderate intentions of the parties who started them. If political actors—whether persons, governments, or nations—are to remain in control of their fate and of their own behavior, positive feedback must be stopped soon, or else it must soon be slowed down to ever smaller increments of behavior, so as to stay within some tolerable limit.

This is to say that positive feedback must be replaced by *negative feedback,* which will reduce or reverse previous behavior enough to limit its outcome. *Negative feedback* is the essential steering process which underlies all keeping of limits and all pursuit of goals. It requires two kinds of information: first, where the goal (or target or limit) is; and second, where and how distant from this goal the actor or acting system is. The feedback of the actual result of the actor's past behavior will then continue or increase his behavior if it is moving him closer to his goal, but will diminish or reverse his current behavior if it is carrying him away from his target.

Negative feedback, then, is the control of behavior at each step or stage, not by good intentions but by its actual results in the stage that went before. In technology, it is at the basis of the thermostats that keep our homes at an even temperature despite a changing climate, and of the automatic control devices that can land a pilotless airplane or guide a missile to its target. In politics, negative feedback implies information that would suggest that a government continue a policy which appears to be bringing it closer to some clearly-defined target state of affairs, but which would signal a change or even a reverse in its actions if they were moving the government away from its goal.

How a State Controls Itself

Although the actual feedback processes in government and politics are multiple and complex, the fundamental concept of feedback is simple enough to be an effective tool to help us recognize, disentangle, and understand the various negative and positive feedback processes we find in practice. And these processes can include more than the direct approach to goals. For example, with the help of data recalled from memory, an actor can pursue a goal around obstacles or through a maze of detours and diversions. To continue approaching a long-range strategic goal throughout a sequence of tactical twists and turns of short-range changes is close to what we call *pursuing a purpose, or purposive behavior*. Recognizing in each case such purposive behavior among states, and discovering specific message flows and communication channels, together with the particular persons, organizations, and material facilities on which it depends, is a major task of political analysis in international affairs. For as soon as these essential key groups and communication channels (persons and facilities for setting and seeking a particular goal) are drastically changed, or put out of operation, then the large organization or the nation-state which contained them may still continue to exist, but this particular purposive behavior will cease, insofar as it depended on their functioning.

The March of History
PURPOSES, CAUSES, AND THE RANDOM-WALK MODEL

Though much of the behavior of political leaders, interest groups, governments, and states is purposive, much of it is not. At all levels—among individuals, groups, and nations—the communication channels and messages directing them toward their goals are not the only ones that impinge on their behavior. Indeed, several goals and several streams of messages, from both without and within, may be competing for the limited available communication channels and for the time and attention of decision-makers. Some of these competing inputs may be relatively random; and all of them may increase the confusion within the decision-making system and the overload on its channels, facilities, and personnel. This can result in making some part of its output relatively random, and hence cause the whole input-output cycle to be much less predictable in the distribution of its results.

Moreover, each actor depends to some extent on his components which may not be wholly under his control; his behavior can be altered when a critical component fails or otherwise changes. For this reason, statesmen continuously depend (and are judged) on their soundness of body and mind, and the temper of their personality and emotional makeup. Witness such American leaders as John Foster Dulles, Dwight Eisenhower, Woodrow Wilson, and James V. Forrestal. Likewise, nations may depend for some of their behavior on crucial subgroups or leaders, and if these fail or change, national and even world history may be changed. The conflict between the army and the Communists in 1966 changed the foreign policy of Indonesia; the deaths of Franklin D. Roosevelt and of John F. Kennedy were followed by far-reaching changes in some of the foreign policies of the United States.

How a State Controls Itself

At the same time, each actor also depends to a significant degree on his environment, which includes the actions of his neighbors, partners, and rivals. In fact, the outcome of the behavior of *any* acting system depends to a considerable extent on the actions of other actors and on the larger suprasystem in which it is located. As a result, though each actor may pursue a purpose, the outcome may be one which none of them intended. At what time an office worker will get home at the end of the day depends not only on his hurrying and on the excellence of his powerful car; it may depend crucially on the flow of traffic at 5 P.M. Similarly, the success or failure of a nation's policy depends not only on its own power and on the intentions of its leaders, but also on the larger political or economic situation then prevailing in the world.

To the extent that we can predict changes in the subsystem or in the suprasystem, or at least account for them in an orderly manner, we are inclined to treat them as causes. We then say that this policy was discontinued "because" of the death of a chief executive, or that some other policy failed "because" of the changed international situation. Conversely, if we cannot explain to our satisfaction just how and why these critical subsystem and suprasystem changes came about, then we tend to call them accidents.

Together, all these various sources of possible elements of randomness, discontinuity, and unexpected change modify (often quite drastically) the progress of policy, and the flow of history; and they also modify the effects of the underlying probabilities, biases, and "mute forces" of history, which in and by themselves often would have indicated a different outcome. As it is, predicting the outcome of international politics often is as hard as predicting the outcome of a game with moderately loaded dice. If they are very heavily loaded, predicting the outcome becomes fairly easy; if their loading is negligible, some few predictions can be made by using randomness as a rule. But if the dice are loaded to a moderate but significant extent without overwhelming all the other factors influencing the outcome, there prediction becomes difficult but interesting. Since just this condition seems to prevail in international politics, a better model than either randomness or determinism is needed for thinking about peace and war.

Such a model is also needed to help us deal with the persuasive but conflicting partial theories that have been developed by great thinkers in the past. The Prussian strategist Clausewitz, drawing on the experience of the Napoleonic wars, stressed the purposiveness of war started and conducted by statesmen as "a continuation of policy by other means." The great Russian writer Leo Tolstoy drew the opposite conclusion from the events of the same epoch: wars and battles to him were long series of accidents, least intelligible to those most immediately involved in them. Finally, to the believers in economic and social causes, such as Plato, Karl Marx, and Charles Beard, wars seemed to be caused (as Plato said) by money, or (as Marx and Beard elaborated) by more complex social class arrangements and group interests.

A helpful tool for dealing with these conflicting theories and facts is the *random walk* model. Imagine a drunken man staggering around the broad, flat ledge of a cliff, taking step after step at random while a horrified but too-busy-to-help mathematician watches him from afar in order to chart and predict his progress. There is an element of determinism in the random walk: the

How a State Controls Itself

drunkard can only move from where he is, and he can take only one step at a time. Combined with this, there is an element of probability: since his steps are random, they are quite unlikely to be all in the same direction; more likely they will change direction often, and sometimes reverse it. As a result the mathematician, using techniques for analyzing what he calls "stochastic" processes, can calculate his progress. He can say how likely the drunkard is, within a certain number of steps, to come back to his starting point, and on which part of the ledge he is most likely to be at any particular time, and how likely he is to overstep the edge, within what period. If, however, the drunkard should happily be tottering instead all over a hillside, the slope of the hill will add some constant downhill bias to his meandering progress. But again, if this slope is not too steep, the random component in the walk will continue to have an appreciable effect on the outcome.

The random walk of the drunkard has more than a little in common with the policies of great nations, and with the march of history on earth. At every step, the walk starts from a position given at that time; it contains an ineradicable random element, which may be either large or small in its effects; and it is subject to modification by persistent deterministic causes, biases, and influences, which can do much to change the distribution of probable outcomes but usually cannot make any single outcome certain. Similarly, national policies and historical processes can only start at one point in time, and from what is given then and there. They too, are subject to persistent influences, biases, and causal processes, ranging from economic conditions and popular preferences to technical constraints and to the power and resources of particular actors, both within and among nations. Of course, they reflect the purposive behavior and often the deliberately chosen strategies of different participants. But they also include many random or nearly random elements: the random behavior of some components within some or all of the interacting subsystems and systems; the conflicts and collisions among different actors whose strategies may frustrate one another and produce results desired by none; and the interplay among the different system levels, combining perhaps the temper or the headache of a statesman in one country with a national crop failure in another; and all of these perhaps with a worldwide business recession or monetary crisis. The disillusioned comment of the author of the Book of Ecclesiastes—"The race is not to the swift nor the battle to the strong, but time and chance happen to them all"—is a fit observation of the properties of random walks and stochastic processes.

Under these conditions men and governments must rely less on *assurance* and more on *insurance*—and even this to only a limited extent. Knowing the limitations of their powers to predict, they can endeavor to provide. They can make provisions for possible risks which they can only very imperfectly estimate; they can strive to make the risks smaller; and they can adapt their aspiration levels in foreign affairs to their actual disposable manpower and material, as weighed against the resources and reserves which each level of foreign-policy goals would require.

Since international politics in today's world includes many aspects of a gamble, the makers of foreign policy—all the way down to the active and interested citizens in a democracy—need to be familiar with the basic idea underlying the mathematical calculation of what is termed *gambler's ruin*. In

How a State Controls Itself

protracted games of chance, gamblers with small reserve are very likely to be wiped out by the fluctuations in their fortunes, even if the constant house odds in favor of the bank should be quite moderate. Once hit by a run of adverse luck, the smaller gambler is apt to be ruined, and hence not able to profit from any later and more favorable run. The bank with its larger reserves, however, or any similarly well-financed player, can survive even long runs of bad luck, and rely on the chance of doing better at some later stage. The greater the risks and the more uncertain and fluctuating the fortunes of the game, the more likely is the ruin of the small player. The gambler—or the country—with the greater resources can afford more accidents and mistakes, and still stay in the game, while the gambler with scant reserves must be very skillful, and even very lucky, to survive. Indeed, if the game lasts long enough, the bank is apt to break him eventually, anyway. This general rule favors large countries against small ones in the uncertainties of conventional warfare. Against the destructive power of nuclear weapons in a major war, however, the reserves of human life even in the largest countries are now quite small.

Rational and responsible policy-makers must work within these limitations. As for their countries, they can try to provide them with more generous resources and reserves for expected or unforeseen contingencies. As to their foreign policies, they can insist on leaving themselves broad margins of safety: the random-walk model suggests that if some of their steps are likely to be random, they had better stay well away from the brink of the abyss. Finally, as to acting toward their adversaries, they can stay mindful of the imperfect knowledge and control and the probable random elements among the actions taken by the other side; and if in doubt about their own actions—which will be often—they can hold to the advice of the great conservative thinker Edmund Burke, that the statesman should be in nothing as economical as in the production of evil.

Models of probabilistic processes can do more for the understanding and making of foreign policy than furnish us with general philosophical advice. They can tell us what initial facts, relationships, probabilities, and rates of change we need to know, or need to estimate as best we can; what model of the process they imply; and, if the model should be reasonably realistic, what most-likely consequences ought to be expected and what less-likely-but-still-quite-possible alternative outcomes ought to be provided for.

Early process models, based on the rates of airplane production and attrition, and on the rates of training losses and recoveries of pilots, were used to predict successfully the outcome of the Battle of Britain in 1940. Other models have been used to simulate the course of electoral campaigns. Such models could be adapted, in the case of an internal civil conflict (using recruitment and attrition rates of guerrillas and government troops, and perhaps also the rates of shift of political sympathies among the rest of the population, and possibly the rate of foreign intervention on one or both sides of the conflict), to estimate the size, duration, and probable outcome of the struggle, and even the probable size, duration, and material and human cost of outside intervention that would be necessary to control it. Where such calculations were not made, or made poorly, or based on grossly unrealistic estimates, men have died needlessly; and frustrating and disappointing wars

85

have been embarked upon that more rational and realistic forethought could have avoided.

Even at best, however, all such calculations will be uncertain and incomplete for a long time to come. Men still will have to make decisions with their hearts and minds; and so we must not underestimate the conceptual and philosophic importance of understanding the random-walk aspects of international politics. It will remind us that in facing the substantial areas of uncertainty that will remain before us, we shall reveal *which of our own values we shall follow when in doubt:* the values of pride and power or the values of moderation and compassion. Men make foreign policy, or accept or reject it, in the light of what they think they know and what they think they like. Their foreign policy is apt to change not only with any major change in their cognitive perception of the world, or in their communication and decision systems, but also with any major change in their salient values.

How a State Controls Itself

How Foreign Policy Is Made

The foreign policy of every country deals first with the preservation
of its independence and security, and second with the pursuit
and protection of its economic interests (particularly
those of its most influential interest groups). Deeply involved with these
interests—in the case of the major powers, at least—are a concern
with resisting any penetration and manipulation by foreign
countries and ideologies, and an unblushing effort to accomplish some
active penetration and manipulation of their own. Finally, closely linked
to the national security, economic, and clandestine warfare interests

of each major power are its policies of economic aid to foreign nations, its efforts to spread its own national and ideological propaganda in foreign countries, and its support of cultural and scientific exchange missions favorable to that end.

The Search for National Security

Each of these activities is to some extent an instrument to further some or all of the others, but each also tends to some extent to become an end in itself. Each in time gives rise to formal bureaucratic organizations and informal public- and private-interest groups. Each generates a more-or-less distinct network of information flows, images, and memories, as well as a network of material expectations and rewards. In fact, there are many networks of rewards, including roles, jobs and careers, appropriations and contracts, and also internalized standards of success and self-respect among the persons involved in this particular branch of the foreign-policy efforts of their country.

The result has been a paradox. The United States and the Soviet Union—and to a significant extent also Communist China, Great Britain, and France—all are powers so large that no one could abolish their national independence, even if anyone were mad enough to try. Yet it is precisely the United States and the Soviet Union that are spending the most money, manpower, resources, and efforts in pursuit of what their governments, elites, and peoples consider their national security. And the three next largest powers follow them closely in their relative levels of expenditure for their national security—although it is not clear who it is that is seriously threatening their national independence.

The explanation is simple. It is a kind of "Parkinson's Law" of national security: a nation's feeling of insecurity expands directly with its power. The larger and more powerful a nation is, the more its leaders, elites, and often its population increase their level of aspirations in international affairs. The more, that is to say, do they see themselves as destined or obliged to put the world's affairs in order, or at least to keep them in some sort of order that seems sound to them. Members of small nations, such as the Norwegians and the Swiss, who have had long experience in preserving their independence, usually have no such idea. It seems natural to them to concentrate their attention and efforts on preserving their own nation in a world whose economics and/or ideologies they do not expect to control in any case. Only the largest and strongest nations can develop some at-least-plausible image of a world which they by their own national efforts might mold, change, or preserve wholly or in large part according to their own desires; and their fears, worries, efforts, and expenditures go up accordingly.

By now, even such large countries as Britain, France, Japan, Italy, and West Germany all have given up the ambition to run the world, and even to gain or retain large empires. They are in fact willing to cooperate with other nations only to a cautious and limited extent, and hope that they do not have to respond (though they will) to a major direct attack on any country that might pose a direct threat to all. The idea of changing or even maintaining the order of the world unilaterally by essentially national decisions and

88

How Foreign Policy Is Made

substantially unaided national efforts ("unilateralism," as the late Professor Charles Lerche called it[1]) cannot be entertained seriously today, even as a tempting thought, by any powers other than the United States, the Soviet Union, and possibly Communist China. And, even of these three giant countries, probably only the United States is in a position to draft and ship hundreds of thousands—possibly millions—of its young men to fight for its world-spanning concept of national security on distant continents. Professor Lerche, commenting on this situation, points out that "few people at present favor American withdrawal from world affairs. The key distinction is between those who prefer maximum American freedom of action, the 'unilateralists,' and those who emphasize the interdependence of nations for purposes of security and prosperity, the 'multilateralists.' "[2]

National-security interests and organizations thus predominate in the foreign-policy activities of any large nation.

Economic Interests in Foreign Policy

Now we move on to the national interest second in importance to security, and very much dependent on it: the economic, sociological, and psychological structures and processes. According to Marx and Lenin, as well as to J. A. Hobson and Charles A. Beard, we ought to expect economic class or group interests to be decisive, but the evidence suggests a far more complex picture. Important as they are, economic interests do not stand alone, but are linked to political interests which may modify or even override their effects.

In the United States, as in other large countries, such matters as the routine protection of the trade, traffic, and travel of a nation's citizens abroad—and the regulation of the activities of foreign nationals in one's own country—takes up only a relatively small part of the activities of the State Department and the other government agencies active in the foreign-affairs sector. More substantial private economic interests in the United States, as in other countries with predominantly private-enterprise economies, are involved in American long-term private investments abroad, such as copper and iron mines, sugar and banana plantations, and telephone companies and other private utilities in Latin America; or oil fields in Venezuela, Libya, Saudi Arabia, and Iran. Professor Raymond Vernon reminds us of the fact that:

. . . nearly half of *Fortune's* 500 largest U.S. companies today have extensive overseas investments in plants, mines, or oil fields, representing an aggregate stake of fifty-billion dollars. A score or two of these large companies now have a third or more of their total assets abroad; even a greater number derive a third or more of their income from foreign sales through one channel or another. If one were to list every large U.S. corporation that owns and controls producing facilities in half a dozen or more countries abroad, the roster would contain about two hundred names. A European list of the same sort would be considerably shorter, covering

[1] Charles O. Lerche, Jr., *The Uncertain South* (Chicago: Quadrangle Books, 1964).

[2] Burton M. Sapin, *The Making of United States Foreign Policy*, Vol. 10 (Washington, D.C.: The Brookings Institution, 1966), p. 48.

How Foreign Policy Is Made

only thirty or so cases. And the overseas stakes of the companies on such a roster would not be as much as one-fifth of the U.S. commitment.[3]

The United States government is expected to protect to a considerable extent the private interests of its citizens abroad; and many of the interest groups just named are sufficiently well organized and politically well connected to make sure that this is done.

The results may be more favorable to United States citizens, however, than they are to foreigners. As private and public loans are repaid by the debtor countries, and as profits from private investments are repatriated, there is a net transfer of wealth from the developing country to the developed one. (For example, in nine of the 10 years between 1952 and 1961, more money moved from Latin America to the United States than flowed in the opposite direction.[4]) This fact is not often perceived by American newspaper readers, who are more aware of the wealth that moves from the United States to the developing countries.

In addition to the international flows of commodities or money, American economic interests abroad include the acquisition of titles of ownership of land, buildings, mineral resources, and productive installations. (Such titles are acquired in foreign countries either by American citizens directly, or indirectly by corporations and holding companies in which American capital or business firms are involved.) Finally, American economic interests may include the preservation or acquisition of particularly favorable conditions for buying, for selling, or for establishing credit for American business firms in those foreign countries which are in some ways relatively dependent on the United States. Thus, in pre-Castro days, Cuba obtained many of its imports, such as textiles, from the United States, although these were not cheap in the world market; and Cuba bought relatively little from Japan, even though Japanese goods of equal quality would have been cheaper. And the Japanese themselves in the late 1950's did not push their exports to Batista's Cuba since, as one of their spokesmen said privately, they did not wish to offend the United States by impinging on our favored market.

Even though such conditions seem to lend some support to the classic theories of imperialism, their evidence must be confronted with a fundamental fact. In the half century since 1913, foreign investments and all foreign economic transactions have formed a declining proportion of the gross national product of all major countries. Similarly, world trade and the international flow of payments have grown more slowly than has the world's industrial production, or its production of services. If the classic theories of imperialism had given an adequate picture of reality, the opposite should be the case. As it is, all economic interests and interest groups oriented to foreign trade and investment command only a small and declining share of the gross national product—and thus probably in the long run, a declining share of political influence and national attention. In the United States in the early 1960's, this share was about 7 per cent; and it was about 5 per cent in the Soviet Union. Even if the latter's collectivist economy had been adapted to

[3] Raymond Vernon, "Multinational Enterprise and National Sovereignty," *Harvard Business Review*, Vol. 45, No. 2 (March-April, 1967), pp. 156, 158.
[4] Paul Rosenstein Rodan, oral communication, M.I.T., 1961.

How Foreign Policy Is Made

the exploitation of its satellite countries, the amounts would have been marginal.

The evidence seems more nearly compatible with what the late economist and sociologist Joseph A. Schumpeter predicted. In all major countries, the national security complex of the armed forces, the propaganda, intelligence, and political warfare services, and the major industries and special technological organizations supplying a substantial part of their output to the national security systems, have tended to form to some extent a self-perpetuating interest group of their own. In the United States, as in some other countries, these groups have included the military, the civilian "defense intellectuals" and strategists, and parts of the arms, aerospace, and electronics industries. There is reason to think that at least some similar congealing of occupational, professional, technological, and ideological interests may also have occurred in some sectors of the elites of the Soviet Union and of Communist China. Similar complexes are observable, though to a much lesser extent, in such middle-rank powers as France and Britain, and additional interest clusters of this kind may be re-emerging in West Germany and in Japan.

Some of the rewards sustaining such a "security complex" in each major country are obviously economic; but to a much larger extent than previously assumed, many of the most salient rewards are sociological and psychological. These are rewards in terms of social status and professional role; of individual and collective self-image and self-respect; of the consistency or "cognitive consonance" of one's previously acquired image of the world; of one's sense of belonging to a group; and of the need to see dignity and meaning in one's past and present actions.

According to Schumpeter, "war hawks" (the "hawks," enemies of the "doves") are a self-perpetuating flock of birds, for he expects that any major interest group with a military or warlike orientation will think up endless rationalizations for warlike policies—that is, for acting out over and over again the patterns of behavior which they have previously learned. President Dwight D. Eisenhower's worried remark in his farewell address about the influence of the "military-industrial complex" in the United States suggests that Schumpeter has not remained alone in his misgivings. Conditions will, it is hoped, improve in the not-too-distant future.

Schumpeter himself distinguished between warlike interest groups which were decisively aided and strengthened by the entire historical, sociological, and ideological structure of their countries and cultures (such as in the cases of Imperial Germany and Japan at the time of World War I) and the far weaker warlike interest groups and elites in such basically democratic countries as Great Britain, where the character of the entire society (in his view) made an early renunciation of empire probable—a prediction which events confirmed. There is little doubt that he would have counted the United States, like Britain, among the basically democratic countries where warlike elite groups would at most be quite shallowly rooted and would not long endure. In any case, there is ample evidence that in the nuclear age most members even of military-industrial coalitions of interest groups are not suicidally inclined. There is also evidence that the executives of large corporations who come to serve in the Department of Defense are most often rather

91

How Foreign Policy Is Made

level-headed personalities; that the whole American political system is irremediably pluralistic; and that it is, therefore, most often likely within one or two decades to encourage compromise and moderation.

Whether the United States and the world will have these next two decades to survive in will depend, however, in large part on the foreign policy that is made here and now. The instruments that make this policy in the United States are, again, plural. Traditionally first among them is the Department of State, which also has the task of producing some coherence among the activities of other government agencies in international affairs.

In the early 1960's, the United States Department of State employed about 24,000 persons. About 14,000 of these were United States citizens, approximately half of whom served abroad, as did the 10,000 foreign nationals employed by the Department. The core of the American personnel was about 3,600 professional Foreign Service officers, supplemented by another 1,200 Foreign Service Reserve officers; and about two-thirds of all these professionals were serving overseas. The State Department in April, 1965, had five geographic bureaus which divided among themselves responsibility for most of the areas of the world, and a number of functional bureaus, with tasks cutting across the geographic regions. The organization is shown in Fig. 1.

Of these bureaus, the geographic ones are the largest and in many ways the most important. Since they deal with different areas and governments, they sometimes develop somewhat different perspectives on certain policy problems. Thus the Bureau of European Affairs and the Bureau of African Affairs each may be aware of somewhat different aspects of the problem of the remaining Portuguese colonies in Africa. And even though both bureaus are expected to agree on basic policy objectives, they may disagree for a long time about tactics—about what should in fact be done. The functional bureaus, such as Economic Affairs, or Educational and Cultural Affairs, have less direct influence on general policy in an area, but they must be consulted where their particular competence is concerned.

The actual decisions are made in stages. (Of course, only an extremely simplified version can be given here.) Some policy alternatives are implicitly stressed, and others perhaps already foreclosed, by the way the United States Ambassador has worded his report from the foreign country where he is stationed. Another stage comes in the evaluation of this report by the desk officer responsible for dealing with the affairs of that country in one of the Department's geographic bureaus; and policy may take shape in the "position paper" (the recommendation for policy or action) which this officer may draft. This draft is then read by the desk officer's superior, who may endorse, revise, or reject it.

If the revised draft moves on, it goes to higher levels. Then functional bureaus may have to be consulted, clearance from other bureaus may have to be obtained, and meetings may have to be held to adjust the remaining differences of viewpoints. If the draft survives all this (as it usually does), an agreed-on version of a policy decision or directive will have been drafted, acceptable in language—and most often also in substance—to all the responsible officials and bureaus concerned, usually including an Assistant Secretary of State or his deputy. If sufficiently important, this version then goes up to the Under Secretary for Political Affairs, or still higher to the Under Secre-

How Foreign Policy Is Made

DEPARTMENT OF STATE

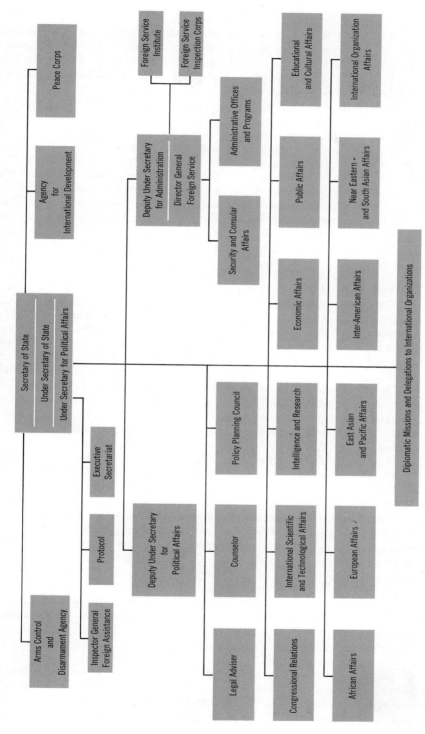

FIGURE 1. *Department of State personnel chart.* (Washington, D.C.: Government Printing Office, 1967–68, p. 622.)

tary of State, or to the Secretary of State himself. Any of these can send the draft back, of course, for further changes, or conceivably could reject it altogether. Otherwise the approved text, with a final checking of its wording, goes to the encoding room and is encoded there and cabled back to the Ambassador.

Within the Department, this whole process resembles less the workings of a pinball machine or other mixed device of chance and skill than that of a carefully arranged set of screens or filters. Tradition and precedent can do much to ensure the consistency of new decisions made in accordance with those taken in the past, and Foreign Service officers and the entire State Department can be relied on to pay them very serious attention. A great deal of policy in all countries consists in "getting on with it"—with completing what has been started, and with repeating what has been done before. There is rarely time even among the top officials for deep thought leading to radically new departures, and the habit is not encouraged among the junior ranks. In addition, State Department officers at all levels are perceptive of consensus, and sensitive to atmosphere. They are usually well aware of unspoken agreements on matters and images that are currently being taken for granted, and that mark the subtle boundary between acceptable and unacceptable policy suggestions. In the light of these, they make only those recommendations they feel will survive the sifting process. Cross-checking with other bureaus makes these restrictions still more narrow. Finally, the heads of bureaus and the higher officers in the Department use their memories and judgment to ensure that the emerging policy is consistent with other policies of the Department and with the current overall policies of the government of the United States. In this manner, the Department most often functions as an assembly line of decisions which turns out a fairly dependable product.

The matter becomes more complicated as other executive agencies have to be consulted, such as the Department of Defense, the Central Intelligence Agency, or the Atomic Energy Commission, each with its own needs and perspectives which may differ somewhat from those of the State Department. The White House staff may add its own viewpoints; and the final policy decision may have to be made in the inter-agency National Security Council or by the President himself.

The results of this larger executive-policy process are less uniform and harder to predict than were those within the State Department. But the matter is not yet ended. Even the President's decision may require an appropriation from Congress to carry it out. Or it may depend for its success on the support of the press and of public opinion (including nowadays even the opinion polls). Or it may require the support or at least the acquiescence of key interest groups, such as big business or labor, or of particular regional or ethnic minorities. And the hard fact is that none of these is under anyone's complete control; they cannot be coerced by even a potent combination of leadership appeal and the skillful use of mass media. If they cooperate, it is only by voluntary consensus.

At this point we may remember the story of the American expert on Soviet affairs who pitied his opposite number in the Soviet Union—for that harried Russian had the much harder task of predicting the next policy moves produced by the inscrutable political processes of the United States. To this

How Foreign Policy Is Made

we must add the consideration that the outcomes of our policies, like those of the policies of other countries, depend often on the support of other nations, and particularly of our major allies, as well as on the moves made by our adversaries—neither of whom we control. The final result of all these processes is the probabilistic combination of firm persistence, careful planning, massive drift, and random accident which is so characteristic of international politics.

Two semiautonomous agencies within the State Department are the Agency for International Development (AID) and the United States Information Agency (USIA). Subordinate to the Secretary of State, each agency has its own head, hierarchy, and geographic and functional subdivisions. In 1962, AID employed about 15,000 persons, and USIA about 11,000. Of these, 7,000 and 4,000, respectively, were United States citizens. A third semiautonomous agency in the State Department, the Arms Control and Disarmament Agency (ACDA), has a smaller staff. All together, the State Department, with these agencies, employed in the mid-1960's over 50,000 persons, divided about half-and-half between American citizens and foreign nationals. Nearly four-fifths of all these, including practically all the foreign nationals, are employed abroad. There seems little doubt that this deployment of manpower abroad has outgrown the comparable efforts by the Soviet Union, as well as those of any other country in the world.

Even with an effort of this size, however, the State Department does not rank first among the agencies employing and deploying American civilians abroad. The Department of Defense in 1962 accounted for 58 per cent of all United States civilians employed abroad by some 28 Federal agencies, as against 37 per cent employed by the State Department and 5 per cent employed by all the rest.[5] In addition, of course, the Department of Defense is responsible for many hundreds of thousands of United States troops stationed abroad, mainly in Asia and Europe.

The geographic distribution abroad of State Department personnel and other United States civilian employees is shown in Table 9.

The rank order of the top 18 countries indicates some of the changes which have occurred since 1945 in the foreign-policy interests and efforts of the United States. Our "special relationship" to England does not seem to be what it once was. Among both State Department employees and other United States civilian overseas personnel, West Germany now takes first place while Britain ranks only eighth. Our interests seem concentrated not so much on stable allies as on countries where an opportunity for United States influence and power is combined with a perception of some insecurity or threat. Thus among our State Department personnel abroad, Italy, France, and the Philippines all outrank England; and Iran and Turkey outrank Canada. In the distribution of all our citizens in federal overseas employment, the emphasis on possible power confrontation and on Asia is even clearer: here Korea outranks Canada, and Thailand outranks India and Mexico. The emphasis in the deployment of most of our personnel abroad seems to be on

[5] Report of the Committee on Foreign Affairs Personnel (Chairman, Christian A. Herter), *Personnel for the New Diplomacy* (Washington, D.C.: Carnegie Endowment for International Peace, December, 1962), p. 5.

How Foreign Policy Is Made

	State Department			All U.S. Agencies	
Rank	Country	Number	Rank	Country	Number
1	Germany	427	1	Germany	4,500
2	France	375	2	Japan	3,200
3	Mexico	243	3	France	2,200
4	Philippines	240	4	Ryukyus	2,100
5	Italy	224	5	Korea	1,400
6	Japan	204	6	Philippines	960
7	Brazil	197	7	Italy	820
8	England	169	8	England	740
9	India	167	9	Spain	560
10	Iran	126	10	Vietnam	560
11	Cyprus	124	11	Turkey	540
12	Turkey	122	12	Brazil	500
13	Greece	122	13	Canada	460
14	Canada	118	14	Thailand	450
15	Switzerland	117	15	Iran	420
16	Lebanon	111	16	Pakistan	410
17	Pakistan	110	17	India	400
18	Thailand	105	18	Mexico	400
19	*Subtotal*	3,301	19	*Subtotal*	17,620
20	*Rest of World*	3,909	20	*Rest of World*	13,000
21	*Grand Total*	7,210	21	*Grand Total*	30,600

Source: Computed from data in Burton M. Sapin, *The Making of United States Foreign Policy* (Washington, D.C.: The Brookings Institution, 1966), Appendix C.

action, rather than on listening to or communicating with powers, no matter how large, over whom our influence is small or lacking. The Soviet Union, the third largest and second most powerful nation on earth, does not even appear on our chart. In 1964 no more than 57 State Department personnel were stationed there; and employees of other agencies brought the total of United States civilians stationed there to only 69.[6]

The corresponding total of State Department personnel stationed among the 480 million people of India is 167; for the 700 million on the mainland of China it is zero. Together the Soviet Union, India, and mainland China comprise nearly half the human race and nearly a quarter of the world's income. Yet these three huge countries in 1964 had stationed in them only about 3 per cent of our State Department personnel abroad; and in the spring of 1967, lengthy deliberations were held in the United States Senate, as to whether it would be safe or wise to agree to the exchange of an additional dozen or so consular officials with the Soviet Union, even though the proposed agreement finally passed that body. Whether a "hot line" of teletype equipment between the White House and the Kremlin can fully compensate for the scarcity of diplomatic and human contacts remains to be seen.

Although the distribution abroad of United States diplomats and other

[6] Sapin, *op. cit.*, Appendix C, next to p. 400.

How Foreign Policy Is Made

government personnel is highly uneven, their numbers are relatively large in all countries where current United States power, influence, and interests are concentrated. Were we to add to the more than 33,000 United States civilian officials abroad the 25,000 businessmen, the 30,000 missionaries, the 10,000 educators and students, and the members of our armed forces, together with their dependents, we would finally arrive at Harlan Cleveland's grand total of about 1.6 million "overseas Americans" who are living abroad in any one year in this new period of American worldwide expansion—in addition to the over 4 million Americans traveling abroad each year.

To these 1.6 million relatively permanent overseas Americans there must be added the nearly 100,000 foreign nationals directly employed by the United States government, not to mention the much larger number of foreign nationals employed by American private individuals and corporations. But even then the count is incomplete, for the Central Intelligence Agency of the United States does not publish either its budget nor the number of its employees, American or foreign. Even the order of magnitude of its aggregate operations can only be guessed at (it has been estimated as being similar to or larger than that of the State Department), though some of its indirect operations, often through unsuspecting American or foreign organizations and individuals, have made headlines around the world.

This United States effort at organized intelligence operations, combined with various forms of clandestine and psychological warfare, has its roots in World War I, and even more in World War II, when the United States, like all major powers, engaged in a wide range of such activities. After World War II, and with the rise of the Cold War, this United States effort was further developed and adapted specifically to offset and overcome the world-wide political pressure of the Soviet Union, its close governmental allies, and its unofficial allies or instruments, the Communist parties of the world. In these parties, together with the international "apparatus" of the Communist International and its successor organizations and in the numerous "front organizations" and "transmission belts," as well as in its own military and civilian intelligence organization, the government of the Soviet Union had at its disposal a powerful range of instruments to influence world politics and the internal events in many developing or crisis-ridden countries. (Despite occasional brief propaganda successes, however, its actual influence in such affluent and stable countries as the United States and Britain, and in the other English-speaking countries, Switzerland, and the Scandinavian countries, was always very small.)

When the United States after 1945 moved into a worldwide contest with these Soviet-directed or otherwise Communist-ruled organizations, it acted as its people usually do in contests: it proceeded enthusiastically to mount a much bigger and better effort than its adversaries. In this, so far as one can see into the dark waters of underground warfare, they have succeeded. Today the intelligence and political warfare efforts of the CIA and related organizations are probably larger and better organized than those of the corresponding Soviet or Chinese organizations which oppose them in the world arena. This success has brought with it its own irony. When Communist penetration and propaganda appeared to be intensely active and increasingly successful, and the United States seemed passive and unconcerned, nationalist sentiment in

How Foreign Policy Is Made

many countries saw Communism as the main threat to national independence. Many nationalists vigorously opposed Soviet or Communist influence and looked to the United States for help. Now that in many countries the United States seems to be the stronger, more active, and much better staffed and financed contestant, many nationalists are sitting back, or even are fearful lest we gain too much influence over their countries.

Here, and in other sectors of world politics, world economics, and world opinion, the very magnitude of our thrust into international affairs has produced some limiting or countervailing responses from the international environment. As in the case of every other superpower in the past, the essentially unilateral expansion of our power and influence in the world may turn out to be a self-limiting process. "The size and obtrusiveness of American representation," testified a former United States Ambassador to the Congo before a subcommittee of the Senate, "sometimes constitute an irritant in our foreign relations that is little recognized by the American public. There are places in which the American mission is as large as the Foreign Office of the host country."[7]

The matter is, of course, not just one of display, such as whether American government personnel in a foreign country are conspicuously concentrated in one large building, (as many of them are in London) or whether they are more discreetly dispersed in several smaller ones (as they are in New Delhi). It is a matter of substance; of the greatly increased actual size and power of the American effort to influence the conduct of foreign nations. Nevertheless, we are continuing this ambitious effort. "Indeed," the same Ambassador continued in his memorandum to the Senate subcommittee, "this writer hesitates even to call attention to the possibility of reduction in force for fear of playing into the hands of those interested not so much in economy as in fleeing from America's obligations as a world power."[8]

What drives us to this effort, and what maintains this image of our obligations? To what extent is it a network of clear-cut treaty obligations with authentic governments of sovereign foreign nations? To what extent is it the automatic logic of the process of international conflict, in which we and our rivals and adversaries are becoming locked ever more tightly? To what extent is it the popular image of a "power vacuum" out there in the developing countries, which is drawing us irresistibly into increasing efforts and commitments? And to what extent is it the result of our domestic political process, together with the domestic effects of our own earlier commitments?

[7] Edmund A. Gullion, "The American Diplomatist in Developing Countries," in Sen. Henry M. Jackson (ed.), *The Secretary of State and the Ambassador*, Jackson Subcommittee Papers on the Conduct of American Foreign Policy (New York: Praeger, 1964), p. 196.
[8] *Ibid.*, p. 197.

How Foreign Policy Is Made

The
Foreign-Policy
Sector

In early 1967, in the words of a well-informed Washington correspondent, the United States Secretary of Defense, Robert S. McNamara, was "in charge of 4 million people and $175 billion worth of property, including 5,000 nuclear warheads."[1] The manpower directly controlled by the Department includes about 3 million members of the armed forces and 1 million civilians. In 1966 it spent nearly $60 billion (not counting at that time the additional funds requested by President

[1] Douglas Kiker, "The Education of Robert McNamara," *The Atlantic* (March, 1967), p. 49.

Johnson for the Vietnam war); and by March, 1967, expenditures for defense stood at $74 billion per year. These sums in each year amounted to more than half the total budget of the federal government of the United States.[2] "The military establishment," wrote Adam Yarmolinsky, a former Deputy Assistant Secretary of Defense for International Security Affairs, in 1967, "is not just the biggest organization in the world; it is bigger by several orders of magnitude . . . than any other government department. In fact, it is bigger than all the other government departments put together."[3]

This huge block of human and economic effort and concern inevitably generates a vast collection of social, political, and economic interests, corresponding to its size. This size, and presumably these interests, equaled in 1967 nearly 10 per cent of the American gross national product. It amounts to considerably more than the total foreign trade of the United States, both exports and imports, which add up to little more than 7 per cent of our GNP; and it is roughly equal to the sum total of all American investments abroad, and about 10 to 20 times as large as the total annual returns from them. Eighty years ago our defense establishment had been considered an instrument for the protection of our interests in the international arena. Today it has itself become the largest interest among them.

The implications have been spelled out by Mr. Yarmolinsky in admirably clear language. All major decisions made by the Secretary of Defense and the other high officials in the Pentagon touching upon matters of policy, procurement, equipment, new weapons systems, strategies, and international arrangements or commitments, Mr. Yarmolinsky reminds us:

. . . involve a balancing of values and risks. These are values and risks not only for the country, and often for the world, but also for interest groups within the Pentagon, across the Potomac, and down Pennsylvania Avenue to the Capitol. The pressures for some accommodation of these competing forces are enormous, and in part because of the complexity of the issues, the opportunities for compromise are not inconsiderable. Even in the first kind of decision, there is room for accommodation. A "yes" on one issue may be balanced by a "no" on a related one. On the other hand, an unbroken series of "no" answers to any bureaucracy tends to inhibit communication altogether, rather like the labor relations concept of failure to bargain in good faith. No Secretary of Defense can regularly reject proposals from his military advisers, particularly where both their professional competence and the lives of American boys are at issue; and no analytical arguments will modify the effect of a blanket rejection on the continuing workable relationship between the Secretary and the generals. Indeed, the remarkable thing is not how many compromise decisions are made in the Pentagon, in the face of all the pressures for compromise, but how few.

It is here, if anywhere, that the so-called military-industrial complex comes into play. When President Eisenhower, as he left office, warned of the growing power of the military-industrial complex, he may only have been giving vent to his frustrations at his inability to hold down the defense budget. At the end of his term, he still thought a President ought to be able to give orders like a general, and when he found the orders were not directly obeyed, he chose to blame it on a conspiracy.

2 Adam Yarmolinsky, "How the Pentagon Works," *The Atlantic Monthly* (March, 1967), p. 56; copyright © 1967 by the Atlantic Monthly Company, Boston, Mass. 02116.
3 Yarmolinsky, *op. cit.,* p. 58.

The Foreign-Policy Sector

Surely the military-industrial-congressional complex is not a conspiracy. But there are coincidences of interest among the military project officer who is looking for a star, the civilian who sees an opening for a new branch chief, the defense contractor who is running out of work, the union business agents who can see layoffs coming, and the congressman who is concerned about the campaign contributions from business and labor as well as about the prosperity of his district. Each of these constellations of interests wants to expand the defense establishment in its own direction. In the early sixties, the Pentagon was an expanding universe, one of the few fortuitous advantages McNamara enjoyed at the beginning of his tenure. Resources that were cut out of unnecessary activities could often find employment in areas that needed to be strengthened. A similar situation prevails today. Until very recently, Army training camps simply were not available for the training of less essential reserves mandated by a congressional lobby, because the training camps were fully utilized readying active forces for Vietnam. But when the war in Vietnam is brought to an end, the pressures of the military-industrial-congressional complex will necessarily be increased.

The pressures can still be resisted, and there is every evidence that they will be. But it is unreasonable to expect any Secretary of Defense to resist them alone, or supported only by the few people within the Department who are entirely his own men. Over the past six years, the Pentagon has developed the kind of organizational and analytical instruments that permit effective communication between the bureaucracy and the responsible political leadership, and among the elements of the bureaucracy with conflicting institutional interests. Yet the Pentagon's administrators themselves cannot determine the role of the military establishment in the United States, and should not be asked to. It took a national debate over a period of years to demonstrate that the military establishment was inadequate to its tasks and needed major structural reform. Those reforms have now given the United States more usable military power. The uses that we choose to make of the military establishment, and the limits that are put on its growth and employment, are a large enough subject again to engage the attention of the nation. . . .[4]

Another Look at the National Decision System

A SIMPLE CASCADE MODEL

The nation, whose attention and decisions are involved here, can be thought of as a national decision system, and for some purposes of analysis we can visualize the flow of communications and decisions in a very simplified image as a cascade of five levels. We can imagine that each level is formed by a distinct reservoir of public or elite opinion. Each of these reservoirs is linked to a particular complex of social institutions and status groups. Communications flow more freely within each level than from one level to the other; and they flow more easily from the higher status and power levels to the lower ones, than they do the other way. The communication and action system at each level can be represented by a simple "black box" with only a few labels attached to parts of it, so as to indicate its chief tasks or functions that interest us here: intake of messages and experiences; memory and recall; decision through combining incoming data with items recalled from memory for determining the output of behavior; and the output of messages and actions

[4] *Ibid.*, p. 61.

The Foreign-Policy Sector

that result, and that may return information to the input side of the system and thus modify the next stages of its behavior.

The first of these levels of opinion reservoirs in any Western country is that of the social and economic elite, corresponding roughly to the top 2 or 3 per cent or so of the population in terms of property, income, and socio-economic status—the major owners, stockholders, employers, investors, and top-management executives in the country, with their families, and their major institutions, such as the main business, banking, and investment corporations. These people and institutions do not form a simple monolithic group, but are connected by a dense net of multiple ties, links, and channels of communication. They share among themselves many memories, preferences, styles, and habit patterns of the subculture of the upper classes, and the views, interests, and behavior styles of more specialized sub-elites are communicated rapidly among them. In addition to its internal communication flow and its shared memories, this elite also receives messages from the rest of the society and from the outside world, and these produce messages and actions directed toward other social groups and to the world outside. We represent it schematically, therefore (Fig. 2), by a "black box" with an intake sector, an output sector, a set of memories available for recall, and a decision system that will at least produce preferences for, or aversions against, particular kinds of output behavior.

The second level in a highly developed Western society is formed by the political and governmental elite. This elite centers primarily around the national government. It, too, however, is not a monolithic bloc. Within it there are subgroups such as the executive-branch personnel, the legislators, and the judges; the higher elected officials and the higher bureaucrats; and (among this latter group) the civilian and the military dignitaries. There are also the distinctions between the political elites at the national center and in the outlying regions, and the differences among the interests and personnel of national, state, and municipal politics. Finally, there are the distinctions between the incumbents of formal government offices, and the individuals whose share in political power rests on their position in the hierarchy or machine of some party; and there is the real distinction between the political "ins" and the "outs"—although these roles may be reversed when power changes hands. Despite all these real cleavages, there is a good deal of cohesion and communication in the political elite, and together with the bureaucratic and military elites, it does form by-and-large the government as well as the most immediate social environment around it. This governmental and political elite again can be represented, therefore, as a communication and decision system with its own memories and decision capabilities, and its own functions of intake and output, similar to the simple scheme shown in Fig. 2.

The third level consists of the media of mass communication—particularly the newspapers, magazines, television, and radio, with advertising agencies and the motion picture, phonograph-record, and book-publishing industries as close appendages. This network of mass media can be treated again as a system with its own intake, output, and memory and decision aspects, and represented by another black box similar to those at the preceding levels.

The communications system at the fourth level is much larger and much

The Foreign-Policy Sector

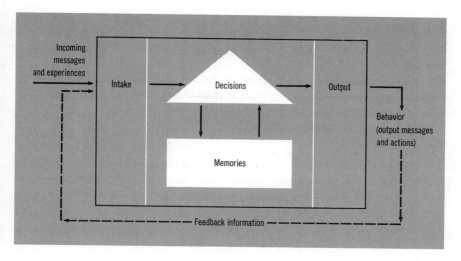

FIGURE 2. *The socio-economic elite level as a decision system.*

less cohesive, but no less important. It can be represented by a similar black box as that at each of the other levels, but we must bear in mind that it differs from them in content. It consists of the network of local opinion leaders—the 5 or 10 per cent of the population who pay continued attention to the mass media, and to some extent to foreign affairs. These are the men and women who mediate much of national and world affairs to their less attentive neighbors who look to them for interpretations and for models of appropriate attitudes and responses to the distant and unfamiliar events which the mass media bring within their range of vision. If the network of local opinion leaders agrees with the messages and interpretations promoted by the mass media, they can do much to reinforce their impact; if they disagree with them, oppose them, or ignore them, they can do much to nullify their effect. Thus the same nationwide telecast on Africa, or on racial integration in the United States' armed forces, could have a very different impact in the North and in the South, depending on the different responses of the opinion leaders (and of the general population) in each region. In mass opinion poll analyses, this "local opinion leader" stratum perhaps can be approximated by segregating the top 5 or 10 per cent of respondents by socio-economic status and education and analyzing their attitudes separately. Alternatively, members of this stratum—or of some subgroup within it, such as local schoolteachers or lawyers—could be identified directly, and a poll taken from a suitable sample among them.

The fifth and largest group formed by the people consists of the politically relevant strata of the population at large, insofar as they are sufficiently accessible, interested, capable, and old enough to have at least a potential influence on politics so that they have to be taken into account in estimating the probable course of political events and the probable outcome of crisis. The politically effective "people" amounts in Western countries to the total

The Foreign-Policy Sector

electorate actually voting; that is, to between 60 and 90 per cent of the adult population. The electorate (or the mass public) again receives messages, calls on its memories, makes decisions, and produces results in the form of messages and actions.

Four streams of information move downward, in cascade fashion, from higher-level communications systems to lower-level ones. The socio-economic elite communicates directly with the government and the political system. Many of its members have access to, and influence in, the legislative and executive branches of the government. Many of them also have such access and influence in the world of the mass media. They have fewer contacts with, and less direct influence over, the bulk of local opinion leaders; and on the mass of the people their direct influence is least. The government has some direct contacts with, and influence on, the mass media; but its communications and influence are weaker with local opinion leaders and the people. The mass media in turn speak most directly and effectively to the local opinion leaders, who then act as their transmitters or confirmers—and only more rarely as their critics—toward the population. They also speak directly to the people, however, and they do so with still more authority and impact

Table 10   A SUMMARY OF 36 INFLUENCE AND INFORMATON FLOWS IN A DEVELOPED COUNTRY
(for Fig. 3A–H)

From:	To:						
	1 Soc.-Econ. Elite	2 Gov't.-Pol. System	3 Mass Media	4 Opinion Leaders	5 Pop. (Mass Opin.)	6 Reality	7 Total Originated
1. Socio-Economic Elite (3B)	Very Strong	Strong	Strong	Strong	Strong	Weak	5 Strong 1 Weak
2. Gov't.-Political System (3C)	Strong	Very Strong	Strong	Strong	Strong	Strong	6 Strong
3. Mass Media (3D)	Strong	Strong	Very Strong	Strong	Strong	Weak	5 Strong 1 Weak
4. Opinion Leaders (3E)	Weak	Strong	Strong	Very Strong	Very Strong	Weak	4 Strong 1 Weak
5. Population (Mass Opinion) (3Fi)	Weak	Strong	Strong	Strong	Very Strong	Strong	5 Strong 1 Weak
6. Reality (Phys., Econ., Int'l., etc.) (3G)	Weak	Strong	Weak	Strong	Very Strong	Very Strong	4 Strong 2 Weak
7. Total Received (3H)	3 Strong 3 Weak	6 Strong	5 Strong 1 Weak	6 Strong	6 Strong	3 Weak 3 Strong	29 Strong 7 Weak

FIGURE 3 (A–H).   *Cascade model of influence and information flows* (pp. 105–109).

The Foreign-Policy Sector

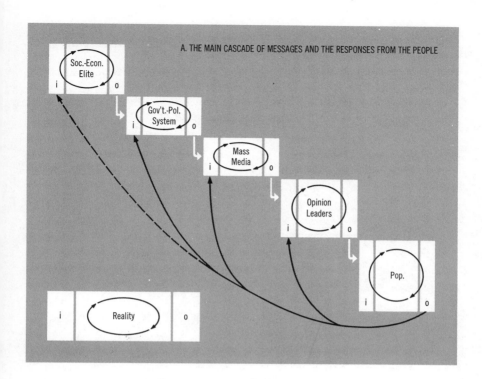

A. THE MAIN CASCADE OF MESSAGES AND THE RESPONSES FROM THE PEOPLE

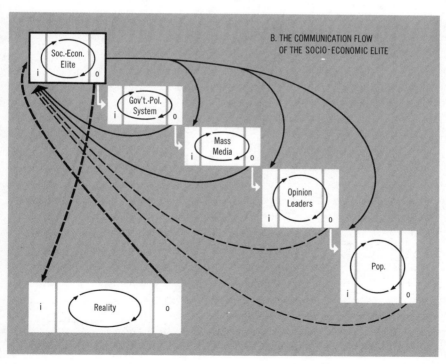

B. THE COMMUNICATION FLOW OF THE SOCIO-ECONOMIC ELITE

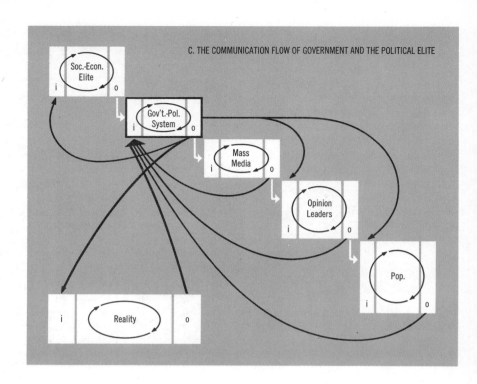

C. THE COMMUNICATION FLOW OF GOVERNMENT AND THE POLITICAL ELITE

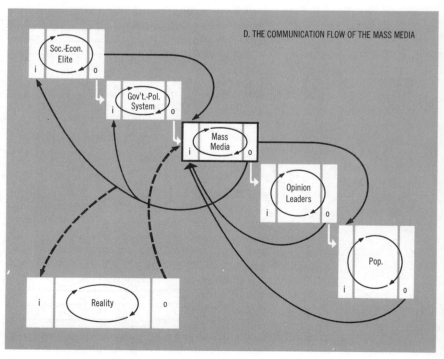

D. THE COMMUNICATION FLOW OF THE MASS MEDIA

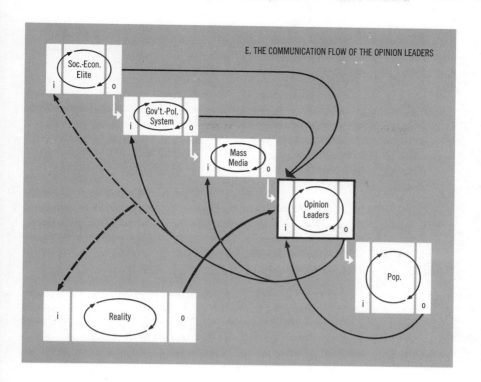

E. THE COMMUNICATION FLOW OF THE OPINION LEADERS

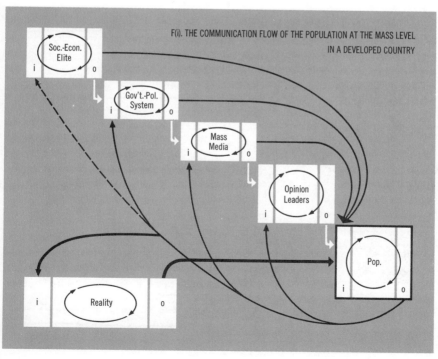

F(i). THE COMMUNICATION FLOW OF THE POPULATION AT THE MASS LEVEL
IN A DEVELOPED COUNTRY

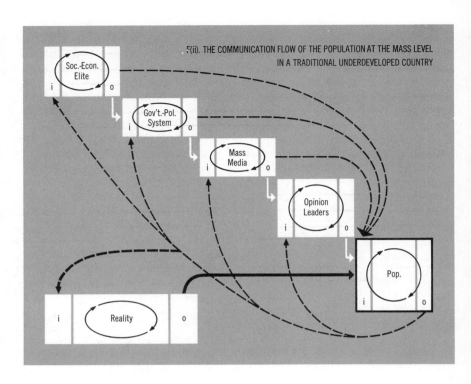

F(ii). THE COMMUNICATION FLOW OF THE POPULATION AT THE MASS LEVEL
IN A TRADITIONAL UNDERDEVELOPED COUNTRY

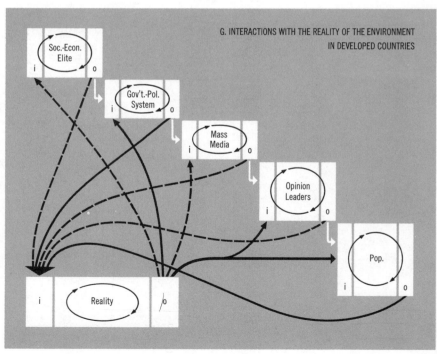

G. INTERACTIONS WITH THE REALITY OF THE ENVIRONMENT
IN DEVELOPED COUNTRIES

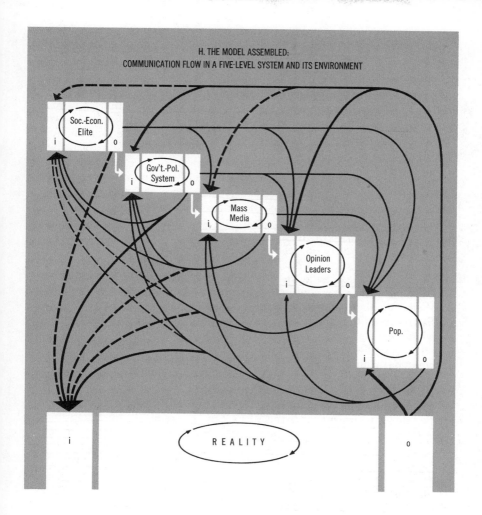

if their messages are paralleled and reinforced by those of the mass media, who often can confer additional status on the local leaders as their spokesmen. The local leaders, finally, communicate directly with the people and exercise their influence in parallel with or in opposition to the politics of the mass media. This is shown in Fig. 3 and summarized in Table 10.

Each of the five groups, however, has its own memories and its own measure of autonomy. Each can reject, ignore, or reinterpret many—perhaps almost all—unpalatable messages. Each is capable of innovation and initiative. And each can also feed back a stream of information upward to some or all of the higher-level groups.

The people respond to the local opinion leaders by increasing or decreasing their attention and deference to them. They respond to the mass media by giving or withholding their attention, subscription, and patronage of each medium and of the firms advertising therein. In a democracy, they have strong channels for communicating upward to the government. They have only

The Foreign-Policy Sector

weak and indirect channels, however, for communication and influence with the socio-economic elite, most of whom do not depend on popular favor for income or position.

The local opinion leaders can support, ignore, or oppose the mass media, and to some extent they have similar choices in their actions toward the government and the political leadership of the country. Usually, however, they cannot do much about the socio-economic elite unless the local and lower-level leaders have become thoroughly alienated from the top elite, or if the top elite should consist largely of conspicuous outsiders or foreigners. But the government and the leaders of the political system *can* do something about the socio-economic elite. They can defend its privileges and make them appear more legitimate, or they can oppose and reduce its power and privileges through legislation, taxation, and national opinion leadership and management, and by means of many acts of administration and policy decision.

All together, every one of the five levels of our cascade model is partly autonomous but also partly interdependent with the other levels. Each level is also open to some extent to the direct impact of external reality. When there is an economic recession and people lose their jobs, then they notice it, and so do their neighbors, almost regardless of what local opinion leaders, mass media, and even the government may be saying. The same is true of situations in which people have experienced hunger or rationing, or the mounting casualty lists of a prolonged war. In all these cases, the media and the local and national political leaders can do something to interpret the experiences of the people, but in time the cumulative weight of experience may (though it need not) outweigh the effects of interpretation.

The same holds for the higher levels. Local opinion leaders, the mass media, the government, and the socio-economic elite all are likely to have some direct experiences with such matters as economic prosperity or depression; the inflow or outflow of gold; the ease or difficulty of emigration; successes or failures in foreign relations or in war; and various advances or frustrations in regard to science, technology, public health, population growth, the improvement or deterioration of the environment, and the conservation or depletion of national resources. Any or all of these can have their effects on the experiences of people at each level of the social communication system, and thus they can influence directly their perceptions of themselves and of the outside world, as well as their trust or distrust of one another. The credibility of a government, a national elite, or a national system of mass media, in the international arena as well as in domestic politics, may well depend in no small part on the extent to which its messages correspond to the actual impact of reality on the populations, groups, and other governments concerned.

Each of these interdependent levels of communication is itself composed of diverse interest groups and institutions, and there are further coalitions among groups at different levels in the communication system. Such coalitions may be found among some national political leaders, some mass media, some local leaders, and some parts of the electorate. All of these may favor a "hard line" or a "soft line" in foreign policy—that is, a greater or lesser willingness to approach the brink of war in the pursuit of their preferred national foreign-policy objectives—while other groups or coalitions may prefer to accord primacy to their domestic goals.

110

The Foreign-Policy Sector

Is There a "Primacy of Foreign Policy"?

Complex political communication systems of this kind are unlikely always to accord primacy to either domestic or foreign policy. The great nineteenth-century historian, Leopold von Ranke, spoke of "the primacy of foreign policy," but this notion was better suited to monarchies than to mass societies. Today the elites still are making policy, but policy—at least its requirements and its results—often also makes elites, or else changes their cohesion and their power, as well as the relationships among elite groups.

A modern political communication and decision system of this type also makes it difficult for a country to maintain a very consistent long-run foreign policy. If a single-level elite or interest group were sure to prevail over all others, and if all these others were to remain relatively passive, then this prevailing body could with no special effort develop and maintain consistent international policies for many years. A pluralistic democracy inevitably finds it much harder constantly to exercise influence over, or consistently to submit to, the influence of another nation.

The more numerous the elements of plurality, communication, and participation are in a system, the harder it is for its elites and interest groups to stay put, and the more apt to shift is the balance among its levels and flows of internal and external political communications and decisions. Modern democracies are not at all well-suited in this respect, to rule or guide other countries for long periods of time, and they are equally ill-suited to submit for long even to the best-intentioned foreign influence or guidance from afar. Britain's relations to the democratic countries of the Commonwealth show something of this difficulty, as do America's experiences since 1954 in trying to influence the policies of France, and our more recent efforts to influence the economic and political course of India.

But what is true of modern democracies is perhaps also true, to a considerable degree, of all other modern countries. All modernization implies more frequent domestic communications, more differentiated and complex internal systems of communication, larger public sectors, increased popular participation beyond the local level, and a greater likelihood of recurring shifts in the communication and power relations within their political systems. Even behind the façade of dictatorship, these shifting processes of politics and communication are at work; they make modern dictatorships no less ill-suited to maintain for very long a tight control over distant foreign countries. The difficulties the Soviet Union has experienced in attempting to retain control of the policies of Czechoslovakia and Rumania, and her loss of control of Yugoslavia and China, show how shifts within the U.S.S.R. have combined with changes in the other countries to weaken or dissolve what earlier had looked at least on the surface like a tightly controlled bloc.

Though modern states find it hard to influence or control other states for long periods, their interests often drive their governments to try. The partial interdependence of countries may add urgency to such efforts without ensuring their success. And where interdependence persists, but control efforts fail, and where opposing interests become prominent, conflicts are likely to arise. Here again, international conflict arises out of the failures of control.

The Foreign-Policy Sector

How Conflicts Arise Among States

No matter what sort of conflict a state works its way into, it finds itself maintaining some degree of control over not only its own behavior, but that of its adversary. The different types of conflicts can be distinguished according to the various amounts and patterns of self-control and mutual control involved. In the terms proposed by the mathematician and game theorist Anatol Rapoport, the three most important types of conflicts can be called "fights," "games," and "debates." Each type has different background conditions, a different pattern of development, and a different distribution of predictable outcomes.

In a "fight" type of conflict, the self-control and mutual control of the actors decline rapidly, for the actions of each actor serve as starting-points for similar counteractions by the other actor. A dog meeting another dog in the street may growl at him; the second dog growls back. The first dog growls louder, and the second still more so. The first dog snarls, and so does the second. In the classic sequence of escalation there follow bared teeth, snaps, and a dogfight. Two small boys at the start of a schoolyard fight may go through a similar sequence: the exchange of taunting looks leads to that of taunting words and gestures, and then to threats, challenges, and counter-challenges, until blows are exchanged and a full-scale fight is under way.

What can be observed among dogs and small boys can also be observed in arms races among nations, and in the confrontations of great powers. One nations's level of armaments or armament expenditure becomes the base line for a second nation, which decides to exceed it by some "safe" margin—say 10 per cent—in order to feel secure. But this new, higher arms level of the second nation now becomes the basis for the security calculations of the first one, which now tries for its part to spend 10 per cent more on weapons than does its rival. Its rival in turn tries to outspend this amount by 10 per cent; and so on in a sequence of escalating armaments until one or both of the rivals are exhausted, or until war breaks out, or until there is some highly improbable last-minute change of policy on either side.

In a great power confrontation, too, each power tries to outbid the other by some margin in its verbal or material commitment at each stage. Moderately worded notes are followed by stiff notes. Notes are followed by movements of ships, troops, or airplanes in locations close to the theater of the quarrel, and perhaps some forces are infiltrated or landed overtly. Shots are fired, followed by a more-than-equal retaliation from the other side. Allied nations step into the picture. And so on, through threat and counter-threat, retaliation and counter-retaliation, right up to the brink of all-out war—and perhaps, across it.

In their essence, such "fight" type conflict processes tend to be automatic and mindless, like the moves of novice checker-players who know less of the game than they think: their every move seems to them obvious and necessary. In fact, often these processes, like the moves of two practiced but still not very skillful checker-players, are so swift that they would be hard to distinguish from a reflex. Thus it is that statesmen start saying "We have no alternative," and that nations that should learn better from experience (as even most novice checker-players often do) find themselves involved in what usually seem (to them) to be unavoidable conflict processes making escape from the evolving sequence of events increasingly more difficult.

In its automatic character, a conflict of this type also resembles a process of nature, and, like certain processes of nature, it can be described by a pair of differential equations. (Mathematical models of such conflict processes have been explored by several natural and social scientists, including Lewis F. Richardson, Nicholas Rashevsky, G. F. Gause, Anatol Rapoport, and Kenneth

Boulding.) Typically, such equations include two kinds of terms. Some terms represent processes of _acceleration_—that is, they stand for the accelerating effects which the moves of each actor have on the moves of the other, and possibly also on his own next steps. The other kind of terms, however, represent the opposite effects, which also occur in many conflict situations. These are the retarding or _decelerating_ effects, and are in particular the effects making for increasing self-restraint on the part of each actor as the conflict mounts. Such effects include those of rising costs (political or economic), or of growing domestic opposition, or of declining resources—or of several of these combined.

Under certain conditions the accelerating factors will prevail; and an appropriate mathematical model will show that the conflict will escalate indefinitely until the destruction or breakdown of some actor or of some part of the system occurs. And it may even show how soon some such limit or point of breakdown will be reached. Under other conditions, however, factors of self-restraint may grow faster than the factors of accelerating conflict. In that event, the rate of conflict escalation will slow down and the whole conflict system may come to rest at some point well short of the breakdown of the system and the destruction of either of the contending parties. Under such conditions, mathematical models will show when and how competing species of beetles in the same bag of flour will continue to coexist indefinitely; or when and how competing missionary religions or political ideologies will continue in a stable state of competitive coexistence; or when and at what levels of expenditure an arms race may come to a halt. If we can discover and strengthen such factors making for greater self-restraint of the competing states, therefore, even the mindless automatism of "fight"-type conflicts may still leave us with some hope.

"Games": Rational Conflicts Characterized by Strategy

A very different type of conflict resembles games in which each player maintains rational control over his own moves, though not necessarily over their outcome; and some of the models of game theory can be applied to them. Many games which we play for recreation, such as poker, bridge, or chess, bear some abstract and limited resemblance to conflict situations in real life—such as business competition, politics, diplomacy, and war; and it is in part for this reason that men have found such games interesting and attractive. In any such game, each player has a scale of utilities, according to which he prefers some outcomes, so long as he plays the game at all. He also has a range of options among different moves which he can make, and he has some set of expectations as to the probable outcome of any move that he may choose.

To play well, therefore, a player must know what he wants, he must know what he knows and what he does not know, and he must know what he can and what he cannot do. His knowledge of the outcome of his actions is uncertain, for in a typical game the results of his own move will depend on the move his opponent makes. Often he will not know completely what his opponent can do (his opponent's capabilities, such as the high or low cards his opponent holds), nor what his opponent may decide or plan to do (his intentions). Faced with such uncertainty, each player must base his moves on

114

the most rational guess or estimate he can make. Napoleon is said to have advised his generals to base their own military moves on their estimates of their adversaries' capabilities, rather than on their necessarily less reliable estimates of their intentions.

As long as he is "playing the game," each player plays to win, or at least not to lose. It is for this purpose that he chooses his single moves and short sequences of moves, which we call *tactics,* as well as his longer patterns and sequences of moves, which we call *strategy* and in which the tactical moves are included as components. The most rational strategy for a player then is the one most likely to produce a winning outcome for him, or—by another criterion—the one most likely to prevent a losing one. If the payoffs can be expressed in quantitative terms, then the most rational strategy is the one that maximizes net gains, or else the one that minimizes net losses.

ZERO-SUM OR FIXED-SUM GAMES

A large class of games are called *zero-sum games,* or, more generally, *fixed-sum games.* In a zero-sum game, the sum of all payoffs to all players equals zero, so that anything any one player wins, some other player or players have to lose. (Chess, bridge, and poker are examples of zero-sum games). In a fixed-sum game, the sum of all payoffs is fixed at some number which need not be zero but may be larger or smaller. (Here, too, however, the gains of any one player necessarily must be always at the expense of other players.) Zero-sum games, therefore, are a subclass of fixed-sum games, but any fixed-sum game can be turned into a zero-sum game by a simple mathematical transformation, for all the important mathematical properties of zero-sum games and other fixed-sum games are identical. What we shall say here of zero-sum games, therefore, will apply to all fixed sum games.

Every zero-sum game represents a pattern of unmixed and unrelieved conflict. In a two-person game of this type, whatever one player wins, the other loses. Whatever is good for one, necessarily is bad for his adversary; and anything that is in any way good for one's adversary inevitably must be to the same extent bad for oneself. More than four centuries before the discovery of game theory, Niccolò Machiavelli used this pattern as a model for his concept of power when he wrote that a prince who advances another's power diminishes his own.[1]

A similar "zero-sum" notion of power and of the competition among rival states, and particularly among rival ideologies, has survived in some of the more fundamentalist versions of Cold War thinking in our time. Whatever is good for, or even acceptable to, the West (some "true believers" in militant Communism may reason in Peking or Moscow) obviously must be bad for Communism; and whatever is good for, or even merely acceptable to, Communism (so reason some of our own "true believers" in militant anti-Communism) must be automatically bad for the United States. Any step toward moderation, mutual accommodation, or compromise between the United States and the Soviet Union, or between the United States and Communist

---

[1] Niccolò Machiavelli, *The Prince and the Discourses* (New York: Modern Library, 1940), p. 14.

How Conflicts Arise Among States

China, on any subject matter, so the "true believers" in the Cold War on both sides think, is nothing but the futile appeasement of an insatiable enemy, and a reasonable sacrifice of the interest of one's own nation.

Strategies and solutions. The world of two-person, zero-sum games is a world of merciless and irreconcilable conflict. By the assumptions of this model, neither the players' motives nor their interest can ever change; they must remain forever hostile. But even this world is ruled by rationality. Each player can calculate his average long-run chances of losing or winning in a sequence of repeated plays of the same game. He can calculate the best strategy he could pursue for this long run; and he can assume, so long as he has no specific information to the contrary, that this strategy will also give him the best chances in a single encounter. His adversary, too, can calculate his own best strategy; each player can also calculate the best strategy of his opponent.

If there is a clear "best strategy" for each player, and if both players can continue to follow their best strategies, we say that the game has "a stable solution." *Solutions* thus are that subclass of strategies from which no player can expect to be able to deviate without loss, and which lead, therefore, to stable outcomes for all rational players.

In fact, it oftens turns out that such a game has more than one such solution, although the number of stable solutions is likely to be small. By contrast, of course, there are usually very many foolish strategies; but it is worth bearing in mind that there may be more than one stable and viable way for dealing with a situation of conflict. If we think of international politics and more generally of human relations as ways of dealing with possible conflict, then this line of reasoning may suggest to us that there may be a plurality of workable ways to deal with them. Whereas it would be an error to be indifferent to all possible foreign policies or ways of life, it is probably realistic to recognize that a few alternative policies, and even ways of life are likely to prove stable and viable even though we are likely to consider *for ourselves* only one such policy and way of life, as most consonant with our own values and traditions. These philosophic implications of game theory favor pluralism but not indifference. They suggest that we may choose a group of viable alternative strategies or policies on completely rational grounds, but that our ultimate choice among them sometimes may have to be based on grounds other than pure rationality.

The minimax concept. Even in the irreconcilable-conflict situation modeled in a two-person, zero-sum game, there may be one or several stable solutions resembling in some ways an automatic equivalent of compromise. These are the so-called *minimax* (or *maximin*) solutions. If a player assumes that his adversary will be as bright as possible and will play to win as much as he can, then there often exists for our own player some strategy (which he can calculate or discover) by which he can hold to a minimum his own losses, and thus the winnings of his adversary. Where such a strategy exists, it usually requires of our player that he accept either the smallest of the gains available (the "MINImum" of the "MAXima"), or else the relatively smallest loss (and hence, from his viewpoint, the relative MAXImum gain) from among all his possible losses (his "MINIma").

Game theorists agree that in irreconcilable conflict game situations the

How Conflicts Arise Among States

safest strategy for a player is to choose either "the best of the worst" or "the worst of the best" of all possible outcomes. They say that where this can be done consistently by a player, the distribution of all possible outcomes of the game for the two players must have at least one "saddle point" at which the minimum of one player's maxima and the maximum of his adversary's minima coincide, and which can be attained by such a strategy. Even in situations where no such "saddle point" exists, a player often can enforce the equivalent of a minimax solution by playing a suitably calculated "mixed" strategy. If he has, say, four possible strategies, it might pay him to alternate randomly between his strategies numbers 1 and 3, but play strategy number 1 twice as often as strategy number 3, and never play his strategies numbers 2 and 4 at all. (These arguments cannot be pursued here beyond the extremely crude hints and sketches that have been offered, but they can be studied in fascinating detail in the works of such game theorists as Martin Shubik, Anatol Rapoport, Duncan Luce, and Howard Raiffa, and, of course, in the classic *Theory of Games and Economic Behavior* by John Von Neumann and Oskar Morgenstern.)

Since this prudent strategy we have been discussing (which offers interesting parallels to certain styles of foreign policy) assumes that one's adversary will do his best, it is not an "offensive" strategy, for it cannot take advantage of any mistakes he may make. Rather, it is essentially defensive. It will protect one player from taking unnecessary risks, and it will represent the best he can do in the long run against the best-playing opponent. It is a relentless strategy of firmness and caution: it gives the player who uses it the best possible payoff against any opponent who is as clever as himself, and in time it may even wear down the opponent. But it can promise no quick victory, and as a (so-called) "no win" policy, when employed in international relations it is likely to be unpopular with action-minded generals and impatient civilians. Unpopularity notwithstanding, however, and in spite of the fact that actual foreign policy is made mainly by politicians and diplomats, and not by game theorists, perhaps something of the style of thought of the minimax policy can be discerned in the United States "containment policy" *vis-à-vis* the Soviet Union. This policy, first formulated by George F. Kennan in 1946 and 1947, was pursued by the United States for the better part of two decades.

VARIABLE-SUM (MIXED-MOTIVE) GAMES

Not all conflict situations, however, either in daily life or international politics, resemble zero-sum games. They more often resemble *variable-sum games*. These are games in which the players not only win something competitively from one another, but also collectively stand to gain or lose something from an *additional* (or *secondary*) player, (whom we may think of as "the banker" in games, or as "reality" or "nature" in certain real-life situations). Such games are, therefore, *mixed-motive games* for their primary players. For these players they are *games of competition*, insofar as these contestants try to win from one another; but they are also *games of coordination*, in that these players will also jointly gain or lose according to their

117

How Conflicts Arise Among States

ability to coordinate their moves in accordance with their common interests against "nature" or "the bank."

A prison revolt, from this point of view, would resemble a game of competition between the prisoners trying to escape, and their guards trying to keep them from doing so. Even a few guards can be successful at this, as long as they can prevent the prisoners, who usually are more numerous, from coordinating their efforts. At the same time the revolt would resemble a game of coordination among the prisoners, insofar as they would have to coordinate their moves against their few guards in order to overpower them. It would also resemble a game of competition among the prisoners, insofar as some of them might side with the guards against their fellows in order to obtain preferential treatment while in prison, or to win a partial remittance of their sentence for being among the first prisoners to throw their support to the guards' side. The basic resemblance of this model to many strikes, mutinies, colonial revolts, popular uprisings, or even revolutions is obvious. So is, in international relations, its general resemblance to some problems of collective security, and of the forming of international coalitions against a major power.

Mutual threats: the game of "chicken." Certain game models of mixed-motive conflict situations have been studied somewhat more thoroughly. One of these is the game called "chicken." In this game (played at some time in the past, according to legend, by some West Coast teen-age gangs in the United States), two players drive their automobiles on a lonely road at high speed, straight toward each other. The first player to swerve from the middle of the road, so as to avoid a collision, is called "chicken" and is held in disgrace by the rest of the gang; and the more reckless driver who refused to swerve is admired by them as a hero. (According to some commentators, this game bears a more-than-casual resemblance to head-on confrontations in world politics between major powers threatening one another with nuclear war.)

A closer look at the game of "chicken" reveals its underlying mathematical pattern. Each of the two players has a choice between two strategies: he can "cooperate" with the other player by swerving so as to avoid collision (but at the risk of being disgraced if he should swerve before his opponent does), or else he can "defect" from their common interest in survival and drive straight on—either to his death, if his opponent does the same, or to a triumph, if his adversary gives in. Each player makes his "move" by deciding whether to cooperate or to defect; but the outcome of his move depends not only on his own decision but also—and crucially—on the decision taken by his adversary.

In the abstract model of this situation there are four possible outcomes: First, both players may "cooperate" (CC) by swerving at the same time, so that neither will be disgraced. Or both may "defect" (DD) by driving straight into a head-on collision that will most likely kill or cripple them. Or player A may cooperate by swerving while B drives straight ahead (CD); then A is disgraced and B is admired by the group. Or, finally, A may "defect" and drive straight on, while B cooperates by swerving (DC); then A is admired and B despised.

When driving at high speed in a "chicken" game, neither player has time to see what his adversary is about to do, so, each must choose in advance his best strategy and act on it. But which is the best strategy, say, for player A? In

118

How Conflicts Arise Among States

Table 11   SOME EXAMPLES OF GAME MODELS

1. "Minimax":

Player B "Column"

Strategies	B–1	B–2

Player A "Row"

	B–1	B–2
A–1	-10 / $+10$	$+20$ / -20
A–2	-10 / $+10$	$+10$ / -10

Matrix of Outcomes: Each cell represents the outcome that follows if *A* and *B* choose the strategies that lead to it. Payoffs to *A* are shown in the bottom left-hand corner, and payoffs to *B*, in the top right-hand corner, of each cell.

"Natural" or Minimax Outcome: A–2, B–2 (−10,+10). A–2 is the best which *A* can do for himself, if *B* does his worst to him; and B–2 is the best *B* can do against *A*'s best strategy.

2. "Chicken":

	B–1 (C)	B–2 (D)
A–1 (C)	-5 / -5	$+10$ / -10
A–2 (D)	-10 / $+10$	-50 / -50

"Natural" or Minimax Outcome: CC (−5, −5)

3. "Prisoner's Dilemma":

	B–1 (C)	B–2 (D)
A–1 (C)	$+10$ / $+10$	$+20$ / -20
A–2 (D)	-20 / $+20$	-10 / -10

"Natural" or Minimax Outcome: DD (−10, −10)

the game of "chicken," it is clearly *C*, for at best, if *B* also cooperates, he will get home unhurt and undisgraced; and at worst, if *B* defects, *A* will still get home alive, even though with diminished standing in his gang. The same applies, of course, to *B*: his best strategy, too, is to choose to cooperate, regardless of his opponent's choice, so long as that choice cannot be reliably foretold. This choice of *C* for each player is unequivocally rational, as long as for each of them the penalty for double defection (*DD*)—which here is being killed or maimed—is clearly greater than the disrepute and chagrin of the "sucker" who trustingly cooperates while his adversary triumphantly defects (*CD*), and as long as the penalty for the outcome (*DD*) is also clearly greater than the temptation for each player to outwit his adversary by letting him cooperate while defecting himself, so as to encompass his adversary's disgrace and his own triumph. Teen-agers, of course, sometimes may be less rational   119

How Conflicts Arise Among States

than game theorists are, but the verdict of game theory is clear. As long as the negative payoff for the outcome DD is greater than any positive or negative payoff for CD or DC outcomes, the game is a genuine game of "chicken." It has a rational solution, which is for each player to choose cooperation over conflict. Where a confrontation in international politics should resemble such a "chicken" game, rational statesmen, according to this theory, should choose a "soft line" rather than a "hard line" policy.

Threats and promises: the "prisoners' dilemma." Unfortunately, however, another game model of international conflict often may be more realistic. This is the "prisoners' dilemma" game. According to the story that goes with an explanation of it, the governor of a prison once had two prisoners whom he could not hang without a voluntary confession from at least one. Accordingly, he summoned one prisoner and offered him his freedom and a sum of money if he would confess at least a day before the second prisoner did so, so that an indictment could be prepared and so that the second prisoner could be hanged. If the latter should confess at least a day before him, however, the first prisoner was told, then that prisoner would be freed and rewarded, and he would be hanged. "And what if we both should confess on the same day, your Excellency?" asked the first prisoner. "Then you each will keep your life but will get 10 years in prison." "And if neither of us should confess, your Excellency?" "Then both of you will be set free—without any reward, of course. But will you bet your neck that your fellowprisoner—that crook—will not hurry to confess and pocket the reward? Now go back to your solitary cell and think about your answer until tomorrow." The second prisoner in his interview was told the same, and each man spent the night alone considering his dilemma.

The mathematical structure of this game resembles in some respects that of the game of "chicken." Each prisoner has two strategies to choose from: cooperate with his fellow by keeping silent (C), or defect from him by producing a confession (D). There are again four possible outcomes: (1) CC—both prisoners keep silent and gain their freedom but no cash; (2) CD—the first prisoner keeps silent, but the second defects, sends him to the gallows, and walks off free with a reward; (3) DC—the first prisoner defects and is freed and rewarded, while the second prisoner cooperates and is hanged for his trust; and (4) DD—both prisoners act as hardheaded realists, confess, and spend 10 years in prison.

Knowing this pattern of possible outcomes but not knowing the decision of his fellow, and with no means of communication or coordination with him, which strategy should each solitary prisoner most rationally choose? Classic game-theory again has a clear answer: he should defect. At best, defection could bring him freedom and money; at worst, 10 years in prison. Cooperation at best promises him freedom without any money, and at worst, its penalty is more severe: the gallows. So long as he cannot rely on his fellow, each prisoner in his own rational self-interest must choose defection, with its higher rewards and lesser penalties. Accordingly, both prisoners do so: they confess—and, since they are equally rational, they do so on the same day. And so, although they could have walked out free if they had kept silent, they now will spend 10 years in prison contemplating the results of their cold-blooded rationality.

How Conflicts Arise Among States

As in the game of "chicken," the two players would be much better off if they could coordinate their strategies and play CC; but in contrast to the game of "chicken," the players in "prisoners' dilemma" find it very hard (and, reasoning as individuals, not rational) to do so. Why?

In "chicken" it is rational to cooperate rather than defect, for the penalty for double defection (DD) is clearly greater than the temptation to defect from a cooperating partner so as to profit from betrayal. In "prisoners' dilemma," however, the "sucker's" penalty for being betrayed while trustingly cooperating is clearly worse than the penalty for double defection. It seems not rational, therefore, to risk betrayal. Situations of arms control and disarmament, or of de-escalation between bitterly opposed ideological adversaries, show somewhat similar characteristics: both sides could reap real gains from mutual trust, but these gains are balanced or outweighed by the rewards for successful cheating and by the penalties for being trustful and cheated.

A single play of the "prisoners' dilemma" game has no convincing rational solution, except the somewhat absurd one that both players, by jointly contriving to choose DD, should put themselves in prison for 10 years. We could drop, however, the "end-of-the-world" assumption which thus far has been implicit in our model, and which made us pretend that in this game nothing more mattered but a single play. If we shift our attention to the best strategy for a series of repeated plays, the beginning of a solution can be discovered.

The approach to this discovery involves a combination of analysis and experiment. If the two prisoners in our game could coordinate their strategies, they could walk out free, but they have no means of communication. In a series of repeated plays, however, they have one such means, for they communicate something to each other, willy-nilly, through every move they make and through the outcome to which it contributes. Anatol Rapoport and his associates at the University of Michigan have conducted experiments with "prisoners' dilemma" games in which two players had to play 300 consecutive plays against each other. Their published findings are based on the experience of about 100,000 plays, and they are of great interest to all students of conflict among persons, groups, and nations.

Only a few points of these findings can be mentioned here. In the initial play of a typical 300-play sequence, the two adversaries succeed in achieving double cooperation (CC) and a joint reward in a little less than 50 per cent of the plays. The next 30 to 40 plays are characterized by seeming disillusionment in which they get tough with one another, and their game then usually becomes more competitive, with mutual cooperation (CC) declining to about 27 per cent, so that both players are now losing heavily. During the next 100 plays, they gradually learn that this cutthroat competition does not pay, and that cooperation does; and during the last 50 plays of the 300-play sequence, they collaborate successfully in achieving the rewarding CC payoffs in about 73 per cent of their plays.

A possible explanation of these findings is that both players in the early stages employ somewhat more cooperation than defection, but that they are very likely to fail to coordinate their cooperative moves. As soon as this happens, the player who made the cooperative move is strongly penalized by the defecting move of his adversary; and he is likely to interpret this as malice

How Conflicts Arise Among States

and betrayal. He retaliates by switching himself to the defecting strategy, and a chain of mutual retaliation follows (from which it takes both sides a long time to recover) until they eventually learn to reach and maintain a substantially higher level of coordination than the one from which they originally started.

The personality of the individual players turns out to have very little to do with the sequence of outcomes of the game. What counts most are outcomes of the first few plays, which seem to produce a powerful "lock-in" effect on further progress of the game. If they set a string of early precedents for hostility, then conflict and mutual penalization will be severe and long, and the recovery of confidence and the learning of more frequent cooperation will be much delayed. If the early moves, on the contrary, have established a setting of cooperation, much of the beneficial effect will tend to persist throughout the later stages.

These findings are suggestive for the prediction and management of international conflict. They would lead us to expect less of an effect from the intentions or the supposed intrinsic characteristics of foreign governments, and to pay more attention to the patterns of mutual interactions among governments, including notably our own. It would then be less important to ask, "What did the government of country X intend by this move toward country Y?" than to ask, "What actually happened to country X and Y as a result of this move made by the government of X and by Y's response to it?"—and to ask further, "What was the possible lock-in effect for the future, generated by this experience?"

The data also confirm what students of politics would have suspected: that both martyrs and cynics will do poorly at this game. A martyr is a player who always plays the cooperative move C, no matter how often his adversary betrays and penalizes him by defecting. The data show that such martyrs tend to be shamelessly exploited by their adversaries; martyrs seem to bring out the worst in the opposition. And martyrs tend to remain losers to the end of the game. Cynics, however, who consistently defect, will fare almost as badly. They will soon provoke retaliation, and if they persist in their strategy of defection, they will remain locked in on the penalty outcomes of the DD type and will be consistent losers. The strategy most likely to succeed, it turns out, is: (a) to initiate cooperation; (b) to persist in making cooperative moves as long as they are reciprocated; and (c) to retaliate without fail whenever repeated or frequent defection is encountered, but (d) to renew from time to time thereafter a sequence of two or three unilateral cooperative moves in order to give the adversary a chance to shift to a sequence of mutual cooperation.

Cooperative behavior doubled in frequency when the payoff matrix was prominently and continuously displayed to both players throughout the game. (This effect was observed, even though all the players had been told of the payoff matrix at the start of the game, and their gains or losses were reported to them after every play.) This finding may add some support to the view of Immanuel Kant and other philosophers, that fuller awareness of their own situation will make men more likely to behave cooperatively and morally.

How Conflicts Arise Among States

By having the adversaries play the "prisoners' dilemma" game through 300 consecutive plays, the game is made more realistic in one crucial aspect. It is no longer an "end-of-the-world" game in which the players have no future and hence no need to consider what future behavior in other players they are inducing by their strategies. Rather, the game is now played more nearly as a *survival game,* in which the reward for success consists in large part in being permitted to continue playing, and the penalty for failure consists in being ruined and having to quit the game—much as in the real-life games of business, party politics, and international relations among governments. The more elaborate game models of the future will have to be conceived of as survival games if they are to resemble real-life business, politics, and international relations, and if they are to be of any use to us in the survival game that all of us are playing for mankind.

Another improvement in the models of game theory is critically needed but will be much more difficult to make. To resemble more nearly the realities of politics, both national and international, improved game-models would have to take explicit account of the *costs of thinking and decision-making.* In classic game-theory, it is assumed that players can calculate all possible moves of their own and of their adversaries, together with all their expectable consequences, and that they can do so instantly, completely, and at no cost in time, effort, or resources. Each player may know all the present pieces and positions of his adversary, as he does in chess; or he may be ignorant of some or all the cards and combinations which his opponent holds, as is the case in many card games, such as poker; but in any case the classic theory of games by Von Neumann and Morgenstern assumes that each player should have no difficulty in thinking through, instantly, all the possible combinations of moves and outcomes which are implied in the facts he sees before him.

In fact, of course, this is not true of either chess or poker. Chess is interesting precisely because the time from one move to the next—often one hour in chess tournaments—is far too short for any player (and his mind would be too limited even if he had a much longer time to think) to go through the whole vast ocean of combinatorial possibilities which the 32 chess pieces on their 64 squares offer; and the universe of possible poker combinations is similarly inexhaustible within the time limits of the game and the human limitations of the players. The best a player then can do is pick a few promising "candidate strategies" or "candidate solutions" by a mixture of rationality, guess, and intuition, and then spend his limited thinking time and calculating resources on analyzing the implications of these few preferred candidate strategies, in the hope that at least one of them will prove acceptable. And he must make his choices at his peril.

A similar limitation holds for politics, and for many other human decision situations. In most of these, the total of combinations of all possible moves and outcomes for all parties concerned is far too great to permit anything like exhaustive calculation within the time available. Under these conditions, it is a delusion to speak of the "optimal" solution (that is, of the **123**

How Conflicts Arise Among States

"best of all possible" solutions) because the complete range of solutions is more than likely to remain unknown to both players and observers within *any* limits of time available for thought and action. So the search for the *absolutely* best ultimate strategy to win becomes transformed into a search for the best *intermediate* strategy to *search* for the relatively best strategy to win—that is, the one considered the best likely to be found within the given limits of time and calculating resources.

Any effort at search, like all other efforts, has its costs. A choice must be made between potentially better solutions that are more costly to search for and less likely to be discovered, and more obvious solutions or strategies which are less good but which are quicker and cheaper to find. In practical politics, both national and international, time and thinking costs are crucial. The search for the supposedly "best" strategy is apt to stop as soon as *any* acceptable strategy is found at tolerable costs in terms of search and computation, provided that no alternative and equally attractive strategy has emerged. Though statesmen and business executives often believe that they are "optimizing" their strategies (in the sense of choosing the best of all), they are actually only doing what social scientist Herbert Simon has called "satisficing," which is to say, picking the most acceptable strategy among the few alternatives they can survey within the time and resources they can or will spend on the search.

In international politics, the result often is something similar to a "law of least mental effort." Foreign policies must be found, or at least approved, by harassed and busy men laboring under severe pressures of time shortage and communication overload. Any policy that is relatively easy to discover and explain, that fits in well with the previously established thought habits of the relevant decision-makers, and that has no obvious major drawbacks, has a good chance to be adopted. Once it has been adopted, moreover, the vast amount of coordination and commitment among very many people, which is needed to implement any major policy, will make it very hard to change. Major foreign policies, therefore, are not always chosen and retained by rational calculation, as the models of classic game-theory would suggest, but rather by a partly rational but also partly random process of limited search and limited evaluation, for which we have as yet no reliable game-theory models.

THREATS AND DETERRENCE AS MIXED-MOTIVE GAMES

A valuable contribution to the better understanding of international politics has been made by Thomas C. Schelling, who has demonstrated that situations of threat and deterrence can be treated as mixed-motive games. The party who makes the threat (the "threatener") and the party who is being threatened (the "threatenee") obviously must have at least one set of clashing interests: the threatenee must be doing something, or about to do something, which the threatener dislikes enough to make his threat to stop, change, or prevent it. Schelling further says that the two parties to the threat also have a common interest in not having the threat carried out. For the threatened action is not only in some sense painful to the threatenee; it is also costly or painful to the threatener. If the threatened action were simply in the threatener's interest, then he should not threaten it but act. The fact that he prefers to threaten

124

How Conflicts Arise Among States

testifies not to his kindness but to his knowledge of and dislike for the expected costs of the threatened act to him. Both threatener and threatenee stand to gain something in common, therefore, if the carrying-out of the threatened act can be avoided.

This analysis has two distinct implications which sometimes contradict each other. The first is that even in situations of threat and deterrence the two sides retain some common interest. This interest increases with the cost of carrying out the threat. If the contestants are about evenly matched, and if this common cost is larger than the matter they are quarreling about, then deterrence becomes similar to the game of "chicken"; if it is large, but smaller than the prize for which they are contesting, deterrence becomes similar to the "prisoners' dilemma" game. If the adversaries remain more or less evenly matched, but the threat between them becomes more intense (either through greater ruthlessness or through more destructive weapons) while the rewards of victory do not increase, then the deterrence contest will tend to move away from the "prisoners' dilemma" to the "chicken" pattern. The greater the intensity of mutual threats, the less *rational* motivation remains for the contestants to carry them out.

Deterrence, therefore, makes the most rational sense against the relatively defenseless. A severe threat against an adversary who cannot inflict the same level of damage in retaliation means to threaten great costs to him at small cost to the threatener. This makes it seem inviting, for example, to threaten naval or aerial bombardment against some recalcitrant smaller or poorer country that has no comparable navy or air force to hit back. The more intense the threat (*e.g.*, by threatening to use more destructive weapons, or to direct attacks against more highly cherished objects or persons, such as cities, children, or the rulers of the country), the more successful it is supposed to be, according to the theory, against a weaker but still rational opponent.

Even according to classic deterrence theory, however, more intense threats (that is, with more devastating weapons, or against more precious targets) have precisely the opposite effect when they are made against an adversary who can retaliate on the same level of frightfulness, or who has firm allies who are likely to retaliate for him. The replacement of atom-bomb warheads in their long-distance missiles by much more powerful hydrogen-bomb warheads in the 1950's, therefore, did not make the Soviet's threats against West Germany or Britain more effective, because both countries continued to count on protection by the retaliatory hydrogen-bomb power of the United States; and in addition, Britain manufactured some hydrogen bombs of her own. Similarly, of course, Communist countries were not overawed by the growing nuclear arsenal of the United States in the 1950's and 1960's, *if* they had great conventional (and soon were also to have nuclear) strength of their own, as did the Soviet Union, and *if* they received Soviet assurances of nuclear protection, as did Cuba in 1962. Neither did they fear if they had vast land armies and at least some Soviet protection, nor if they had acquired some nuclear weapons capabilities, as did China in 1964. There is little reason to doubt that intensified threats of chemical or biological warfare among the great powers would be similarly useless in extracting any political concessions. As long as both sides remain rational and able to inflict great damage on each other, any intensification of threats will merely decrease

How Conflicts Arise Among States

their motivation to carry them into effect. Since each side knows this of the other, more intense mutual threats under these conditions decline in credibility and become less effective.

The second implication of Schelling's model deals with just this point. The effectiveness of a threat, according to Schelling, depends not only on its intensity but also on its *credibility;* and this credibility is a distinct aspect of the threat which can be manipulated separately by an astute threatener. Such a threatener, says Schelling, can make his threat more credible by appearing to be partly irrational, and by acting in a partly irrational manner. He does this by making more reckless gestures, and by committing himself to more reckless acts, than strict rationality would permit. In one of Schelling's examples, if two automobiles contest for the right of way at an intersection, success is likely to go to the driver who first speeds up his car so much that he could not stop in time to avoid a collision even if he tried to. This irrational behavior, says Schelling, should force the other driver to slow down to avoid a collision—unless, of course, the other driver (presumably having read Schelling, or at least following the Schelling rationale) also commits himself to speeding up until he cannot stop before hitting his antagonist or someone else. In the game of "chicken," by the same reasoning, victory could be gained by the player who throws away the steering wheel of his car, or who flings a black cloth over his windshield, while driving straight ahead—unless, again, his adversary has resorted to the same tactics.

In essence, the tactics studied by Schelling depend on the deliberate creation of a shared risk between the two adversaries. The greater the shared risk created by reckless tactics or by some device that leaves some of the threat to chance (such as by launching a nuclear-armed satellite into orbit, controlled by a roulette wheel; or by engaging in a limited but escalating war which everybody knows could easily get out of hand), the more credible the threat becomes. (And the greater is the rational interest of both parties to escape from this dangerous situation. And, since the threatener has committed himself to an irrational persistence in his course, the greater now, in Schelling's view, is the rational interest of the threatened party to give in.

The theory of deterrence contains no specific term for the size of the stakes of the contest, which may be momentous or petty, and the hazard of which may be immediate or remote. To the extent that it is true, the theory applies to deterrence confrontations among powers quarreling about some marginal interests, as well as among powers struggling for the existence of their central regions and institutions. It also applies to international conflicts involving merely the goals of particular elites or special-interest groups, as well as to those involving the survival of entire regimes, states, or populations. Indeed, in its stress on the potential usefulness of irrational behavior as an aid to the credibility of threats, the theory puts a premium on the ability of a government or nation in such a contest to overrepresent and overestimate its interests at stake. The more credible its overestimation and self-deception about these interests, the more effective may become its threats. Here the theory of deterrence comes close to becoming a theory of self-deception.

The theory of deterrence is interesting and important, but it has grave and potentially fatal gaps. It seems to be widely believed by influential statesmen, military leaders, and segments of public opinion in many countries;

126

How Conflicts Arise Among States

and it summarizes and synthesizes elegantly and wittily many of the folk beliefs held by these groups. In any case, it has done much to improve thinking on these matters. It has replaced the spirit of crusading with the spirit of gamesmanship and calculation; it has taught people always to look at both sides of the gaming board and to consider the real capabilities and possible strategies of their adversary; it has replaced self-righteous fervor with critical reason; and it has taught adversaries to pay attention to possible shared interests as well as to opposing ones.

At the same time, the deterrence theory has created its own dangers, both emotional and cognitive. It has encouraged some people to play in their imagination with the lives and deaths of millions, to "think the unthinkable" (as Hermann Kahn has put it), and to contemplate almost as easily the "spending" of a "megadeath" (a million lives) as that of a "megabuck" (a million dollars). Among various people it has encouraged some callousness, some hardening of sensibilities, some belief that the end justifies all means, and some willingness to lower emotional barriers against considering the admitted equivalents of mass slaughter and torture as potential means of public policy. In all these respects, it has posed a serious challenge to our most central religious and ethical traditions.

Its cognitive dangers are greater still, because in its present state it is shot through with intellectual weaknesses. Eight of these weaknesses seem worth listing here. Three of these could be remedied relatively easily by a better use of the intellectual possibilities offered by game theory, even in its present state; the other five defects of current deterrence theories seem likely to require more far-reaching changes in our thinking.

The current deterrence-theory has a bias for short-run thinking. First, it tends to treat the capabilities of the contestants as fixed, and to neglect the opportunity costs of conflict to each of them. It spends much more attention on what each can take from the other at the points of contact and conflict, than on what each could obtain for the same resources if the conflict were avoided or else limited rigorously for the time being to a holding operation, and the resources saved there were invested more productively elsewhere. In the second place, it often tends to treat the immediate stakes of most of the major international conflicts as bigger than the costs of nuclear war; it thus tends to treat these conflicts as more similar to the "prisoners' dilemma" (which suggests strong motives for distrust and hostility) than to the "chicken" game, although the latter model in some cases may be more realistic.

Third, much of current deterrence-theory stresses single encounters or confrontations more than repeated ones, even though the rational tactics for one-shot or "end-of-the-world" games are different from those for survival games. For instance, negotiating after an adversary has started the bombardment of one's territory might seem rational at the moment, but this might invite the adversary to repeat these tactics at the time of the next dispute and thus open the door to a sequence of successive acts of intimidation and stepwise surrender. So, the most rational tactic for any yet undefeated nation might be a flat refusal to negotiate under duress. And, as a matter of fact, for more than a century this has indeed been the customary tactic of most nations not already defeated or hopelessly isolated and overawed into submission.

The five remaining shortcomings of the deterrence theory are more

How Conflicts Arise Among States

serious. First, current theory assumes that both threatener and threatenee have complete control of their behavior. But this assumption is quite often false. To the extent that the threatener acts irrationally in order to increase the credibility of his threats, he will thereby almost inevitably decrease the credibility of his *reassurance* that he will certainly not carry out his threat if the threatenee complies with his demands. If he uses reckless tactics, the threatener usually cannot control his threats and his reassurances at the same time. But if the threatenee concludes that the terrifyingly reckless and irrational threatener will do his worst to him in *any* case, then the threatenee loses his motive to comply; he might as well be hung for a sheep as for a lamb, he may conclude, and, having nothing to lose, may now defy the threatener. By 1939, Hitler had become more credible than he had been in 1936, but now his threats failed to stop France and Britain from going to war against him—not because their governments did not take them seriously (they did), but because they had lost faith in his reassurances.

The threatenee, however, may have even less control over his own behavior. Classic deterrence theory neglects to take into account the *autonomous probability* of the behavior that is to be deterred—that is, which the threatener wishes to prohibit. If this prohibited behavior of the threatenee is quite unlikely to occur in any case, then deterrence may work easily, or at least it may seem to do so. But if the behavior to be deterred is ordinarily very probable and frequent, or otherwise backed by strong motives, as in a religious movement or a social revolution, then deterrence would have to be extremely powerful to bar it completely; and such attempts at deterrence are most likely to fail.

Second, deterrence theory often neglects to calculate *cumulative risk.* Schelling's reckless driver is likely to get the right of way at the first intersection, and thus to pass it quickly alive. Let us suppose that his chances of survival are 0.9 or 90 per cent. Let us then suppose that he continues his reckless tactics and that his chances of survival and success at every following encounter at intersections are likewise 90 per cent. In that case, his chances of being alive after two encounters are 90 per cent of 90 per cent, or $.90^2$, which is 81 per cent. His chances of surviving three such encounters are $.90^3$ or 72.9 per cent; for four encounters they are about 66 per cent, for five encounters they are about 59 per cent, for seven encounters they are less than 48 per cent, and they will be halved again for every additional seven encounters. Hence 21 successive encounters would offer our high-risk player only one chance out of eight to stay alive, 49 would give him less than one chance in 100; and 70 would leave him less than one chance in 1,000. The fact that each single encounter offered him nine chances out of 10 to live is almost irrelevant compared to the deadly effect of cumulative risks. The foreign affairs of nations and states which intend to continue for long periods of time must be governed by methods that more likely than not will let them survive for generations and centuries, and hence through scores of foreign-policy encounters, fraught with some risk of war.

Classic deterrence theory is still more dangerous in its third basic assumption: that both threatener and threatenee—that is, the governments and elites of both countries in a deterrence confrontation—will remain completely *rational under stress* (such as in a crisis involving threats, fear,

How Conflicts Arise Among States

uncertainty, fatigue, and communication overload). Experience, as well as a good deal of research in psychology, suggest the contrary; tense, frightened, and exhausted men—including statesmen and military men—tend to become irritable and aggressive, while their perceptions become less accurate and their judgment becomes poorer. In short, they become *less* rational—even though deterrence theory may advise the threatener to stake his own survival, just like theirs, on their rational responses to his threats.

The fourth of the basic but dubious assumptions of deterrence theory is a hidden one. It is the implicit assumption of some significant *asymmetry* between the threatener and threatenee, particularly when the writer's own country is involved in the contest. American writers on deterrence, as well as some American political and military leaders, assume that foreigners can be intimidated by threats or by demonstrations of ruthlessness which could only infuriate Americans: the foreigner often is assumed almost automatically to be weaker in his capabilities, or in his motivation to see the conflict through, or in his nerve and tolerance of risk. In our age of nationalism, this is a well-known and more-or-less international illusion, much encouraged by almost every government among its citizens. But it can be deadly in a policy of nuclear deterrence.

The fifth basic assumption of deterrence theory is perhaps the most fundamental of all; and it is one which extends to the entire larger class of game models. It is the familiar assumption of *unchanging motives* of the players throughout the game. Rational players, by assumption, must want to win, and they must want nothing else, from start to finish of the game. But this assumption is inappropriate for human affairs, and particularly for politics. We know that individuals, groups, parties, governments, and nations all change their minds; they often do so during some conflict in which they are involved; and some of these changes may be induced by the course of the conflict itself.

This assumption of unchanging motives is particularly important for calculating the probable success of the deterrence through calculated recklessness and partial irrationality—the threats that deliberately leave something to chance—that have been studied by Schelling. If both the cognitive perceptions and the values of the threatenee remain unchanged while he is being subjected to such tactics, then indeed it would be rational for him to give in to them. But this assumption is not plausible. The threatenee's perceptions of the threatener may change. If a threatener tries to present himself as partially irrational—by speeding up his automobile at intersections, by turning off his hearing-aid during negotiations, by pretending to be staggering or drunk while carrying high explosives past his adversary, or perhaps, in the case of the leader of a nation, by deliberately inflaming his domestic mass opinion—then it is rather likely that his adversary will *perceive* him as being largely or entirely irrational and thus as a blind menace which must be destroyed as soon as possible, at almost any risk. Seemingly irrational or imperfectly controlled threats with nuclear weapons, for instance, might most likely invite a "pre-emptive" nuclear attack from any threatened party that had the capability for one.

A shift in the *values* of the party who received the reckless threat might work in the same direction. The "Schelling-type" threats work best in situa-

How Conflicts Arise Among States

tions resembling "chicken" games; that is, situations in which the penalties for mutual non-cooperation are clearly much higher than the penalties to either side for giving in; and this is precisely why the more reckless threatener who speeded up his car, or who otherwise committed himself early in some irrevocable manner, may expect that his opponent, for reasons of self-interest, will give in to him about the less valuable point which is at issue in this encounter. In fact, however, the threatenee's values may now drastically change. What matters to him now is no longer the relatively trivial subject of the original dispute—such as the right of way at the original intersection, or, among governments, some barren and relatively worthless strip of disputed territory in a border conflict—but he may now assign an extremely high value to *not being subjected to such high-pressure tactics.* "I'll get that road hog if it's the last thing I do," an incensed motorist may mutter, even though he had been in no particular hurry at that intersection; and the government and mass opinion of a threatened country may now prefer to run the highest risks rather than to submit to threats even in an originally trivial dispute. In mathematical terms, the change in the scale of the threatenee's utilities has transformed the original "chicken"-type conflict into a genuine prisoners' dilemma, at least for one player, in which the penalty for unilateral giving in (CD) has become for him decisively larger than his share of the joint penalty for mutual conflict (DD). If and when this happens, "Schelling-type" threats through irrevocable commitments or deliberate partial loss of control are likely to become self-defeating and potentially self-destructive, and the erstwhile reckless threatener now may be able to save himself only by a quick return to tactics of moderation and mutual cooperation.

In the early stages of a deterrence conflict, therefore, both threatener and threatenee can, by their behavior, change to some extent each other's values and perceptions, as well as their own; and they can enlarge or diminish the proportion of interests which they have in common. To the extent that they are thus changing one another's motivations, their contest becomes less of a game and more of a genuine debate.

Debates: Contests that Permit Changes of Images and Motivations

Conflicts in which the adversaries are changing each other's motives, values, or cognitive images of reality, may be called "debates" in the strict sense of the term. Not all exchanges of words or messages, nor all events labeled as "debates," are genuine debates in this sense. Commonly, two high-school debating teams are not trying to change each other's minds on the debating topic which happens to be allotted to them; rather, they are engaged in a game in which they compete in impressing the judges of the debate, and perhaps the audience. In this game, they play to win; if a team announced in mid-"debate" that its adversaries had won it over by their arguments, its members might have learned about the topic under discussion, but they would have lost the game. Adversary proceedings in law courts usually have a similar gamelike character. Prosecutor and defense counsel are not trying to convince each other, nor are the lawyers for opposite parties in civil law suits trying to do so. In each case, they are trying to win their case, usually by impressing a judge or a jury; and to the extent that one side wins a verdict, the other side loses.

How Conflicts Arise Among States

Only the judge or the jury are expected to change their minds as a result of such adversary pleadings; between them, it is assumed (generally with good reason) that the contending parties will do a better job in bringing out all the relevant facts for the judge than any single and supposedly impartial investigating officer would be apt to do.

Debates in legislatures have a better chance of becoming genuine debates, and so have negotiations among diplomats representing governments, and the debates of government representatives in international organizations. In each of these cases, of course, the legislators, diplomats, or government delegates are trying to win something for the interests, parties, groups, or governments and nations which they represent. Often they must win something for the interests they represent at the expense of any interests opposed to them, and hence at the expense of other groups or governments. But often it is not entirely known which outcomes or solutions would in fact be most beneficial to the respective interests which each negotiator represents; and the outcomes most favorable to each, and perhaps jointly favorable to several or all of the parties concerned, may yet have to be discovered, and if discovered, then presented for acceptance and agreement.

Genuine negotiations, therefore, are a mixture of a competitive game with a joint voyage of discovery and with a mutual campaign of education toward a mutual appreciation and adjustment of the perceptions and preferences of several or all parties concerned. The long negotiations that led to the partial nuclear test-ban treaty of 1963 between the United States and the Soviet Union—which then was subscribed to by most of the nations of the world with the exception of France and Communist China—are an example of such a genuine debate. Soberly, in the course of it, in addition to the several persistent competitive interests of the various powers, a set of common perceptions and interests also developed, strong enough to lead to a decision which was accepted by almost all countries as being in their interests.

Though it seems that genuine debates, national or international, cannot well be represented by game models, nor indeed by any of the dumb, quasi-automatic "fight" processes discussed earlier, the precise nature of such debates is not well understood. However, there is a good deal of empirical experience about debates; and elements of insight and practical wisdom have been derived from it. One of these could be called the principle of *mutually acceptable restatement*. According to this principle, a debate is more likely to lead to the discovery of a mutually acceptable and beneficial solution if each side finds out what the other side is actually saying—that is, if it learns to state for itself the case of its adversaries in a form so clear and appealing as to be acceptable to these adversaries themselves.

Another essential step is for each side to find out on what grounds the other side could possibly be convinced of the truth of its own views. After one side has found out what views or pictures of reality its adversaries hold in their minds, they must try to discover the *domain of validity* of each such view. In a dispute between a newly emerged ex-colonial country and its former "mother country," spokesmen for the new nation are likely to complain about their earlier oppression or exploitation by their colonial masters, while spokesmen for the former imperial country will tend to stress the former colony's original poverty and the improvements and benefits which their colonial rule brought to the colony's people. Each of these views is likely to be valid for some limited range of facts, but invalid for others. If each side learns to discover the domain of validity, however small, of the seemingly preposterous views of its adversaries, and if they also discover the limits of the validity of their own (seemingly so reasonable) notions, then the likelihood—though not the certainty—of a genuine debate with an eventual fruitful and mutually rewarding outcome is increased.

As these examples suggest, many actual encounters among contending interest-groups, parties, nations, or ideologies may have many of the characteristics of debates. If so, then we may expect that time, events, and the results of their own behavior eventually will change not only the fortunes but also the outlook, goals, and values of the contestants. Somewhat in this vein, John Dewey once observed that men do not decide many of their controversies, but get over them. Apart from such small bits of wisdom, however, adequate formal models for genuine debates have yet to be developed.

Actual conflicts among states often resemble mixtures of fights, games, and debates, with this or that element predominating in the combination at different times and places. The art of statesmen, governments, and responsible citizens then consists in managing these international conflicts so as to keep them within tolerable bounds; to safeguard as far as practicable the current national interests while these interests themselves continue to evolve and change; to gain time and strength; and to ensure the national survival.

How Conflicts Arise Among States

Diplomacy
and
Coalitions

Any two states in conflict with each other invariably find themselves
peculiarly dependent on each other, even though their interests are at odds.
This comes about because the government of neither state can get
everything it wants without some cooperation (whether voluntary or
involuntary) on the part of the other. That is, the one state cannot make
(and legitimately claim) a gain against the other unless the other
allows (and tacitly admits to) a corresponding loss. Under such conflict
conditions, the rulers of each state will, of course,
try to make the other state do (and concede the doing of) what they

want, by whatever means that seem to suit the situation at the time—and the less embarrassing and costly the means, the better.

Diplomacy

First of all, of course, states can negotiate and bargain through the normal channels of diplomacy. Their ambassadors, foreign ministers, and other high-level diplomatic personnel usually are experienced negotiators. They know that to get a favor one may have to give or promise a favor in return; and they know that sometimes they also can put into the scales of bargaining polite suggestions that favors granted earlier to the other country are more likely to be continued if their own government's present wishes are accommodated.

Bargaining of this kind often resembles a game of diplomacy according to the rules of which the perceptions and interests of both parties are treated as given. The diplomats on both sides first have to figure out the most promising strategy for their *own* side, in the light of their estimate of the probable strategy of the *other* side. They then play the negotiating game from move to move, from proposal to counter-proposal, as best they can, until either an outcome acceptable to both sides is achieved, or the negotiations fail and are adjourned or terminated.

Sometimes, as we have seen in the preceding chapter, such negotiations even may take on some of the character of a genuine debate or dialogue between the two governments and nations. Each country and government then stands to learn something in the course of the negotiating process. And each party's images of the other, and of external reality, may therefore change somewhat, and so may even some of their initial preferences and values. If these changes tend to make the current interests of each country more compatible with those of the other, then their negotiating positions may converge, and a mutually satisfactory agreement between them become more likely. In international politics, however, each nation usually acts as if it had an interest in influencing this process in such a way as to induce as much change as possible in the other nation's views, while accepting as little change as possible in its own. As a rule, each nation prefers to talk rather than to listen; to teach rather than to learn. Each nation thus tries to induce much change in its adversaries or partners, while accepting as little change as possible for itself. (This sort of behavior was defined as the exercise of power—specifically, of net power—in an earlier section of this book.)

The relatively gentlest instruments of this pursuit of power over one or several other countries are *influence* and *propaganda*. Members of foreign elites can be made somewhat more receptive to the wishes of one's own country if they are educated there, especially in its prestige schools and universities. The influencing country may offer such bait as various honors and prizes to members of the elite of the target country, scholarships to their gifted students, and subsidies to some of their cherished but impecunious cultural institutions. Cultural-exchange programs, libraries, hospitals, visits by eminent poets or scientists may be provided for the same implicit purpose.

Beyond this, more massive efforts at influence may be directed at the mass media of the target country. They may be provided with a flow of

Diplomacy and Coalitions

suitable news, features, or pictures, free or at low prices; or they may be induced to commit themselves to take most of their international news from one of the more-or-less monopolistic news agencies of one of the great powers, such as Reuter's of Britain, Agence France-Presse of France, Japan's Kyodo News Service, Germany's DNB, the Soviet Union's TASS, and Associated Press (AP) and United Press International (UPI) for the United States. A glance at the initials of the worldwide news agency supplying most of its international news items to the major newspapers of a developing country often is enough to suggest which of the major powers probably exercises most influence in the country.

Other mass media can be used in the same way. For instance, by supplying a large share of the motion pictures shown in a country (usually on the basis of some specific trade or cultural agreement), or a substantial share of its television or radio programs, a large country can greatly increase its indirect influence over a smaller one.

Some methods of influence are more direct. For example, partial control of some foreign mass-media can be acquired through manipulation of advertising, or through purchase of ownership or stock. Editors of newspapers can be invited on extended and well-publicized official visits; or editors, like newspapers, can be subsidized discreetly in a variety of ways. Something similar can be done in some countries about some politicians, interest groups, or political factions or parties, and even about some members of the civil service, the military, the police, or the government itself. If any of these are for sale, often there are many ways of buying them quietly, or at least supporting their ambitions; or if their favors are offered freely, they still can be subsidized so as to make them more effective. At these points, of course, influence and propaganda are shading over into corruption, infiltration, subversion, and other disreputable forms of political warfare—but this has rarely stopped governments from resorting to such methods against countries which seemed vulnerable to them, and where major interests seemed to be at stake. All such attempts may backfire badly, however, if the target government discovers them in time, and if its nation, once aroused, is capable of strong resistance.

Supplementing such efforts at influencing a country from within are ways of subjecting it to propaganda and various forms of pressure from without. The mass media in the influencer country may launch a barrage or a sustained campaign of propaganda against the target government, so as to try to make it yield on some matter in dispute. Broadcasts may be beamed from abroad at its population; and even the booming of loudspeakers may be added at some border points. Pamphlets and leaflets may be mailed in, or smuggled in, or dropped from airplanes or balloons; or personal letter-writing campaigns may be organized in the influencer country, directed at presumably susceptible groups among the target population.

Rarely do such propaganda methods accomplish very much unless the target country's policy or government is already on the verge of changing. As a rule, it is far more effective to gain major positions of control or influence within the target country, or to acquire some really major levers for pressure on it from without. For this purpose, it may sometimes help a great deal to have control of major industries or business enterprises in the target country, with all the contacts and channels of economic, political, and social influence

135

Diplomacy and Coalitions

that go with them. The influencer country may also gain a power position within the target country by supplying essential weapons or communications equipment to the local military or police—who then must send some of their future key officers to the influencer country for training in their use, and who thereafter remain dependent on it for spare parts and for help in the more complex problems of both regular maintenance and periodical updating against obsolescence.

Promising but delaying or denying such supplies and help can be a powerful instrument of pressure, particularly in a crisis. So also can be the offer or the refusal (depending on the circumstances) to buy some exports of the target country, which are otherwise hard to sell; or the granting or withholding of a much-needed loan in a time of financial stringency; or the speeding-up or slowing-down of grain deliveries, after a crop failure in the target country has put a part of its population on the verge of famine.

But there are even more drastic means of pressure. Military aircraft of the influencer country may begin to stray more often across the boundaries of the target country, or engage in more extended overflights. In so doing, the influencer's aircraft not only can gather useful intelligence by photographing military onjectives, but can show their presence, demonstrate their (and thus their country's) prowess and the target country's timidity or inability to stop them, and encourage the local adherents of the influencer country while demoralizing their opponents. Similar effects can be obtained by warships; they have often been used to "show the flag" and to engage in various naval demonstrations off the coast of some recalcitrant country to be overawed, or of some precarious ally to be strengthened.

Unfortunately, perhaps, influence over a foreign country can be achieved only to a certain point by mere promises and threats. Beyond that point it is practically impossible of achievement without resorting to some form and degree of war. Before we survey these forms and degrees, however, it may be worthwhile to summarize in Table 12 the various situations that can create within the government of a potential influencer nation a demand for influence over the actions of the government of a potential target country.

In all these situations shown in Table 12, promises can be used to good advantage if they can be made relevant and credible for B, the country whose actions are to be influenced. Threats may help in six of the eight cases, and "perhaps" also in the other two, if B's future compliance seems dubious or tardy. Whether threats will succeed or backfire, however, depends not only on A's strength but also on all the conditions and limitations of deterrence theory discussed in the previous chapter. Similar limitations hold for actual rewards or penalties, for these, too, function among nations as implicit messages, and hence as promises or threats of future actions.

Coalitions

Often a state can make its promises and threats more credible, and its arsenal of possible actual rewards and penalties larger, by joining a coalition or by organizing one. More generally speaking, coalitions are an essential instrument for exercising influence and power, in international no less than in

Diplomacy and Coalitions

Table 12 OCCASIONS FOR COUNTRY "A" TO EXERCISE INFLUENCE OVER COUNTRY "B"

A prefers B to	Perform X Persuasion Situations				Avoid X ("perform" O) Dissuasion Situations			
	1	2	3	4	5	6	7	8
A prefers	X	X	X	X	O	O	O	O
A perceives B as now doing	O	O	X	X	X	X	O	O
A expects B to do later	O	X	O	X	X	O	X	O
A wants to *reinforce* or *modify* B's present behavior	M	M	R	R	M	M	R	R
A should:								
Punish	Yes	Perhaps*	No	No	Yes	Perhaps*	No	No
Reward	No	No	Yes	Yes	No	No	Yes	Yes
Threaten	Yes	Yes	Yes	Perhaps*	Yes	Yes	Yes	Perhaps*
Promise	Yes	Yes	Yes	Yes	Yes	Yes	Yes	Yes

* *A* should punish or threaten only if he doubts his own predictions about *B*'s future action, or if he doubts that *B*'s autonomous change will come soon enough.

Source: Adapted from J. David Singer, "Inter-Nation Influences: A Formal Model," *The American Political Science Review*, Vol. 57, No. 2 (June, 1963), p. 427.

domestic politics. Most often no single person, group, or nation is strong enough to prevail alone in a major decision; most often each can prevail only with the help of a coalition, or not prevail at all.

Political scientist William H. Riker has developed important theories about such coalitions. He sees politics, elections, legislative voting, and warfare all as decision situations which produce at least two alternative outcomes that are of different value to each participant. Every *politically rational* participant, says Riker, prefers the outcome that is more valuable to himself—that is, he wants to win. Where there are winners, he adds, there must be losers; and therefore, the best model for politics and war is a zero-sum game (which was discussed in the preceding chapter). But whereas money or utilities can be divided in a zero-sum game of economics, this cannot be done in the decisive contests of politics and war; "victory," as Riker sees it, "is an indivisible unit."[1] The rational man, then, is the one who always chooses the outcome with the biggest payoff for himself and who greatly wants to win.

[1] W. H. Riker, *The Theory of Political Coalitions* (New Haven: Yale University Press, 1967), pp. 29–31, 174.

Diplomacy and Coalitions

How can such dedicated egotists form coalitions? They will do so whenever this pays them more than staying in isolation does. For though victory, according to Riker, cannot be divided, often its spoils can be. In that case, the *rationality principle* predicts that each political actor will join—or try to organize—that coalition that promises him the biggest payoff. Clearly, this must be first of all a winning coalition, because without victory there are no spoils. Among several potential winning coalitions, however, that coalition will be preferable which can distribute the largest amount of spoils, and which can do so among the smallest number of partners.

Political rationality, therefore, as Riker understands it, will lead the political actors to the *size principle:* they will form and re-form tentative "proto-coalitions" in the process of bargaining, and search until some of them finally succeed in forming a *smallest winning coalition,* just big enough to win but small enough to allow no unnecessary allies to claim any part of the spoils.

Since there may be more than one such possible smallest winning coalition, the process of bargaining and search is likely to be long and complex. Rational political men, such as professional politicians or diplomats, will often spend extra time on negotiations and maneuvering if they have reason to expect that this will give them a better chance of ending up in a more favorable coalition. The direction of their maneuvers is predicted by Riker's *strategic principle: in the final stages of the coalition-forming process, the participants will move toward a minimal winning coalition.* When there are two large proto-coalitions of almost winning size in the "last-but-one" stage of the bargaining, therefore, they probably will not join forces, because the resulting coalition would be too big to offer sufficiently attractive payoffs to its members. Rather, according to Riker, one of the smaller proto-coalitions, or even a single participant, may suffice to turn one of the two large proto-coalitions into a minimal winning coalition. And this small but *pivotal* ally may be paid a share of the coalition's winnings quite out of proportion to his size or weight, but corresponding to the value of his strategic position in this particular sequence of the coalition-forming process.

Often, when the fruits of a victory cannot be readily divided, one of the participants to whom they are particularly valuable may offer various *side-payments* to prospective coalition partners, so as to purchase their support. Some of these side-payments may come out of the profits of the expected victory: they may consist of changes in a bill or treaty to be enacted, or in commitments to future policies, appointments, contracts, or concessions in the particular territories soon to be acquired by the coalition. Other payments may come out of what Riker calls the leader's "working capital," such as his present time, effort, and resources or commitments involved in other decisions of his, beyond the immediate victory now aimed at; and still other payments may come out of what Riker likens to his "fixed assets," such as the credibility of his threats, or his positive prestige, or his *charisma.*[2]

All such side payments have in some sense their costs to the leader: he

[2] A leader's charisma is his power to elicit spontaneous admiration and compliance from some significant audience or constituency, whose members are habituated or predisposed to respond in this manner to his presence, example, and messages.

Diplomacy and Coalitions

has to give up some things or efforts which have some value to him. As his side payments to prospective allies go up, therefore, the cumulative value of these payments may become higher than the content of the victory is worth to him. In that case, a rational leader ought to stop—if it were not for the probability, according to Riker, that winning in itself has acquired a value for the leader, almost regardless of the content or object of the victory. Indeed, says Riker, competitive politics selects the kind of opportunistic leader or statesman who has this compulsive habit and desire to win, not for a principle or ideology, but for the sake of winning.

The result is that coalition leaders almost inevitably tend to overspend. They will pay out in side payments more than the spoils of victory are worth to them. Thus they will eventually weaken themselves and build up their overpaid allies. In the end, as Riker sees it, each coalition leader ruins himself, because the intangible value to him of winning cannot replace the gradual depletion of the tangible assets he wastes on building or maintaining a materially unprofitable empire or coalition. This is one reason, in Riker's view, why empires decline, and why the United States and the Soviet Union will lose in the future a large part of the power they now hold in world politics: sooner or later they will be weakened by this fatal tendency of coalition leaders to overspend on allies.

It might be noted here that the tendency to overspend, according to Riker, is also one of the reasons for the basic instability of the international system of sovereign states. A second reason for this instability is the tendency of such an insatiably competitive system to eliminate some of its essential actors.

Coalition Theory and the Instability of Balance-of-Power

According to the classic *balance-of-power theory* (as reformulated in modern terms by political scientist Morton A. Kaplan), there ought to be at least five great powers, or "essential actors," in the world (since with fewer powers there would not be enough different coalitions to keep the system flexible); and each of these powers would have to obey certain essential rules. A somewhat modified and simplified version of these rules might read:

A. *Rationality:*
  1. Always act to increase capabilities.
  2. Negotiate rather than fight; but fight rather than pass up an increase in capabilities.
B. *Preservation of actors:*
  3. Stop fighting rather than eliminate an essential actor.
  4. Permit any defeated essential actor to reenter as a possible partner; or replace him by elevating a previously nonessential actor (*i.e.*, a smaller power) in his place; and treat all essential actors as acceptable potential allies.
C. *Preservation of the system:*
  5. Act to oppose any actor or coalition who tends to become predominant within the system. (Hence, if one proto-coalition is close to victory, neutral actors ought to join the strongest of its weaker opponents.)
  6. Act to constrain actors who subscribe to supranational organizing principles.

Working by these rules, says Kaplan, such a system can preserve itself for a long time; but such a system, says Riker, *cannot* work. Rational actors want to win; they will not support a balance-of-power system, when they have an opportunity instead to join a winning coalition; and among five powers, sooner or later there will be such opportunities. Moreover, a rational actor certainly will act to increase his capabilities. He will not stop to spare a defeated essential actor, if there is no other way to get a payoff for himself. Hence, as payoffs in the contest become scarcer, restraints will become ineffective. The same holds for all restraints in rules 3–6: they are based on international morality or long-run self-interest, but both of these are likely to weaken or fade away when immediate decision pressures mount. The competitive system of politics, says Riker, rewards and selects leaders who overreach and overspend, and who care more for winning than for principles. Such leaders cannot be expected to care much for any principles by which a balance-of-power system would have to be preserved.

Riker concludes that all such politics are characterized by a *disequilibrium principle*. Political systems whose members act in accordance with the principles of size and strategy must be unstable. They contain forces pressing toward decision regardless of the stakes or content of the decision, and hence toward the elimination of participants, and potentially of the whole system.

Riker's analysis is penetrating but one-sided. In order to highlight some aspects of politics, he has chosen to represent all coalition politics by the zero-sum game rather than by the more realistic variable-sum model. He has emphasized short-run victory and "winning" as single values in themselves, far beyond their substantive content, and remote from the actual context of all other basic values—which are no less important in man's social and political behavior. He has paid a heavy price for this extreme degree of abstraction. In his theory, every victory is final in regard to its spoils. These spoils are grasped by the victors, but no attention is paid to the question of how these spoils were produced in the first place or how they are to be reproduced in the future, for the next round of the process. Where modern economics and sociology, and much of political science, deal with circular flows or feedback processes of messages, services, or values, in Riker's world, transfers of spoils are terminal and one-way only: to the victors. Thus he has written a theory of the politics of appropriation, but not of the politics of production, of cooperation, and of growth—all of which are no less vital.

Regardless of its limits, however, Riker's theory of coalitions represents a considerable intellectual achievement. It offers a model of the process by which coalitions may be formed; it permits the identification of strategic possibilities in this process; it contributes an important criticism of the balance-of-power theory; and it reveals deep-seated sources of instability in the behavior of statesmen, national coalition leaders, and leading governments and nations in the international arena.

Diplomacy and Coalitions

Failures of Controls, and Forms of War

CHAPTER THIRTEEN

If neither national means of influence, nor the added influence of an international coalition, suffices to change the behavior of a target country, then the power trying to influence it may have to resort to force. The least violent use of force is the blockade—either by land, as imposed by the Soviet Union on West Berlin in 1948, or by sea, as used briefly by the United States against Cuba in 1962.

Limited Violence as a Means of Pressure

If a blockade is not challenged by another power, its enforcement may succeed without bloodshed. But if it is challenged, or if its enforcement fails, or if, though enforced, it fails to change the behavior of the target country, then the would-be influencer nation may either have to abandon its attempt at putting pressure on the target country, or move up higher on the ladder of escalating conflict. And from this level of conflict on upward, some people are likely to be killed.

An obvious way of stepping up the pressure on the target country is the infiltration of saboteurs and guerrillas, who mine roads, blow up weakly-guarded installations, and attack isolated officials or local agencies or minor centers of the government. Even if such infiltrators find no significant support among the population, as was the case of Arabs infiltrating into Israel before 1967 from Syria and the United Arab Republic, they can maintain an atmosphere of insecurity and harassment, at least in areas close to the border. And if the infiltrators carry more powerful equipment and get some support from among the local population, they can strike more deeply, as did some of the British commando raiders against Nazi-occupied France in World War II and as Arab raiders could do in the Israeli-occupied part of Jordan after the 1967 war.

The greatest effects of infiltration are obtained, however, in situations where the infiltrators serve merely as supplements or catalysts for local guerrilla forces recruited—and, if possible, led wholly or in part—from within the target country and its population. Here the foreign input of radio, propaganda, armed agents, special equipment, technical expertise, and (perhaps) troops, can augment or sustain or even trigger a genuine domestic civil war.

Foreign Intervention and Internal Wars

Foreign pressure or interference can have several different purposes. It can aim at making the government of the target country do something which it otherwise would not do; or it can try to prevent the target government from doing something which it otherwise would do. (The first of these aims was called "X" and the second "O" in Table 12.) But the influencer country may have more far-reaching aims. It may wish to change the composition of the target country's government, or some of its basic institutions, or to take over part of its territory, or to end its independence altogether. Thus, a Communist government may wish to pressure a neighboring target country into admitting local Communists to its new coalition government, which alone can end (it is suggested) the foreign-supported violence on its soil; or its pressure may even aim at installing there a full-fledged Communist regime, either locally recruited or partly imported from abroad. Conversely, an anti-Communist power might put pressure on a Communist-ruled target country to relax its dictatorial controls and to grant more freedom and influence to non-Communist or anti-Communist domestic groups; or to concede greater local

Failures of Controls, and Forms of War

autonomy to border regions where non-Communist or anti-Communist sentiments might prevail; or to overthrow entirely the target country's Communist government and replace it with an anti-Communist regime, perhaps one allied to the West. Soviet Russian, Bulgarian, and Yugoslav support for Greek Communist guerrillas in the mid-1940's, and North Vietnamese pressure on Laos and South Vietnam in the 1950's and 1960's, exemplified problems of the first kind; United States support for anti-Communist Cuban guerrillas at the time of the Bay of Pigs invasion in 1961 raised problems of the second kind.

The outcome of such efforts depends most often on three things:

1. The sympathies, activity, and vigor of the domestic population of the target country in supporting or opposing its government;
2. The sheer size, kind, and persistence of the foreign input and pressure against the target country or regime;
3. The intervention or nonintervention of additional countries on either side of the conflict.

The relative weight of each of these three factors varies in part with the size of the target country. The larger its population, the larger will tend to be the cost of foreign intervention, and the smaller its effect. In large countries (such as those with over 30 million inhabitants), foreign intervention is particularly costly and unpromising, and the attitudes and actions of the domestic population are apt to be decisive to the outcome of political contests. In small countries (such as those with less than 10 million population); outside intervention, disguised or open, is more likely to carry the day, as it did in Guatemala in 1954, in Lebanon in 1958, and in the Dominican Republic in 1965. It takes an unusually well-entrenched government, or usually strong motivation among a large part of the population, for a small country to retain a type of government that puts it at odds with a powerful next-door neighbor, but at different times and in various ways Switzerland, Israel, Finland, Afghanistan, and Cuba all have shown that it can be done, particularly since a vigorously defended small country may not be worth (to its bigger neighbor) the probable costs of intervention on a scale large enough to bring down its government or end its independence.

Serious international problems are most likely to arise in the case of middle-sized countries (perhaps those between 10 and 30 million in population) such as Algeria, both Vietnams, Yugoslavia, Czechoslovakia, and Egypt, which may seem small enough to look like easy targets of intervention, yet big enough to appear profitable. If a country of this tempting middle size becomes divided by internal group conflict or incipient revolt or civil war, one or several outside powers may be strongly drawn to intervene, clandestinely or openly, in the hope of some quick gain in the international power contest. Such hopes, however, are likely to be disappointed, particularly if a substantial part of the country's population is strongly motivated to take part in its political struggles. In such cases, the balance of domestic political forces is likely to contribute most to determining the outcome; and the scale of the conflict is apt to be so large as to make outside intervention very long and drawn-out, costly, and ultimately unrewarding. Even if the domestic allies of the intervening power should prevail in a country of this inviting but

Failures of Controls, and Forms of War

unmanageable middle size, they are likely to conclude quite soon, and often correctly, that they won chiefly by their own efforts, and they may eventually astonish their former protectors by their ingratitude.

In countries of any appreciable size, the relative strength of the three basic factors—the numbers and activity of the domestic population, the size and skill of intervention by the outside power, and the abstention or intervention of other foreign powers—will generate one of three main types of conflict:

1. A civil war, fought and sustained mainly by forces from within the target country, with foreign inputs and pressures playing only a marginal part (as they did in the Russian Civil War of 1917–1921);

2. A foreign attack, carried out primarily by outside troops invading across a national frontier or across the demarcation line of a part of a divided country, with only short-lived and marginal support from local sympathizers and guerrillas (as in the case of the North Korean invasion of South Korea in 1950);

3. A mixed type of war, in which large domestic rebel forces are fighting against the government of the target country in the manner of a genuine civil war, while at the same time receiving substantial and sustained support from at least one outside power (as did the Viet Cong guerrillas in South Vietnam, who were estimated in 1967 by the U.S. Department of Defense to consist of about 230,000 South Vietnamese and 50,000 individuals and troops from North Vietnam).

Most of the time since 1945, United States policy toward the first two types of conflict has been clear and relatively simple. It has been to avoid any heavy involvement in genuine civil wars abroad, such as the Chinese Civil War, but to oppose vigorously, and even at great cost, any massive aggression across an international boundary or demarcation line, as in Korea in 1950. Both these policies have been reasonably popular, within the United States as well as in most of the non-Communist world, where opposition to them has remained minor.

But there is no simple policy for dealing with the third (mixed) type of war, such as the Vietnam war in the 1960's. When simple policies were tried in that case, it soon became evident that they did not work particularly well. Successive administrations in the United States, and particularly President Johnson's administration from 1964 onward, tended to describe this conflict as primarily a matter of North Vietnamese aggression against South Vietnam. Domestic and foreign critics, on the contrary, pointing to the four-fifths of South Vietnamese among the Viet Cong, tended to see the contest mainly as a civil war, disregarding the one-fifth of Viet Cong troops coming from North Vietnam, and the presumably much larger share of Viet Cong firepower and equipment supplied from there or from other Communist countries. A succession of hard-pressed South Vietnamese governments, all of them already dependent on American support, soon called for ever larger numbers of troops to help them against their foreign and domestic enemies. By May, 1967, about 450,000 United States troops were engaged in South Vietnam, outnumbering by then its North Vietnamese infiltrators roughly 9:1. Also by then, United States air and naval forces had subjected much of North Vietnam to steadily extending bombardment for more than two years (since February, 1965). But the government of North Vietnam showed no signs of yielding, and the war in South Vietnam showed no signs of abating—indeed, the overall conflict in

144

Failures of Controls, and Forms of War

the area was continuing to escalate. A war of this kind, it appeared, was unlikely to be settled by either a clean-cut doctrinal definition or clear military victory, but rather by a long and drawn-out sequence of attrition, exhaustion, and eventual compromise—unless it were to be swallowed up in the cataclysm of a much larger war among the great powers.

The Ladder of Escalation

As pictured by Herman Kahn (and shown in Table 13), a limited war of the type fought in Vietnam early in 1967—that is, a war stopping short of all-out bombardment, massive land invasions, and the use of nuclear weapons—offers only a temporary resting place on the long ladder of escalation.

In almost every limited war in our time, the great powers are directly or indirectly involved. If all of them accept the outcome of the local limited conflict—win, lose, or draw—then this war becomes for them an "agreed battle." Within its explicit or tacitly accepted rules, the major powers then are free to test both their policies and their (conventional) weapons, as well as the capabilities and motivations of their local outcome and to pursue thereafter their interests there and elsewhere in its light.

If at least one major power refuses to accept this local outcome, however, then it will break some of the limiting rules rather than accept loss of face or influence for itself, or defeat for its local allies. In that case, it will escalate the war; and unless every great power on the opposing side is much weaker, or much more cowardly, or much more pacifistic, the other side will do the same; and escalation will proceed beyond this major halting-point.

From here on, halting-points are fewer, and each of them will be less likely to have much effect. Limited conventional war now tends to give way to all-out conventional war, with no limits on military targets in the field. But all-out conventional war strongly favors the rise of a conventional war psychology of the kind familiar from World Wars I and II. Ever more extreme weapons will seem attractive to the elite and mass opinion in the main contending countries, with the ancient rationalization that the most ruthless tactics are now expected to be the most merciful, since they are to knock out the enemy quickly, and thus to save lives. But this logic tends to appeal to both sides; or else the side that first was less ruthless soon resorts to retaliation. The war thus gets ever more destructive, and its survivors on both sides more embittered. Now the resort to nuclear weapons may seem only a question of time, and each side may become determined to snatch every possible advantage by doing sooner what they now think in any case is inevitable.

At first, even nuclear war may remain local. Only tactical nuclear weapons may be used, and only on the battlefield. Soon, however, rocket-borne intermediate-range nuclear weapons may be used to attack the seaports, railroad centers, and airfields of each side behind the local front, destroying in the process much of the civilian population in their vicinity. (Public opinion may be less shocked at this stage. People already may have become used at earlier stages of the war to large-scale conventional air attacks on civilian populations, and they may not yet be fully aware of the other side's capabilities for nuclear retaliation.)

Failures of Controls, and Forms of War

Table 13   AN ESCALATION LADDER: A Generalized (or Abstract) Scenario

AFTERMATHS

Civilian	44.	Spasm or Insensate War
Central	43.	Some Other Kinds of Controlled General War
Wars	42.	Civilian Devastation Attack
	41.	Augmented Disarming Attack
	40.	Countervalue Salvo
	39.	Slow-Motion Countercity War

(CITY TARGETING THRESHOLD)

Military	38.	Unmodified Counterforce Attack
Central	37.	Counterforce-with-Avoidance Attack
Wars	36.	Constrained Disarming Attack
	35.	Constrained Force-Reduction Salvo
	34.	Slow-Motion Counterforce War
	33.	Slow-Motion Counter-"Property" War
	32.	Formal Declaration of "General" War

(CENTRAL WAR THRESHOLD)

Exemplary	31.	Reciprocal Reprisals
Central	30.	Complete Evacuation (Approximately 95 per cent)
Attacks	29.	Exemplary Attacks on Population
	28.	Exemplary Attacks Against Property
	27.	Exemplary Attack on Military
	26.	Demonstration Attack on Zone of Interior

(CENTRAL SANCTUARY THRESHOLD)

Bizarre	25.	Evacuation (Approximately 70 per cent)
Crises	24.	Unusual, Provocative, and Significant Countermeasures
	23.	Local Nuclear War—Military
	22.	Declaration of Limited Nuclear War
	21.	Local Nuclear War—Exemplary

(NO NUCLEAR USE THRESHOLD)

Intense	20.	"Peaceful" World-Wide Embargo or Blockade
Crises	19.	"Justifiable" Counterforce Attack
	18.	Spectacular Show or Demonstration of Force
	17.	Limited Evacuation (Approximately 20 per cent)
	16.	Nuclear "Ultimatums"
	15.	Barely Nuclear War
	14.	Declaration of Limited Conventional War
	13.	Large Compound Escalation
	12.	Large Conventional War (or Actions)
	11.	Super-Ready Status
	10.	Provocative Breaking Off of Diplomatic Relations

(NUCLEAR WAR IS UNTHINKABLE THRESHOLD)

Traditional	9.	Dramatic Military Confrontations
Crises	8.	Harassing Acts of Violence
	7.	"Legal" Harassment—Retortions
	6.	Significant Mobilization
	5.	Show of Force
	4.	Hardening of Positions—Confrontation of Wills

(DON'T ROCK THE BOAT THRESHOLD)

Subcrisis	3.	Solemn and Formal Declarations
Maneuvering	2.	Political, Economic, and Diplomatic Gestures
	1.	Ostensible Crisis

DISAGREEMENT—COLD WAR

Source: On Escalation: Metaphors and Scenarios by Herman Kahn, published by Frederick A. Praeger, Inc., Publishers, New York and Pall Mall Press, London, 1965.

Failures of Controls, and Forms of War

As one side gets the worst in the local nuclear contest, however, its leaders will be tempted to attack the enemy power's (or coalition's) "central sanctuary"—that is, his main national territory with its central regions and main cities. The first attacks from either side may well be mere demonstrations, or they may be "exemplary" attacks, designed to devastate a few specific military targets, industrial installations, or population centers, in order to demonstrate the power of its weapons. From the point of view of the technician, the destruction of the cities of Hiroshima and Nagasaki in August, 1945, were such "exemplary" attacks, against which the Japanese then had no power to retaliate. But in today's world, both sides in any major war would have nuclear weapons, and as demonstration or "exemplary" attacks are answered by retaliation rather than surrender, escalation would very likely continue.

Now that each side has demonstrated the terror of its weapons, and its own readiness to use them ruthlessly, it has a very strong motive to destroy as many as possible of the weapons of the other before they can be used. Here the escalating war may enter the stage of "military central wars," with nuclear attacks on military targets in the central territory of each of the contending powers. These may be "counterforce" or "first strike" attacks, aimed at quickly destroying on the ground many of the bombers and missiles of the adversary before they can be launched; here each power may try to beat the other to the draw. But no "first strike" is likely to eliminate all the nuclear weapons of a major power, and its surviving force, for a retaliatory "second strike" against the attacker may be devastating.

At this stage, "counterforce" war, directed against airfields and missile sites, may give way to "countercity" war directed against people. According to the calculations of some strategists, it would be most rational for each side to destroy at first only one or a few of the cities of its adversary, so as to impress upon him that his surviving cities now are hostages. But the same rational strategic calculations will suggest to him that he should do the same: destroy one or a few cities of the enemy nation, so as to hold their remaining cities as hostages. The results may be a "countercity" war in slow motion, in which the two great powers destroy each other's cities, one after the other, in a stately minuet of death, until one of them decides to escalate the war further.

For there is still room for escalation. There are some cities which a nation may treasure more highly than others, because they contain sacred religious objects, treasured national relics, irreplaceable art treasures, or many members of the families of the nation's governing elite. And there are, most important in our age of mass politics, the large concentrations of population containing the lives of many millions of the nation. Any or all of these could become targets at this stage for "countervalue" attacks or reprisals. If all or most of them should be attacked, we may speak of a "civilian devastation attack," and if all restraints, and indeed all further efforts at rational political control should cease, and a country should fire all its remaining weapons at its enemy, there would be what some writers speak of as "spasm, or insensate, war." After this—after the last weapon had been fired and the last military resource exhausted—there would be nothing left but the prospect of a lingering death in a vast, poisoned wasteland for most if not all of whatever survivors there might be.

Failures of Controls, and Forms of War

Crucial Links in the Processes

Our survey began with the effort of one state to put pressure on another. It then surveyed the rising scale of international conflict until the level of limited war had been reached, and then traced its possible escalation to all-out war and the destruction of the major contestants, together with much of their environment. The processes that can link these successive stages of mounting conflict into a fateful chain of events are failures of *perception, foresight,* and *control.*

Failures of perception are familiar to us from our earlier discussion of mass images, media, and the role of governments, which first may strengthen these images and then themselves become influenced by them in their decisions. Attachment to established images of one's own nation and of foreign countries, desire for cognitive consonance, rejection and denial of information that does not fit accepted preconceptions—all these can add up to the equivalent of sleep or blindness for governments and nations. They may fail to see realistically the attitudes and capabilities of foreign populations, and the interests, policies, capabilities, and commitments of foreign governments, until they are on a full collision course with them, and on the way to escalation.

On its way toward collision, a government may be thought of, in a manner similar to that of a ship's captain or an automobile driver, as passing a point of surprise and a point of no escape. The *point of surprise* in an automobile accident, according to a scheme developed for the accident research of insurance companies, is that point in the progress of a vehicle at which its operator first becomes aware that he is moving toward a collision or other major accident. The *point of no escape* is that point in his progress toward the accident when nothing further he can do can prevent the crash. If the point of surprise comes before the point of no escape, the operator can still prevent the crash and save himself and his vehicle; if it comes afterward, awareness comes too late and catastrophe has become inevitable.

The same sequences have been traced in the catastrophic collisions of world politics, such as the start of World War I. Some governments in 1914 discovered that they were moving toward a big war, not a small one, at a time when they still could do something to avert it (although, as it happened, they did not do enough). But other governments, such as those of Imperial Germany, Russia, and Austria-Hungary, discovered only too late where events were taking them, and were unable to stop their countries' journey to destruction.

If the process of escalation is slower and drawn out over more intermediate stages, the point of no escape comes later. If the rulers of at least one country discover in time that the entire "conflict system" of the contending countries is moving toward catastrophe, they may still succeed in halting escalation. But even if they realize their danger in time, the process of escalation itself may impair their capacity for rational decision-making, or in part even destroy it. The national decision-makers are now exposed to the tension caused by fear and resentment of the foreign adversary; to the impact of his

148

Failures of Controls, and Forms of War

threatening, provocative, or hostile actions; and to the impact of domestic mass opinion and their own patriotic and almost inevitably inflammatory propaganda. Under these pressures, the values and perceptions of the decision-makers may change in the direction of more intense conflict, or else the decision-makers themselves may now be replaced by others who have fewer inhibitions about vigorously prosecuting and aggravating the conflict.

Eventually, as in a limited war, pro-war or pro-conflict sentiment among the elite, as well as among the masses, may reach a peak level at which it may become stabilized for a time while the limited war is being pressed forward. From this peak level, there are three exits. The limited war may be won, and the pro-conflict sentiment ends in triumph; or the conflict escalates to all-out nuclear destruction; or else the conflict drags on without victory, and there eventually follows a stage of weariness, exhaustion, or reorientation of desires on the home front. After many young men have been killed, the lives of those who survive often have seemed more valuable; and the aims or demands of the opening phase of a conflict sometimes have seemed curiously irrelevant to those who were still living near its end.

At this stage, domestic political consensus may break down. While some groups are likely to continue to press the war, other groups now may come to oppose it and to press for peace. Alternatively, domestic opinion among all groups and levels may move more-or-less in step, so that domestic conflict is avoided as the foreign war gradually becomes less popular. In either case, elite and mass opinion may now shift toward compromise and accommodation.

In the case of a badly exhausted and defeated country, elite and mass opinion may shift further. They may now accept large concessions to the adversary, as many Russians did in early 1918 at the time of the Peace of Brest-Litovsk with Germany. In extreme cases, they even may favor outright surrender, if further resistance against a greatly superior enemy appears hopeless, and if life under the predictable post-surrender conditions appears preferable, as it did to the German and Japanese military leaders who surrendered to the United States and to the other Allies in 1945.

Such a surrender still was an implicit bargain. The defeated country traded its residual capacity to inflict damage on the victor for terms which it expected to be significantly better than it was likely to receive otherwise. Such a surrender, however, requires an effective victor capable of enforcing terms; and it seems unlikely that after any all-out nuclear war between great powers any victor of this kind will be left. Since any great power also seems quite unlikely to surrender short of extreme—and mutual—destruction, discussions about "strategic surrender" are likely to remain quite academic. Discussions of de-escalation, and conflict limitation at early stages of great power conflict, should be far more practical.

Failures of Controls, and Forms of War

Some Alternatives to Escalation and Warfare

CHAPTER FOURTEEN

Even where one state has not succeeded in controlling the behavior of another, escalation toward all-out conflict still can be either slowed down or halted—perhaps even reversed. Under certain conditions (to be discussed later) it can in fact be avoided altogether. It is possible to make conflicts rare and weak, even between closely interdependent countries or peoples, and to make collaboration so frequent and rewarding that it may initiate a chain of events leading to some form of stable and lasting political integration.

One class of strategy to de-escalate tense conflict situations has been proposed by the social psychologists Charles E. Osgood and Morton Deutsch and the sociologist Amitai Etzioni. In their view, any government wishing to mitigate a conflict should make a limited but unmistakable unilateral concession or gesture of conciliation, or even a small number of such acts or gestures. If the adversary nation should reciprocate by some counter-concession or conciliatory gesture, the first country should initiate another small but clear step toward improved relations; and if this were answered in kind, still another step should be initiated, until the entire conflict has been reduced to a safe level, or even until it has been replaced by some degree of mutual tolerance, cooperation, and—eventually—friendliness.

If the first initiative toward de-escalation or greater friendliness should be rebuffed, this theory suggests that the more conciliatory country should under no circumstances escalate the conflict, but merely wait for a time. If attacked, it should defend its interests at the existing level of contention or hostility; but it should soon seek and take another limited unilateral initiative toward conciliation. The basic idea is similar to the one suggested by Anatol Rapoport's experimental data for the prisoners' dilemma game. It is to avoid both martyrdom and cynicism: to resist attack, but to continue offering the adversary clear and repeated opportunities to shift to a sequence of mutually cooperative moves.

Though this strategy may work sometimes in international relations, as it has worked in labor relations and in some other relatively small-scale conflict situations, its success at the present stage of international politics cannot be relied on. After all, drives toward conflict most often have existed in *both* states. Usually they have been embodied in much of their social and political structure, in their earlier economic decisions and investments, in the commitments of their political and military leaders and elites, in the images in the minds of their elites and their masses, and in the expectations and trains of actions to which all these have given rise. To stop these trains of actions, to undo commitments, to reverse specific orders and major policies, to cancel government contracts, to take back political promises, to disengage the reputations of parties and leaders, to disappoint expectations and interests, to upset domestic and international compromises and policy agreements—all this is painful, costly, and often fraught with severe risk. The country that is suddenly trying to de-escalate a foreign conflict may find itself subjected to severe domestic strains and conflicts; and its rulers and elites may fear the domestic costs of "giving in," or even of de-escalation, in a foreign conflict, more than they fear the political and military costs of a mounting foreign confrontation.

These domestic dangers are greater if the unilateral concessions to a foreign adversary are large or sudden, and they are still greater if these are not matched fairly soon by some visible concessions by him. Repeated limited step-by-step initiatives, tempered by waiting for counter-concessions and by resistance to, and limited retaliation for, any new attacks by the foreign adversary, may go far to reduce the risks of bringing on a domestic political crisis, but may not eliminate it altogether. For success, genuine good will to de-escalate abroad would have to be combined with skill and competence in domestic leadership.

Some Alternatives to Escalation and Warfare

Internal Transformation of One or Both Parties to the Conflict

Since conflicts are often brought on by processes implicit in the internal structures of one or both of the clashing countries, a change of these structures might end such conflicts and also end their recurrence. Radical internal transformation of competing countries has often been advocated, therefore, as the best way—and by some, as the only way—to abolish war. Jean Jacques Rousseau believed that absolute princely rule in the states of eighteenth-century Europe was the root cause of wars. He rejected, therefore, as impracticable the project of his contemporary, the Abbe St. Pierre, for a League of Princes to keep the peace; only by abolishing the absolute monarchial regimes, Rousseau thought, could peace be made secure. (Alexander Hamilton would not have believed this. He pointed out in *The Federalist* that in history, "commercial republics," such as Carthage and Venice, had proved as warlike as, or more warlike than, aristocratic monarchies.) In due course, absolute monarchies disappeared from most of Europe and the rest of the world, but the nation-states that succeeded them proved no more peaceful than their predecessors.

Whereas Rousseau had hoped to abolish war by abolishing absolute monarchies, Marx and Lenin hoped to end all wars by abolishing the capitalist economic system—and with it, as they expected, eventually all class rule. With the end of conflicts among classes, Marx believed, there would be an end to conflicts among nations. Since 1945, a plurality of Communist states has emerged, and this hope, too, has begun to be tested by experience. Although Communist governments usually claim that class conflicts within their countries have been largely ended, and that their relations to other Communist countries are fraternal, the dictatorial state machinery in each of the countries has not yet "withered away," nor does it show any signs of soon doing so; too, international relations among Communist countries, particularly those with different shades of Communist doctrine, have been rich in political and economic conflicts, although by mid-1967 no wars had broken out among them. The Communist hope to avoid short-of-war conflicts among Communist states has thus been disappointed—as in the 1968 Soviet occupation of Czechoslovakia—but the verdict on their hopes to avoid major inter-Communist warfare indefinitely still remained open.

If no radical internal transformation of states thus far has abolished the danger of war, the fear of such radical transformations often has made the danger worse. Threatened elites and favored minorities (such as those of Germany, Italy, and Japan in the 1930's) sometimes have deliberately preferred conflict abroad to the prospect of intolerable change at home. Their fears and resentments of threatening domestic changes have made them irrationally defensive and aggressive, seeing everywhere around them conspiracies and threats and striking out finally in blind panic and fury against some foreign rival or target.

From the viewpoint of preserving peace, less sweeping changes in the domestic social systems and politics of states might be both safer and more effective, particularly if such limited changes can be carried forward unremit-

Some Alternatives to Escalation and Warfare

tingly. Such limited changes would have to be generally in the direction of increasing the capabilities of each nation for conflict tolerance and conflict management. They would have to aim within each country at increasing the adaptability and cohesion of its political system, at its capability for integration and for the effective change of at least some of the nation's goals, and perhaps even at its capability for further national self-transformation and development.

Such limited and partial internal transformations of states and nations (toward more effective conflict management and the pursuit of less dangerous and more rewarding goals) have been more frequent in history than one might think. England had been embroiled in land wars on the European continent from the thirteenth to the fifteenth centuries, holding during much of the time such port cities as Bordeaux and Calais, winning resounding victories at Crecy and Agincourt, burning Joan of Arc and devastating France, and spending considerable manpower and treasure in the process. The English military and political commitment to the Continent may well have seemed irreversible to many of her leaders. As late as the mid-sixteenth century, Queen Mary the Catholic was said to have died with the word "Calais" on her lips. Yet in fact the commitment was by then almost ended. Calais, and with it the last English strong-point in France, was soon abandoned, and England turned away from the pursuit of land power on the continent to the more rewarding pursuit of sea power all around the world.

This shift was immensely beneficial for England, to whom it brought four centuries of unprecedented growth, power, and prosperity. But the shift was made possible, or at least easier, only by the coming to power in England in 1485 of a new dynasty, the Tudors, with a greater interest in ships and naval affairs, a new coalition of supporters (based on Wales and some of the formerly less influential elite groups and families in England), and a new view of administration and government. Later on, after 1536, the shift was further aided by the rise of a new issue, the Protestant Reformation, which overshadowed the old images of an English commitment to the Continent. The shift became complete when in 1555 English Protestantism finally triumphed with the accession of Queen Elizabeth I.

Other examples cannot be traced in detail. But the shift of the Swiss Confederation in 1515, from an exhausting pursuit of power over Lombardy to a less costly and more rewarding policy of neutrality, limited westward expansion, and internal development would show a similar pattern. Here, too, the shift was facilitated by a relative shift in influence in favor of those old and new members of the Confederacy (such as Bern, Fribourg, Solothurn, Basel, Schaffhausen, and Appensell) who had little interest in Lombardy, along with a relative decline of influence over the Confederation as a whole on the part of Cantons (such as Uri and Schwyz) most immediately concerned with the affairs of Lombardy. Here, too, eventually, the Reformation brought in a new set of problems and conflicts which made the earlier Swiss commitment to power politics in Lombardy soon seem unimportant and even irrelevant.

Sweden's abandonment in the eighteenth century of her former great power policies in the Baltic area and at the edge of the land mass of Russia was similarly prompted by the mounting costs of unending land wars against Russia. And the United States' efforts to bring Canada into the Union, **153**

Some Alternatives to Escalation and Warfare

pursued in fits and starts from the American Revolution and the Articles of Confederation until the War of 1812, were abandoned after that war and its unsuccessful campaign against Canada. The United States–Canadian frontier was demilitarized in 1819 and remained substantially unchallenged thereafter, while United States policy shifted fully to the more rewarding pursuit of westward expansion.

The conflict between France and the Arab nationalists of Algeria may have been de-escalated by a similar process. France shifted from protracted and unrewarding land warfare in Algeria to a more effective pursuit of her interests in much of the rest of Africa and in Europe, as well as to the economic and technological development of France herself and the nuclear equipment of the French armed forces. This shift was made easier by the partial replacement of the institutions and leadership groups of the Fourth French Republic by those of the Fifth, including notably President de Gaulle and his party, and by the replacement of some of the old colonial-war-minded generals by new and more technically oriented military leaders.

The United States in the late 1960's was beginning to face the possibility of a choice between increasing pursuit of land power in Asia and a more vigorous pursuit of European and Atlantic integration, more economic aid to developing countries, and expansion into outer space, with an attendant growth in its over-all scientific and technological capabilities and resources. Under its Constitution and the two-party system, such a shift could be easily and smoothly accomplished, once public opinion at the mass and elite levels should come to demand it; but by mid-1968 the choice had not been made.

Reduction of Mutual Contacts

As the schematic presentation in Fig. 4 suggests, conflicts tend to arise among countries which have a high degree of interdependence and mutual trans-action, but who have opposite interests, so that there is a "negative covariance" in their rewards: many outcomes which are rewarding for one country are frustrating or penalizing for the other. Conflicts among such countries can be reduced by reducing the extent of their mutual interdependence, and by cutting down the flow of transactions among them. As mutual contacts decline, so may occasions for quarrels.

The traditional policies of ancient China seem to have followed some such principle when its rulers built the Great Wall and kept down most contacts with the outside world until the early nineteenth century. Japan's rulers under the Tokugawa Dynasty from the sixteenth to the nineteenth centuries pursued a similar policy of isolation from the outside world. In the course of the nineteenth century, both China and Japan had to give up these policies of seclusion, but until that time they had enabled both countries to avoid major external wars for several centuries, in striking contrast to the far more warlike history of the countries of contemporary Europe.

In the Western world such policies of conflict-reduction by the reduction of the absolute level (or at least the relative importance) of contacts among potential enemy countries have been used more rarely. Some sentiments of this kind may have contributed to the mood of George Washington's Farewell Address in 1797, when he realistically advised his countrymen to keep clear of

Some Alternatives to Escalation and Warfare

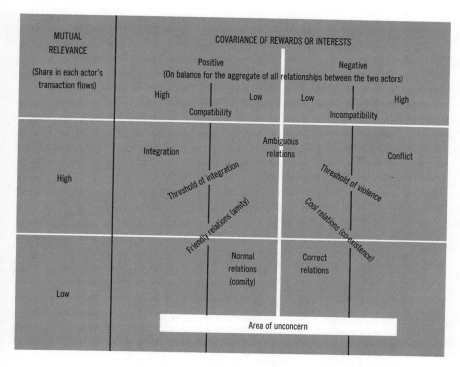

FIGURE 4. *Covariance of rewards or interests between countries.* (Reproduced from K. W. Deutsch, "Power and Communication in International Society," in *Conflict in Society*, Ciba Foundation Symposium, A.V.S. de Reuck and Julie Knight, eds., London, 1966, p. 302.)

the contemporary political quarrels and entanglements of the Old World; and they were revived once more under very different circumstances in the isolationist mood of many Americans between 1932 and 1941, with less fortunate results. Communist governments have been more inclined to reduce contact across the boundaries of their countries—a particularly dramatic example of this was the building of the Berlin Wall in August, 1961—but they have done this less to reduce foreign conflicts and more to maintain and tighten their domestic control within each of their countries. It is possible, however (though not certain) that this policy may have prevented at least some international frictions and clashes which otherwise might have occurred. Divided Berlin, at least in the mid-1960's, seemed a somewhat calmer city that it had been in the preceding decade.

Reduction of Antagonistic Interests and Strengthening of Consonant Interests

If mutual contacts cannot or ought not be reduced, conflicts can be made less probable by reducing some or all of the mutually opposed interests in the **155**

Some Alternatives to Escalation and Warfare

countries concerned. How and at what price this can be done depends on the nature of each interest. Countries engaged in keen economic competition can each shift to a different line of specialization, or to a different market or geographic area of primary interest. Political objectives can be readjusted, and alternative and less conflict-laden foci of attention can be created for public opinion in each country.

Threats and grievances can be removed, as the Soviet intermediate-range ballistic missiles were removed from Cuba in late 1962, at United States insistence; and real or pretended fears can be calmed, as were Cuban and Soviet fears by United States assurances, given at the same time, that there would not be any further United States–supported invasion attempt against Cuba, following the abortive one at the Bay of Pigs in 1961. After these de-escalation measures (and with a continuing low level of United States–Cuban contacts), tension in the vicinity of Cuba in 1962–1967 was markedly reduced.

Even if neither contacts nor clashing interests can be reduced significantly, conflicts still can be reduced by increasing the salience and weight of parallel or interlocking interests among the countries concerned. Within each country, such positive bonds of interest to the other country often can be made to outweigh the negative and mutually clashing interests that make for separation or hostility. Where such common interests can be found and can be made to predominate in the relation between two countries, these countries are apt to move toward friendly mutual relations, and perhaps even toward some higher stage or degree of political integration.

The best hope for moving in this direction may be in a combined strategy of both internal and external change for the countries that may remain locked in conflict or move toward correct relations or even integration. Among the concerned, such an approach would imply making dissonant interests less weighty and salient, while making consonant ones more clearly perceived and stronger. It would require shifting the foci of public attention away from conflict and, if possible, toward cooperation. Within each country, it would mean isolating and weakening all groups, elites, institutions, and interests making for aggravated conflicts, while strengthening and joining into coalitions all those groups and interests making for international peaceful adjustment and cooperation.

All this may well imply considerable political change within most or all of the countries concerned, and within some of them these changes would have to reach fairly deep into their political structure. Yet these changes may be most effective for peace if they stop well short of total revolution, and if they avoid arousing extreme and potentially war-engendering fears and resentments in hitherto favored but now threatened elites and interest groups.

Most of all, such a strategy of conflict-reduction and potential integration would have to aim at increasing each nation-state's capability for conflict management, for tolerance of threats and ambiguity, and for goal-change and self-transformation with loss of identity and of essential values and traditions. This would require a redefinition of a nation's role in international politics, as well as a redefinition of many political roles within each country. Most often it also would require a redefinition of the image of the world, held by a nation, or by its leaders and its politically relevant strata; and it usually would

Some Alternatives to Escalation and Warfare

require some change in national self-perception—that is, in the politically and culturally accepted image which a nation has of itself, its values, and its goals.

In the course of history, as we have seen, a few nations have succeeded in undergoing such partial transformations and reducing the threat of some (though not all) international conflicts to their existence or prosperity. But today, such successes are necessary for many nations, more reliably and sooner. New or improved instruments may now be available to attain these results, and deserve to be studied; and most promising among these potential instruments are international law, international organizations, and the various forms of federalism and supranational integration.

Some Alternatives to Escalation and Warfare

Integration:
International
and
Supranational

C H A P T E R   F I F T E E N

To *integrate* generally means to make a whole out of parts—that is,
to turn previously separate units into components of a coherent system.
The essential characteristic of any *system*, we may recall,
is a significant degree of interdependence among its components,
and *interdependence* between any two components or units consists in the
probability that a change in one of them—or an operation performed
upon one of them—will produce a predictable change in the other.
(In this sense, a lock and a key that fits it form an integrated system:
turning the key will "turn" the lock.) Usually, a system

as a whole also has *system properties* which are absent in any one of its components alone. (A proper lock-and-key system can be used to control the opening and locking of a door; a lock by itself or a key by itself cannot.)

Integration, then, is a relationship among units in which they are mutually interdependent and jointly produce system properties which they would separately lack. Sometimes, however, the word "integration" is also used to describe the *integrative process* by which such a relationship or state of affairs among formerly separate units is attained.

Political integration is the integration of political actors or political units, such as individuals, groups, municipalities, regions, or countries, in regard to their political behavior. In politics, integration is a relationship in which the behavior of such political actors, units, or components is modified from what it otherwise would be (*i.e.*, if these components were not integrated). In this respect, integration can be compared to *power,* for we recall that power can be thought of as a relationship in which at least one actor is made to act differently from the way he would act otherwise (*i.e.*, if this power were absent).

The *domain* of integration, like that of power, consists of the populations of the geographic areas integrated. Like power, integration also has *scope,* which is the collection of different aspects of behavior to which this integrated relationship applies. Thus England and Wales are integrated not only politically by means of all the many policies of a modern welfare state, but also in regard to religion through the Church of England, which is supported by their common state and headed by its monarch. But in the United States (which are integrated in very many other respects) there is no such official religious integration among the states (which may have as different traditions as have Massachusetts, Maryland, Utah, Nevada, and New York). And the members of the United Nations are integrated in regard to a still much smaller set of tasks.

Political integration also may be compared to power in regard to its *range.* We may think of this range of integration as consisting of the range of rewards and deprivations for the component units, by which an integrated relationship is maintained among them. This range may be moderate in the case of some minor international organization which is only of marginal importance to its members, so that its success can bring them little gain, and its dissolution, or their secession from it, only little loss. Or this range of positive and negative integrative sanctions can be large, including vast joint rewards and prospects in case of success, and severe penalties for failure or secession. This was the case from 1776 onward, when the populations and elites of the states of the United States faced—and won—the rewards of integration in terms of independence and the joint settlement of the western lands, and eventually of a continent. A failure of integration, on the other hand, would have threatened them with the loss of independence, the establishment and persistence of different European colonial regimes in various parts of the divided continent, and the ravages of both civil war and international wars waged within their territory.

Whether a given range of rewards and penalties will actually prevail in a given political environment is, of course, another matter. In the case of power, as we recall, we spoke of the *weight* of the power of an actor as his probability of overcoming resistance, and as his ability to shift the probability of relevant

Integration: International and Supranational

outcomes in his environment (see pp. 25–29). The case of integration—the notion of the weight of power—is paralleled by the concept of *cohesion*, or *cohesiveness*.

An integrated system is *cohesive* to the extent that it can withstand stress and strain, support disequilibrium, and resist disruptions. Its cohesion, or cohesive power, could also be measured by the sustained shift which the system produces in the probabilities of the behavior of its components (as against the way in which they probably would behave if they were not integrated in the system). The greater the strains an integrated system can survive, the greater we may estimate to be its cohesion. Thus the cohesiveness, or consolidation, attained by Germany and Italy, respectively, after the national unification of each in the nineteenth century, is indicated by the fact that none of their component regions tried to secede after the disastrous sufferings of either World War I or World War II, while comparable strains contributed in 1918 to the breakup of both Austria-Hungary and of the British-Irish union.

Differences in these four dimensions of integration—domain, scope, range, and weight—help us to distinguish different types of integrated political communities:

A community with a general domain we call *universal*, such as the Universal Postal Union in principle, and nearly so in practice, in contrast to a *particular* community, whose membership is restricted to particular countries (such as the Arab League, or Benelux customs union of Belgium, the Netherlands, and Luxembourg). In terms of *scope* we distinguish *specific* communities, communities limited to some specific subject-matter or service, as against *diffuse* communities, each of which is expected to do more or less whatever is needed or demanded by its members. Usually, the limited capabilities of international organization force a choice. An organization can perform a specific service for a universal clientele, such as the International Telecommunication Union (ITU), which coordinates international telegraph services among a large number of countries, and which is open to all qualified nations who apply. Or else an organization or community can undertake a diffuse responsibility for a wide variety of services limited to a particular group of regions, states, or countries. The United States, under the Articles of Confederation (1781–1791), was a community of the latter kind, and it became still more so under its federal Constitution (ratified in 1791).

Before we survey some of the different types of international organizations or communities which are generated by such differences in domain and scope, we must first be clear about the meaning of the concept of "political community." A *political community* is a collection of political actors whose interdependence is sufficient to make a substantial difference to the outcome of some of each other's relevant decisions. According to this minimal definition, community is simply a relevant degree of interdependence, and hence an objective fact, regardless of whether the governments or populations involved are aware of it or not. Two players in a game, or two states in competition or conflict, are members of one political community in this minimal but real

Integration: International and Supranational

sense, and, whether they like it or not, the outcome of what each of them does will depend to a significant extent upon the actions of the other.

If the two units, groups, or states concerned are aware of their interdependence, and perhaps also of its limits, they may modify their behavior accordingly. They may then act as members of a community and adopt the competitive and/or cooperative roles appropriate to the particular kind of interdependence—economic, strategic, or political—in which they find themselves involved. If it is mainly a *community of conflict,* so that outcomes rewarding for country *A* are frustrating or penalizing for country *B,* they may act as rivals or adversaries; if their rewards run parallel and depend on the coordination of their actions, they are in a positive *community of interest,* and may try to cooperate. Whether in cooperation or in conflict, however, they will now act as members of a community—rather differently from the way they would otherwise have acted.

Communities of conflict lock their members (whether individuals, groups, or nations) in a relationship in which mutual conflict predominates either wholly or to a large extent. Interestingly, however, although usually they produce little or no integration among the "traditional" or "hereditary" adversaries within them, it turns out (as many students of history and psychology have observed) that men and nations tend to copy in many ways the very things they hate. Some of the most Anglicized Irishmen, the Irish patriot George Russell (who wrote under the pen name "AE") once pointed out, were those who professed the greatest hatred of England.

Most often, nations are involved with one another in a community characterized by a variable-sum or mixed-motive contest. Their interests are then in some important respects opposed, but in other respects they stand to gain from coordinating their behavior. In such cases, it helps both parties if there is some conspicuous "prominent solution," acceptable to both, around which they can coordinate their expectations and their actions. A simple form of such coordination often is supplied by international custom and international law.

International Law

A *law* is a general rule which covers a specific class of cases, and which is backed by a probable sanction, stated in advance and widely accepted as legitimate among the population concerned. *National law* usually derives its sanction from the enforcement machinery of the nation-state, and its legitimacy from the community of communication, memories, and political culture upon which popular acceptance and support of each nation-state are based. Within the nation-state, enforcement machinery and sentiments of legitimacy are available *for general purposes* (that is, for whatever purpose or need that may arise) and thus are diffuse in scope. Within the international system, they are not.

International law can be thought of, therefore, as both the most universal and the most specific form of international organization. Like all law, it applies only to specific matters. But as a rule, it has no dependable permanent machinery behind it. There is also (ordinarily) much less of a common international political culture, except at most within a thin top layer of diplomats, international lawyers, and some other elite members particularly concerned with international affairs. National messages, symbols, and perceived interests are much more salient to most members of the general population of every country. As a result, perceptions of the legitimacy of international law tend to be relatively weak, and perceptions of national law and interest relatively strong. Nonetheless, international law has not only survived, but actually has increased, over several centuries, and in general it cannot be broken without serious consequences. International law gets its sanction—that is, the equivalent of a significant probability of enforcement—from the significant probable cost of breaking it.

The boundary between international law and international custom is blurred, therefore—unlike the sharper boundary between legal and political custom and statutory law within each nation, but still somewhat like the earlier blurred boundary between unwritten customary law and written law or precedent found in the early stages of development of many legal systems (such as Roman Law and the English Common Law), and in the law of contemporary developing countries in transition from traditional to full-fledged modern law.

Custom saves time, trouble, and uncertainty. It prefabricates many decisions; it reduces the burdens of communication and decision-making; it coordinates the expectations of different actors; and it helps to make the future more predictable. Law is custom which is widely perceived as being legitimate, and which is backed by probable sanctions against a few transgressors. Law does what custom does, only more so—more precisely, more intensely, more reliably. Moreover, law is explicit, and it is usually rational (that is, retraceable in its operations, step by step). It is, therefore, usually amenable to logic and often to combinatorial manipulation which permits its elements or rules to be put together in new ways so as to cover new problems. From the outset, it creates classes of cases included or excluded by its provisions. Therefore, it can be used to include new cases under old categories, or it can be extended by analogy to new classes of cases. Law is, therefore, not only potentially more powerful and more precise than custom, but also more flexible and more capable of development.

International law has all these properties and possibilities. Whether arising out of custom or out of treaties, it serves the nations to coordinate their mutual expectations and behavior *in their own interest*. The first and foremost sanction behind it is not merely the self-restraint of the actors but also the realization of the much greater cost and trouble for all parties concerned if international law did not exist, or if it were generally disregarded. The situation resembles that of the matter of traffic rules, such as driving on the right-hand side of the road, which are usually more troublesome and dangerous to disobey than to obey. The ancient rule of international law which provides that the persons of ambassadors must remain inviolate is a good example. Ancient tyrants sometimes executed foreign ambassadors whose messages displeased them. Usually the rule of such tyrants did not last long. Any modern nation that would dare to execute ambassadors would have to expect that no foreign nation would send them ambassadors in the future, and also that its own ambassadors might have to expect similar treatment abroad (which doubtless would make a career in their diplomatic service rather

162

unattractive). In short, ill-treatment of foreign ambassadors and other diplomats leads to much more trouble than it is worth (as Communist China and India were in the process of discovering in 1967); and thus the rule of respecting ambassadors has held for more than a thousand years, with very few exceptions, even though there has been no world government or world court and police in existence to enforce it. The self-enforcing aspects of this rule have on the whole proved sufficient.

As a rule, however, the self-enforcing character of international law requires either an *approximate equality* in the power positions of the parties (permitting tit-for-tat tactics between them), or else an expectation of possible future *role reversal* between them (permitting tit-for-tat tactics in the probable future). If the two sides in an international cause are about equally strong, each can retaliate effectively for what the other may do. In repeated encounters under such conditions of approximate symmetry, simple self-interest will reward actors who learn to coordinate their behavior and to avoid mutually penalizing clashes.

Even if the two sides are not roughly symmetrical in power and position, they may have to expect that in the future their roles may become reversed. Nazi Germany had air superiority in 1939 and 1940, and exploited this superiority in bombing the cities of Warsaw and Rotterdam, with their civilian populations, in disregard of the international law which then prevailed. Within a short time, from 1942 onward, Germany had lost her air superiority; the precedent of the heavy bombing of cities which she had so recently established now turned heavily against her, and American, British, and much of world opinion now accepted the saturation bombing of Hamburg and other German cities (which had little military effect but claimed about half a million German civilian victims).

In general, most nations do well to consider the possibility, and indeed the probability, of role reversal in the future. The nation that stresses its sovereign right to stop and/or search all ships in its coastal waters, and is tempted to extend its own definition of "coastal waters" to beyond the traditional three-mile limit as far as 12 miles out (as the United States did back in the Prohibition days of the 1920's), may find later on that this principle, if adopted by other countries, can work against the interests of its own fishing industry. More serious examples apply to international legal restraints on warfare, such as the treatment of prisoners or of civilian settlements, or the use of chemical or bacteriological weapons. Whatever weapons or methods of warfare one nation uses, particularly if it uses them repeatedly, are likely to be used some day against its own people. The long-run advantages of having been the first to disregard an international legal restraint usually turn out to be much smaller than they seemed at first, and the long-run costs and disadvantages are belatedly discovered to be far more heavy. The biblical rules which warned "It must needs be that offense comes, but woe to him through whom it comes," and "As you measure unto others, so it shall be measured unto you," had a thousand years of political experience behind them when they were written; and the experiences of the many empires and kingdoms that have risen and fallen in the thousands of years since then have only served to confirm their long-run validity.

It is perhaps more difficult for Americans than for others to appreciate

163

Integration: International and Supranational

the full weight of the biblical consideration, history-proven though it be, because their own historical experience thus far has been so different, and indeed in large part exceptional. Much of the early American experience was against the Indians, who usually were inferior in strength, and against Britain (in 1776–1783 and 1812–1815), which was too distant and preoccupied to apply her full strength. The wars of 1848 against Mexico, and 1898 against Spain, were waged against conspicuously weaker countries, while World Wars I and II against Germany were waged in alliance, so that in each case the American troops met the German forces on the ground relatively late in the war, when much of the German strength was already weakened or occupied elsewhere, and the American push could force an early decision at a relatively low cost in casualties. The fight against Japan in World War II was perhaps the most bitterly fought American war of the past 100 years; and here, too, the United States defeated a country that had only about half its population and less than one-twentieth of its capacity to produce steel. In no foreign war since 1815 has the United States mainland been invaded or its cities bombed. The vast majority of Americans have no personal experience of seeing their own cities and houses become a battleground, an experience that has been unhappily commonplace in other countries.

It seems natural to many Americans, therefore, to think of all-out war as meaning victory and not disaster; and to call for a bigger war and for the use of ever more destructive weapons when they feel frustrated in some limited war far from their shores; and to feel impatient of all international legal and diplomatic restraints on what they believe to be their country's powers, while paying little or no realistic attention to the long-run costs. This is indeed a natural response to the unique experiences of our past, and it seems most popular among those groups in Congress and among our electorate who are most strongly oriented to the past—but in the last decades of the twentieth century this response could be suicidal. For in the age of intercontinental ballistic missiles, the entire mainland of the United States is within range of thermonuclear warheads; and for every disaster that we could inflict upon the Soviet Union, some no-less-intolerable disaster could be inflicted upon us. Many of our past international power relationships were asymmetrical and left us with memories making many of us impatient of international law and national policies of self-restraint. But today our most important power relationship, that to the Soviet Union, is a symmetrical one for many practical purposes; and as time goes on and other nations acquire larger stocks of nuclear weapons and the means for their delivery, international law and national policies of self-restraint will become increasingly relevant to everyone's survival.

Self-enforcement through bitter experience, and self-restraint through exercising foresight, however, are not the only sanctions behind international law. Lesser but not negligible sanctions are the pressure of world opinion (which German governments ignored to their sorrow in two world wars), and the revulsion of domestic opinion from deeds of their own government, which are perceived as illegitimate and which may lead to a quiet but effective withdrawal of popular support and of the support of important sections of the country's social, cultural, political, and technological elites. In addition, flagrant violations of international law may bring about adverse actions by

Integration: International and Supranational

third countries, and various disadvantages and penalties in international organizations. No responsible government could afford for long to ignore the cumulative effect of all these processes.

All this does not mean, however, that it is always easy to determine just what the international law is in a given case, any more than one can always determine easily the content of national law (or "municipal law," as the international lawyers call it) on a disputed point. Much of international law is laid down in international treaties and conventions. These bind directly, of course, only those nations whose governments have signed and ratified each document; but if sufficiently widely accepted, notably by all the great powers, they also indicate the consensus of the international community of states. Beyond this, there are codes and collections of international law, the consensus of experts, and the precedents created by earlier international awards or acts of adjudication.

Disputed points may be settled by *direct diplomacy*—that is, by negotiation and bargaining among the parties directly concerned. If this process fails and leads to deadlock and the danger of escalating conflict, third countries may be brought in. Their participation may be limited to *good offices,* such as providing hospitality and a neutral meeting-ground for the next round of negotiations. Or they may act through *mediation,* offering suggestions or proposals for a possible compromise. These latter are listened to by the contending parties in proportion not only to their perceived intrinsic merit but also to the power of the nation whose government proposes them.

If the two parties to a dispute bind themselves in advance to accept the decision of a third party, mediation is replaced by *arbitration*. The arbitrator may be a government, or a panel of individual arbitrators. Often three or five arbitrators are chosen by the two parties from some existing list of trusted experts. Such a list is maintained as the Permanent Court of International Arbitration at The Hague (which is, therefore, not a court of law). The powers of the arbitrators and the limits of the case to be decided are established in each case by an agreement among the parties to submit this case, or sometimes this class of cases, to the arbitrators. The same agreement also states the principles according to which they are to decide—such as strict law, or considerations of equity.

If the case is to be decided by *strict law,* it is most often submitted to the International Court of Justice (ICJ). This Court, in the words of the United Nations Charter, is "the principal judicial organ of the United Nations." It is the almost unchanged successor of the former Permanent Court of International Justice, and thus it has been functioning in effect since 1920. Members of the United Nations are bound by the statutes of the Court, but the Court's jurisdiction depends in many cases upon the consent of the parties, and is further limited by many reservations by the member nations. The Court has no means to enforce its judgments, but once states submit to its jurisdiction, they usually obey its decisions, though there have been some exceptions in cases involving either the Cold War or the Union of South Africa.

Efforts to extend drastically the compulsory jurisdiction of the Court   **165**

Integration: International and Supranational

have been resisted by the United States as well as by the Soviet Union and many other countries, and they have thus far failed. If such efforts should succeed at some time in the future, they would turn the World Court into a more general-purpose instrument of control, and thus make it far more diffuse in scope. If the Court at the same time would retain or expand the universality of its domain, it would require much greater capabilities in order to cope with its expanded tasks in both domain and scope; and such greater political capabilities at the international level have yet to be developed.

Functionalism: International Organizations for Specific Purposes

Functionally specific international organizations open to all or nearly all nations differ from international law in their stronger permanent machinery, in their greater stress both on making limited new rules and decisions, and on the implementation and administration of policies. Some of these are nongovernmental organizations (NGOs), such as the International Red Cross (stemming from the first International Red Cross Conference at Geneva in 1863), which concerns itself among other things with disaster relief, the furnishing of emergency medical supplies, and the care of prisoners of war.

Most of the important international organizations of this kind, however, are composed of governments. Such governmental organizations include the Universal Postal Union (UPU, 1874), the International Telecommunication Union (ITU, 1932; successor to the International Telegraph Union, 1865), the International Civil Aviation Organization (ICAO), and others. Somewhat broader functions are exercised by such organizations as the International Labor Organization (ILO, 1919), the Food and Agriculture Organization (FAO, 1945), the World Health Organization (WHO, 1948), and the United Nations Educational, Scientific and Cultural Organization (UNESCO, 1946). These and several other "specialized" agencies of the United Nations are coordinated, very loosely to be sure, by the United Nations Economic and Social Council (ECOSOC). This council, which also has the task of discussing basic economic and social issues, has sponsored some important departures toward setting new standards of national and international behavior through its Convention Against Genocide, and its Human Rights Convention, both of which many countries have yet to ratify.

The theory of *functionalism* in international relations is based on the hope that by delegating more and more common tasks to such specific functional organizations, the world's nations will gradually become integrated into a single community within which war will be impossible. But this hope seems rather uncertain. All these organizations are limited mainly to the exchange of views and of knowledge, the making of studies, the drafting of recommendations, and the rendering of technical assistance to governments requesting it. They cannot legislate. Although the old principle of unanimity usually has been replaced in these organizations by majority voting, their decisions do not bind any government until it has ratified them. (Only some technical agencies have a limited rule-making power; thus air-safety standards set by ICAO, and regulations by WHO to prevent the spread of epidemics, become binding on their member nations unless they give notice to the contrary within a specified time.)

Integration: International and Supranational

Neither do these agencies have the power to tax, nor do most of them have any effective power of sanctions. Their governing bodies are composed of instructed delegates of governments who must say what their governments have ordered them to say. Unlike members of a national legislature, these delegates, even if they should arrive at a consensus, cannot vote a decision, and bind by it those who sent them. They are, so to speak, one-way representatives. They represent their governments to the international organization, but they cannot also represent effectively the will of this organization to their constituents, as national legislators can and sometimes do.

Perhaps most importantly, classic functionalism, as formulated by David Mitrany, envisaged the treatment of these international or supranational functions and services as technical matters, nonpolitical in nature, and well removed from the clamor and pressures of interest groups, nations, and the masses of the populations. But this view is more likely to prove a source of political weakness than of strength. Most of the time, the present international organizations can do no more than communicate with governments which remain free to deny their international officials all access to their territories at any time. Except for technical assistance missions in the field, the international civil servants cannot deal directly with the people whom they are to serve. They are hampered in receiving and answering direct communications from the public, and even more in doing anything about them. Under these conditions, popular loyalties to international agencies and symbols are unlikely to grow, and the appeal of nationalist images and symbols is unlikely to weaken.

Most of the national elites prefer it just this way. Their members have no desire to weaken their own power over their national societies by permitting the serious promotion of any competing international loyalties by which their own domestic power could be weakened. UNESCO soon was discouraged from following through on its original assignment to create a new international ideology and set of symbols. Neither the Soviet leaders nor the major Western governments cherished the thought of fostering potential competition.

Similarly, the Food and Agriculture Organization was refused in 1947, at that time chiefly by the Western countries, the effective powers over international food prices and supplies. It has remained an organization devoted to studies, recommendations, and a modest amount of technical assistance, while the decisions about the allocation of the world's grain and other foodstuffs, and the potential political power that goes with them, have remained in the hands of the governments of the main food-exporting countries, such as the United States.

The greater the potential power of an international organization, the broader and more functionally diffuse becomes its potential influence; and the greater usually also becomes the resistance of national societies and elites to let this potential international power grow. The closer an international agency comes to touching the core of the sovereignty of a nation, the more severe this problem may become. The International Monetary Fund (IMF) and the International Bank for Reconstruction and Development (IBRD) touch upon the freedom of each nation to manage its national currency as each national government sees fit. The Fund even has some power of sanctions, since, under

Integration: International and Supranational

certain conditions, it can refuse financial support to, and even block the credit of, uncooperative governments. The United States, as the largest financial contributor, has 50 per cent of the votes in the IMF, and it can usually count on the votes of several other nations with like-minded banking leaders. But just for these reasons, further extensions of the powers of the IMF to act and to bind its members, at the price of a further cut in their sovereignty, are apt to be quite difficult to accomplish. The hope for a "spill-over" effect, which would lead from one specific integrated service or function to a widening demand for creating additional international institutions and integrating additional functions and services, has not been fulfilled to any large extent among organizations of this type.

Classic functionalism, to be sure, had a different ideal. Highly specific functional agencies, Mitrany hoped, would enter into direct contact with the people they served in each country. Their services would somehow remain nonpolitical, but they would win, through their performance, both increasing elite acceptance and popular support. Among the universal and functionally specific international agencies, as we have seen, to date very few, if any—except perhaps the World Health Organization—have moved very far in this direction.

Integration: International and Supranational

Universal General-Purpose Organizations

Among the many goals which individuals and governments pursue, the broadest and most common is *security*. It is the basic mode in which most other values, such as wealth, wellbeing, affection, and "the rest," are enjoyed with the expectation that they will last for at least some time; and to many people it is also a value in itself. But since it is both a manner of and a condition for enjoying many other values, its meaning often is ambiguous.

Most often and most obviously, security to most people means the security of life and limb for themselves and their loved ones; and thus it means peace and the maintenance of peace. But security can also mean the security of wealth and property, even if this wealth should be based on a partial but real conflict of interest between creditor and debtor, landlord and tenant, employer and employee—a conflict which may reach the intensity of a latent war in some developing countries. Or security can mean the security of symbols and institutions, of positions of class and role, of images and habits, of ideology and culture, of claims to respect and self-respect. To most people, some or all of these seem worth defending; and since the nation-state so often has been manifestly inadequate to safeguard these, people have turned their hopes to international organizations for their protection.

To preserve the peace requires the ability either to forestall force or to overcome it; and to safeguard the security of other values usually requires the same ability. To preserve security thus means to control and organize power, and hence to have the capacity to influence the allocation of many values and the pursuit of many purposes.

A federal or international organization to preserve "only" peace and security, therefore, may look like a special-purpose organization in form, but it would be a general-purpose organization in substance. Its charter and its personnel may solemnly promise that it will not interfere in the "domestic" or "internal" affairs of its member states, but in the long run, its intentions are less important than its capabilities. If it is weaker than one or several of its members, the organization will not be able to keep or restore peace in the face of their defiance, but if the organization is stronger than its members, it is likely to be strong enough to intervene from time to time in any and all of their affairs as it may choose. If there is disagreement as to just what are "domestic" matters, a stronger federal or international organization will be more apt to make its view prevail; and its superior strength may eventually determine how gaps or disputed passages in its charter or constitution are to be interpreted.

Thus far, the main problem of every international organization for the maintenance of peace and security has been its weakness rather than its strength. In each case the organization has remained weak precisely because most of its members feared its strength, and because they feared the possibility that this international or federal organization might become a mere instrument for the power and hegemony of one or a few of its strongest members, somewhat as the holding company often serves as an instrument to enhance and multiply the power of a well-organized minority of stockholders against all the rest.

In international organizations aiming at a worldwide membership, the differences among members are apt to be greatest, and so are their mutual fears. Accordingly, though projects for peace-keeping organizations or alliances including most or all states have been recurring ever since Pierre Dubois proposed such a project in 1310, and international congresses advocating such ideas have been held since the 1840's, it was only after World War I that an actual organization of this kind, the League of Nations, came into existence. Only then did governments and nations begin to be more afraid of war and

Universal General-Purpose Organizations

international upheaval than of one another, and only intermittently and fitfully since the founding of the League have they continued to do so.

Collective Security and the League of Nations

The League of Nations was founded after World War I in order to protect peace and the new international distribution of rights and territories that had resulted from the global upheaval. Article 10 in its Covenant obligated the members to defend the independence and territorial integrity of each of them, but it ultimately left each nation to decide whether and how to fulfill this obligation.

According to the principle of *collective security,* all members of the League were to act together in resisting any peace-breaking nation by imposing economic and, if necessary, military sanctions on it. They were to do this regardless of whose ally the peace-breakers might have been; for the defense of the new status quo through collective security, so it was hoped, was going to replace the old system of alliances and the balance of power, which had led to World War I. During the two decades that followed, almost every then-sovereign nation at one time or another joined the League. The handful of exceptions included Afghanistan, Bhutan, Nepal, Yemen—and the United States.

The United States, under the leadership of President Woodrow Wilson, had since April, 1917, actually been one of the chief sponsors of the League and of its Covenant, of which a preliminary draft was published in February, 1919, at the Paris Peace Conference. Concessions to nationalist sentiment in the United States, and particularly in the Senate, soon seemed to be essential. In accordance with proposals by former United States President William Howard Taft, the draft Covenant of the proposed League was modified to protect the domestic jurisdiction of members, to require unanimity for all political decisions, to assure to each nation the right of withdrawal, and to reserve the Monroe Doctrine and thus to keep the worldwide organization and the non-American members of the League out of the settlement of any disputes within the Western Hemisphere. Each of these modifications was designed to reduce the legal powers of the world organization and to preserve and strengthen those of the nation-states of which it was composed. Nonetheless, President Wilson failed to obtain ratification of the Covenant in the Senate. With the defeat of Wilson and the Democratic Party by President Warren G. Harding and the Republicans in 1920, the project died. The United States never became a member.

The League was governed by a Council in which the great powers predominated. These were primarily France and Britain, but they were joined by such other "permanent members" as Italy, Japan, and eventually Germany (1926) and the Soviet Union (1934), and by nine nonpermanent members elected by the Assembly of the League, so as to represent all the main geographical areas of the world. The Assembly, including all members, was the other chief organ of the League; and there was a secretariat with a staff of about 750, headed by a Secretary General.

In the course of its existence, 66 political disputes were submitted to the League. It dealt successfully with 35 of them, but failed in the most important

171

Universal General-Purpose Organizations

ones. Successes predominated in the early years of the League (1920–1925) and in its heyday (1925–1932). Though the United States remained outside, it drew somewhat closer to the League from 1927 onward, when France and the United States launched the Briand-Kellogg Pact, by which each signatory nation solemnly renounced war as an instrument of national policy. The pact was joined by many other nations, and marked a new low for the declining moral prestige of war, though not yet a turning point in its continuing occurrence.

The members of the League remained profoundly divided by their interests and ideologies. France and Britain wished to retain the territories and privileges they had won in World War I. France, which had gained Alsace-Lorraine and (temporarily) the Saar basin on the European continent, wanted collective security arrangements to be tight and rigid; Britain, whose gains were overseas, preferred such arrangements to be loose and flexible; and in their rivalry the two countries succeeded, between the two World Wars, in destroying most of one another's influence on the continent of Europe. Germany's elites and a majority of her voters wanted her to make new and larger gains, and after Hitler's seizure of power in 1933 a militant German policy was directed toward these ends. The leaders of Italy, particularly after the Fascist seizure of power under Benito Mussolini in 1922, and the leaders of Japan desired territorial gains which their countries had failed to make in World War I. These three "Axis powers," as well as some lesser powers, strove to upset the status quo which the League was to defend against all threats of "external aggression."

The Soviet Union's attitude was more ambiguous. For the time being, its rulers were willing to accept the diminished frontiers of their country as they had emerged from World War I. They hoped for greater gains in the future from the growing economic and military strength of their vast and rapidly industrializing country, and from the eventual appeal of its revolutionary ideology to the poverty-stricken masses of China, the rest of Asia, and other developing regions—and even some day (so they hoped) to the workers of a depression-ridden Western world. The Soviet government thus had no interest in defending the status quo, but it was in no hurry to risk an all-out attack on it. Rather, it felt more immediately threatened by the new militancy of Germany and Japan, and by joining the League in 1934, it sought an alliance with the status-quo powers.

The original concept of "collective security" as an alternative to the old system of alliance politics soon faded out. As an end in itself, collective security never was salient enough for governments and peoples to override national interests and cost considerations of each nation-state. And as a means to other ends, alliances seemed better suited. Soon "collective security" became a mere label attached to any alliance system opposed to any other (which of course was similarly labeled by its members).

But all alliances remained precarious. Germany, Italy, and Japan insisted on revision of the territorial status quo. France and Britain alternated between attempts at resistance and moves toward "appeasement" through buying off the revisionist powers by concessions, or through deflecting their expansionist pressures in the direction of third countries. The United States, with no substantial territorial interests at stake, long remained aloof; and between the

172

Universal General-Purpose Organizations

Soviet Union and the Western powers there remained an abyss of ideological hostility and mutual suspicion.

The League could not be stronger than the unity of the great powers who between them made up most of its strength. From 1931 onward, the major failures of the League began. In that year, it failed to take effective action against Japan's attack on China in Manchuria. In 1935, it voted to impose limited economic sanctions on Fascist Italy, whose armies were invading Ethiopia, but it did not even vote to try to stop the flow of oil to the Italian war machine; and the feeble sanctions ended in failure by 1936.

Although not all observers saw it at the time, the years 1935–1937 were the turning point in the fate of the League. In those years, it was the focus of world attention. It could have become the rallying point and the unifying symbol for world opinion and for the coordinated action of many powerful governments against the threat and practice of aggressive war by the revisionist powers (Germany, Italy, and Japan). For reasons of its own, the Soviet Union in that period was interested in collaborating with the Western powers, and the aggressor powers at that time were much less strong, relative to the West (as well as to Russia), than they were to become later in 1938–1941. If the League had succeeded in those crucial years of 1935–1937, World War II could have been prevented, or at least it could have been stopped by defeating the aggressors much sooner, with much less loss of life than eventually occurred.

But for reasons of their own in each country, both governments and mass opinion in all major Western countries hesitated throughout the period of 1935 to 1938, until the years of opportunity were lost. President Franklin D. Roosevelt, in a famous speech at Chicago in 1937, called for "quarantining the aggressors," but neither mass opinion nor elite opinion backed him up, and he had to wait another four years for majority opinion to come closer to his view.

Thus the League failed, and the world moved step by step to World War II and the 50 million deaths it was to claim. The League did nothing to stop the massive intervention of Italy and Germany in their attempt to overthrow the Spanish Republic in the Spanish Civil War (1936–1938), nor did it do anything about Japan's attack on Shanghai in 1937, or about Hitler's forcible absorption of Austria and Czechoslovakia in 1938 and 1939, nor about Hitler's all-out attack on Poland in the latter year, which started World War II. By then the Soviet Union, too, had come to disregard the paralyzed League. Abandoning the frustrating search for an alliance with the West, Stalin in August, 1939, concluded a sudden and utterly opportunistic "nonaggression pact" with Hitler; and in the fall and winter of 1939–1940 his armies occupied parts of eastern Poland, the Baltic countries of Esthonia, Latvia, and Lithuania, and finally eastern Finland, all on the grounds of either "liberating" their populations or of safeguarding Soviet national security. The Finns fought back, and this time the League acted by "expelling" Russia. It was a gesture without effect, its moral force destroyed in advance by the League's passivity in the face of the far more extended and spectacular aggressions of the Axis powers.

Thereafter, the League became politically insignificant. The alliance between the Western powers and the Soviet Union, vital to their interests,

Universal General-Purpose Organizations

did not come about until France had been overrun, German bombs had fallen on London, and attacking German tanks had reached the vicinity of Leningrad and Moscow. By then, in late 1941, the United States was moving toward increasing aid to the allies; but it remained for Japanese bombs falling on Pearl Harbor, and for a German declaration of war on the United States on the next day, to make the United States a full, and soon a leading, member of the alliance which in time was to give rise to the United Nations.

The United Nations: World Assembly or World Government?

When the formal organization of the United Nations was founded in June, 1945, its general purposes were stated in the preamble to its charter. There, in language bearing traces of many compromises, "We the peoples of the United Nations" declared themselves "determined" to pursue four major aims:

1. "To save succeeding generations from the scourge of war"
2. "To reaffirm faith in fundamental human rights, in the dignity and worth of the human person, in the equal right of men and women and of nations large and small"
3. To maintain "justice and respect for the obligations arising from treaties and other sources of international law"
4. "To promote social progress and better standards of life in larger freedom"

The first two aims, peace and human rights, appealed to human desires aroused by the war in almost all countries. The third, "justice and respect for obligations," could be understood to protect the new status quo to be established by the peace treaties, and also perhaps property rights in foreign countries on the part of nations, business firms, and individuals, insofar as such rights were covered by international law. (But the actual words of the preamble only said that the signers were determined "to establish conditions" under which such justice and respect for international obligations "can be" maintained.) The last aim linked the "social progress" and higher living standards, emphasized by the Soviet Union and some of the poorer countries, to "larger freedom," stressed by the Western powers. More than the League of Nations, the United Nations showed the marks of the ideological compromises characteristic of the era of the modern welfare state.

The United Nations, of course, was not a superstate. Like the League of Nations before it, it left untouched the sovereignty of its members. Article 2 of its Charter described the organization as "based on the principle of the sovereign equality of all its Members" (Art. 2.1), and explicitly denied to it any authority "to intervene in matters which are essentially within the domestic jurisdiction of any state" (Art. 2.7). Just what matters were "essentially within" this domestic jurisdiction was left undefined; in practice the government of each member state insisted on making this judgment for itself whenever it became involved in a case which it considered important.

THE GENERAL ASSEMBLY

In contrast to the League, the Assembly of the United Nations has the power to make decisions by majority vote. "Important questions," such as the

Universal General-Purpose Organizations

admission or expulsion of member states, the suspension of their rights and privileges, the election of member states to major United Nations bodies, and the making of "recommendations" to member states and/or to the Security Council "with respect to the maintenance of international peace and security," require a two-thirds majority of the members present and voting (Art. 18.2). Other questions, "including the determination of additional categories of questions to be decided by a two-thirds majority," are to be made by a simple majority of the members present and voting (Art. 18.3).

About the crucial questions of war and peace, the Assembly cannot act. It can only consider, debate, and recommend, and it may not even make recommendations concerning any matters of international peace and security while they are being dealt with by the Security Council. In the fall of 1950, during the Korean War, the Assembly passed a United States–supported resolution, "Uniting for Peace," which was designed to enable the Assembly to initiate action by its members, if the Security Council should be deadlocked by disagreement among the great powers. As more new states have entered the United Nations, however, the majorities in the Assembly have been more often led by the countries uncommitted between the United States and the Soviet Union; and its majority votes on such issues as the remnants of colonialism, or the racial policies of the Union of South Africa or of Rhodesia, often have become inconvenient to the Western powers who have then, predictably, shown little inclination to act on them. In general, each great power has professed great zeal in implementing Assembly votes or recommendations when they suited its national policies, but no zeal at all when they did not. By mid-1968, the Assembly had not yet moved very far toward becoming a more effective instrument than it had been two decades earlier.

Similarly, the Assembly's power to "consider and approve the budget of the Organization" (Art. 17.1), and to apportion "the expenses of the Organization" among the members (Art. 17.2), has not developed into any full-fledged power to tax. When the Assembly voted for the intervention in 1961–1962 by a United Nations force in the troubled affairs of the Congo (Leopoldville)—i.e., the former Belgian Congo—the United States approved of the action, exercised considerable influence in its execution, and favored the assessment of each member of the United Nations with a proportionate share of the cost. France and the Soviet Union refused to pay, on the grounds that the action (which they had opposed) could have been taken legally only by the Security Council (where their adverse votes would have stopped it), and that it was illegal to assess them for an action taken in a manner circumventing their veto right in the Security Council. The United States for a time tried to get an Assembly vote which eventually would have suspended from voting in the Assembly all nations not paying their assessment, just as if they had failed to pay their regular dues (Art. 19). Many of the Assembly members, however, were reluctant to accept this new interpretation of the Charter; and the United States itself had to consider what its response would be if some day an Assembly majority, perhaps a coalition of developing countries and the Soviet bloc, should authorize some governments to start some expensive undertaking in the name of the United Nations, and then assess the United States for a substantial portion of the cost. In any case, by 1967 the project of having the Assembly assess unwilling great powers for

Universal General-Purpose Organizations

special enterprises backed by it had been quietly abandoned. An international organization with an effective taxing power (which in the end would fall most heavily upon the richest countries) was at best still in the future.

The heart of the United Nations' capacity to act is in the Security Council. United Nations members "confer on the Security Council primary responsibility for the maintenance of international peace and security, and agree that in carrying out its duties . . . the Security Council acts on their behalf" (Art. 24.1). If the Council can act, the United Nations can; if it cannot, they cannot do more than make gestures. This was foreseen from the start. While the Assembly was to debate, the Council was to act. The Charter speaks of the Assembly as making "recommendations"; it empowers the Council to make "decisions" (Arts. 25, 27, 39, 41, 44, and 48).

Under the Charter, these decisions include decisions about life and death. The Council has the power to "determine the existence of any threat to the peace, breach of the peace, or act of aggression," and to "decide what measures shall be taken . . . to maintain or restore international peace and security" (Art. 39). Such measures, as envisaged by the Charter, include "complete or partial interruption of economic relations and of rail, sea, air, postal, telegraphic, radio and other means of communication, and the severance of diplomatic relations" (Art. 41). These measures are to be carried out by the member states, when called upon to do so by the Council. "Should the Security Council consider," however, that these measures "would be inadequate," it has the right to act directly. "It may take such action by air, sea or land forces," says the Charter, "as may be necessary to maintain or restore international peace and security" (Art. 42). In short, the Council has the legal power to enforce its decisions, if need be, by warfare. For this purpose, all members "undertake to make available to the Security Council, on its call and in accordance with . . . special . . . agreements," suitable armed forces and facilities (Art. 43.1), and: "In order to enable the United Nations to take urgent military measures, members shall hold immediately available national air-force contingents for combined international enforcement action" (Art. 45).

All this legalized enforcement machinery can be set in motion, moreover, to enforce any political disposition or solution on which the Security Council may decide in dealing with any situation which in its judgment is threatening the peace. The Security Council, to be sure, "shall act in accordance with the purposes and principles of the United Nations" (Art. 24.2), but it is its own judge in this matter. No other body within or outside the United Nations can override its decisions. Indeed, the United Nations General Assembly is explicitly barred even from making any recommendation about any situation (e.g., political or military) while the Security Council is dealing with it, "unless the Security Council so requests" (Art. 12.1).

Taken together, these are extremely sweeping powers, almost wholly unchecked from outside, but checked from within the Security Council, almost to the point of paralyzing it, by the inability of its members to agree on many decisions of importance.

Universal General-Purpose Organizations

The crucial dilemmas of world politics are realistically reflected in the voting procedures of the Council. The Council has five permanent members (the United States, the U.S.S.R., the United Kingdom, France, and China), and since its 1963 enlargement, 10 nonpermanent members elected by the Assembly for two-year terms. The permanent members were the actual or potential great powers of 1945; and by 1965, they had become the five powers possessing nuclear weapons, albeit still in very unequal amounts. The heart of the functioning of the Security Council, as envisaged by the Charter, is in the unanimity of the five permanent members. The "concurring votes" of all the permanent members are essential for all decisions of the Security Council except procedural ones, which may be carried by the affirmative votes of any nine Council members (Art. 27).

Due to this "principle of unanimity" among the great powers, each permanent member has a *veto right* built into the Charter. Against its vote, or even without its concurrence, no substantive action may be taken. The Soviet Union, most likely to be in a minority in a Council vote, has used its veto right most often by far, but the Western powers, too, have used it on occasion.

This voting arrangement reflects a basic fact, not only of the world of 1945, but also of the world of the late 1960's. Then, as now, it has been manifestly impractical to coerce either the United States or the Soviet Union to do anything important against their will; and it seemed clear that Britain, France, and China were similarly uncoercible, or soon would be. But if these five powers can agree, and if they care enough, so the drafters of the United Nations reasoned, they can muster enough force to stop quickly any war or threat of war anywhere in the world. The age-old problem of stopping or controlling the warlike propensities of all men and all states was thus replaced by the much smaller problem of discovering ways of producing coordination among only five countries—a problem which, though still very difficult, clearly seemed more manageable.

EAST-WEST CONFLICTS IN UNITED NATIONS POLITICS

The potentialities for collaboration among the major powers, envisaged by the designers of the United Nations Charter, to date have been realized to only a small extent. The Cold War has kept the United States and the Soviet Union on opposite sides on most questions, and each power has used the United Nations primarily as an instrument to serve its own interests in that struggle.

Neither of these two superpowers, nor indeed most other members of the United Nations, has thus far shown any deep commitment to United Nations intervention or United Nations supranationalism as ends in themselves. Western powers have favored United Nations intervention in countries and situations where it has seemed likely to weaken Communist influence, or forestall its extension, such as in the cases of northern Iran (1946), Greece (1946–1948), Korea (1947–1953), Hungary (1956), Lebanon (1958), and the Congo (Leopoldville; 1960–1963). But where the Assembly majority has urged United Nations measures against the colonial policies of a Western ally, such as Portugal, or against the racial unrest of regimes closely linked to the Western financial and economic system, such as Rhodesia and the Union of

171

Universal General-Purpose Organizations

South Africa (in the 1960's), Western powers have been far more reluctant. The Soviet Union, of course, has generally tended to take the opposite side in each question, modified by its general distaste for supranationalist institutions which would be dominated almost inevitably by non-Communist majorities. Even where the United States and the Soviet Union have found themselves in limited agreement in the United Nations, as they did in such cases as those of Palestine and Israel (1947–1949), the independence of Indonesia (1947–1949), and the Suez War (1956), antagonistic East-versus-West alignments eventually have recurred in these regions.

All things considered, East-West conflicts have increased in United Nations voting. A recent study shows that in 1947 they dominated about 45 per cent of votes in the Assembly; this rose to about 65 per cent in 1961, and was expected to reach over 70 per cent by 1967. During the same period, so-called "North-South" issues between developed and underdeveloped countries declined from about 20 per cent of the Assembly votes in 1947 to about 12 per cent in 1961, and was expected to fall below 10 per cent in 1967.[1]

This growing bipolarity in terms of East-West issues has been accompanied, however, by a growing multipolarity of interests and of voting successes on the part of different voting blocs. More often than in the early years of the United Nations, the great powers now are finding it expedient to make alliances with special-interest blocs of lesser powers, by accommodating them on particular issues most salient to them. As a result Arab, African, and Soviet groups in recent years have been more often successful in the Assembly, and perhaps also in other organs of the United Nations.[2] To the extent that this has happened, the United Nations may be moving toward a kind of two-party system in which the leading powers of the West and East blocs respectively must compete by offering concessions to lesser powers in order to hold their coalitions together and to attract needed additional support. Under such conditions the great powers can destroy the United Nations through rigid and closed-minded policies, or they can save the organization and develop it by increasing their powers of perceptiveness and flexibility.

THE KEY POSITION OF THE SECRETARY GENERAL

The changing position of the United Nations Secretary General will be one indicator of the direction in which the world organization will be moving; the universality of membership and representation in the United Nations may well be another. The first Secretary General, Trygve Lie of Norway, incurred the hostility of the Soviet Union in 1950 for favoring an interpretation of the United Nations charter which was substantively attractive but legally doubtful. Then (at the time of the North Korean attack on South Korea) Lie as Secretary General had accepted a crucial vote of the Security Council deputizing the United States, in effect, to resist the attack on behalf of the United Nations. But this vote had been taken in the absence of the Soviet

---

[1] Hayward R. Alker, Jr., and Bruce M. Russett, *World Politics in the General Assembly* (New Haven: Yale University Press, 1965), pp. 134–137, 276–279, and 289–293.

[2] *Ibid.,* pp. 293–297.

178

Universal General-Purpose Organizations

delegate (who was then boycotting the meeting in protest against the non-recognition of Communist China); and thus, lacking the "concurring vote" of a permanent member of the Council, as prescribed in the charter, it was considered illegal not only by the Soviet Union, but by jurists in many countries, including some highly respected international lawyers in the United States.[3] At the time, the view of Lie and the Council majority prevailed. The Korean war was fought under the United Nations flag, and the North Korean attack was thwarted; the cease-fire and armistice of 1953–1954 left the territories of both North and South Korea substantially unchanged; and no Soviet delegate has absented himself since then from a meeting of the Security Council. But at the end of his term, Trygve Lie was not acceptable to the Soviet Union for reelection.

Lie's successor, Dag Hammarskjold, was acceptable to all the great powers. During his term of office, the membership of the United Nations was greatly enlarged, and issues of rapid decolonization came to the fore, as did the use of United Nations forces to keep the peace in local conflicts. The first force of this kind was used in the Gaza Strip between Egypt and Israel, from 1956 to 1967. A larger United Nations force, drawn from India, Ireland, Sweden, Yugoslavia, and a number of African nations, was used in the Congo, where Hammarskjold lost his life in an airplane crash.

The third Secretary General, U Thant of Burma, was the first non-Westerner to become the chief executive officer of the world organization. As in the case of his predecessors, the degree of support which his recommendations in international disputes receive from the great powers indicate the degree to which they wish the United Nations to become a true world organization with a leadership and a common will reaching beyond any of the nations constituting it. By mid-1968, these prospects did not look good. The United States had turned down U Thant's repeated calls for a unilateral halt in its bombing of North Vietnam—a halt which he hoped might open the way (as he saw it) to an early cease-fire and to negotiations to settle the Vietnam conflict; nor had the government of North Vietnam made any effort to encourage a United Nations settlement of the conflict; and U Thant announced publicly his fear that the world might be well on the way to World War III.

ISSUES FOR THE FUTURE: MEMBERSHIP AND TASKS OF THE UNITED NATIONS

Neither North Vietnam nor South Vietnam are members of the United Nations. The same is true of the two Koreas, North and South, and the two Germanies, the German Federal Republic in the West and the Communist-ruled German Democratic Republic in the East. Of the "two Chinas," only the anti-Communist government on the island of Taiwan is recognized as the government of China, while the Communist government of the Chinese mainland with over 700 million population has been denied United Nations recognition for nearly two decades. Every Secretary General of the United

Not so

Red China is a member

---

[3] For a good example of the controversy, see Leo Gross, "Voting in the Security Council: Abstention from Voting and Absence from Meetings," and Myres S. McDougal and Richard N. Gardner, "The Veto and the Charter: An Interpretation for Survival," *Yale Law Journal*, Vol. 60, No. 2 (February, 1951), pp. 209–257, 258–292.

Universal General-Purpose Organizations

Nations thus far has recommended the adoption of the principle of universality, according to which every government in effective control of a country ought to be a member of the United Nations, but the Western powers, and particularly an influential part of domestic opinion in the United States, have been extremely reluctant to recognize any Communist regimes established after World War II. Several Communist governments (Albania, Bulgaria, Hungary, and Rumania) were admitted to the United Nations in 1955, along with the anti-Communist dictatorships of Spain and Portugal, but by 1967 the problems of United Nations representation of the divided countries—China, Germany, Korea, and Vietnam—had not been solved.

Throughout the history of the United Nations, two themes can be traced: the search for centralizing power and the search for pluralistic communication and accommodation. Greater centralizing power would require strengthening majority rule, abolishing the great powers' vetoes, increasing the powers of the Secretary General, and widening the compulsory jurisdiction of the Permanent Court of International Justice. It also would require the development of a United Nations military force, and of United Nations powers of taxation. However, as long as the nations of the world are as different from one another as they are now, the nation exercising paramount influence in the United Nations, whether it happened to be the United States or any other, in effect would rule the world.

There is no realistic prospect that anything like this will happen in the near future. But there is a second way, suggested by the late Senator Arthur Vandenberg in 1945. It is to make the United Nations the town meeting of the world, where all issues can be brought out into the open, and where governments can learn how to manage differences of interest and ideology, and how to avoid head-on collisions. Here the United Nations also can help newly emerging nations to learn their new roles in world politics and to become, so to speak, "socialized" into the international system. In these respects, the United Nations since 1945 has been remarkably successful. If one recalls the bloody emergence of the Balkan nations in the nineteenth century, and contrasts it with the United Nations era since 1945, one may realize the contrast. Never before in history have so many new nations emerged as now, with so relatively little loss of life (Nigeria's civil war in 1968 was a major tragic exception).

All these considerations show that a worldwide general-purpose organization is still far away. Even the United Nations is neither quite worldwide nor fully able to serve general purposes. It includes only about three-quarters of mankind; and it is so limited in its actual tasks, resources, powers, and support that it cannot be called supranational, only international. It is at best the common servant of most of the major national governments in the world, and it is the master of none. Nor has it replaced all of them completely in any one major political task or function. In order to find genuine supranational government (responsible for many or all major tasks of government and empowered to override the component governments on at least some matters of importance), or for the full-fledged delegation of at least some important task or function of government to an international organization, we must turn to particularistic international organizations.

Universal General-Purpose Organizations

Regional Organizations as a Path to Integration

CHAPTER SEVENTEEN

Particularistic international organizations are usually limited in their domain to something vaguely called a "region"—that is, to a few countries united by some geographic, cultural, or historical associations, or by economic and financial ties, or by political liberal-mindedness and similarity of social institutions, or by some combination of all these. Experience in creating and developing such "regional" and/or "functional" associations, it has been hoped, may teach governments and peoples to appreciate the benefits of international integration, and to develop

181

the integrative political habits and skills necessary to practice it successfully on a larger scale and for a broader range of tasks.

Quite a few such regional organizations are now in existence. Each of them deals with a small number of functions for a limited number of countries—usually not many more countries nor many more functions than the ones with which they started. Perhaps in the early stages of each such organization, a few countries and/or functions were added, and sometimes there were confident expectations of their continued growth. In fact, however, growth usually soon either stopped or slowed down greatly. Eventually each organization reached some kind of plateau on which it continued to function and survive (except for a few regional organizations which became dormant or defunct—such as, for example, the Balkan Entente of the 1930's). Occasionally, some regional organizations later on entered again into another phase of growth in membership or scope, or both; and some regional organizations may achieve such phases of new growth again in the future.

Perhaps the largest and most important regional organizations were those formed after World War II in Western Europe. The *Organization for European Economic Cooperation* (OEEC) was founded in 1948 to provide a forum in which the plans for using the American Marshall Plan and for the national economic reconstruction and development of 16 European nations could be coordinated. Its successor, the *Organization for Economic Cooperation and Development* (OECD) is larger, since it also includes the United States and Canada, but its powers are limited to the making of studies and recommendations. OEEC and OECD are special-purpose organizations, limited to economic matters. Even thus limited, however, perhaps they have helped, together with other international organizations, to prepare the groundwork for successive reductions of tariff barriers between the United States and Western Europe. By 1967, the so-called "Kennedy Round" of negotiations had brought agreements, not yet ratified, to reduce these barriers on the average by about one-fourth of their original amounts.

The North Atlantic Treaty Organization

An international body with a smaller domain but somewhat greater powers is the *North Atlantic Treaty Organization* (NATO) which comprises the United States, Canada, Britain, and 13 continental European countries including some rather far from the Atlantic Ocean, such as Greece and Turkey. The main concern of NATO is the military influence of its members, and hence the management of power. To some extent, therefore, it could become an organization serving general purposes. When it was founded in 1948, its main task was to coordinate the armed forces of its members in order to ward off any possible Soviet attack upon Western Europe, whether in the form of military invasion, escalating border conflicts, or Soviet-supported international revolts. Its core was in a kind of exchange of military commitments. The United States promised to use its nuclear weapons (which then were still a United States monopoly) to protect its European allies; and these allies committed themselves to furnishing much of the manpower and part of the conventional equipment, as well as the territorial bases and facilities, for the joint defense effort under a joint command.

182

Regional Organizations as a Path to Integration

In practice, this joint command was most responsive to the policies of the United States, which continued to control the main part of the nuclear "sword" of the alliance. At the same time, however, NATO provided the political and legal framework for the rearmament of Western Germany. By the late 1950's, the German Federal Republic had come to supply the largest single ingredient of NATO's "shield" of conventionally armed ground troops. A lesser but substantial contribution to both "sword" and "shield" has come from Britain, while France gradually withdrew her cooperation from NATO to the point where by 1968 the Organization had been compelled to remove its troops and installations from French soil, and to move its headquarters from Paris to a small town near Brussels, Belgium.

From the outset, NATO had considerable powers to plan, coordinate, and arrange agreements with its member governments for the deployment of troops, ships, and aircraft; to conduct maneuvers; to provide a common NATO command for the forces put at its disposal by its member nations, and to propose agreements to these members for the raising and upkeep of such forces. NATO has no power, however, to compel any country to provide the forces for which the Organization may ask. The target level of 30 divisions in Europe under NATO command, agreed on in the early 1950's, has not been reached to date, and there seems little prospect that it will be in the foreseeable future. During the years of NATO's existence since 1948, however, no European country has fallen under Communist rule, or has been the victim of a major Communist attack or Communist-supported internal uprising. If all these things were quite unlikely to happen in any case, then the efforts put into NATO could have been put to better use elsewhere; but if it is believed that at some time between 1948 and 1968 intense Soviet pressure on a Western European country undefended by NATO would have been likely to occur, then NATO may claim some of the credit for having prevented it.

In any case, the likelihood of a direct Soviet attack on Western Europe seemed remote by the late 1960's. Once the United States and the Soviet Union could inflict intolerable damage on each other, both governments seemed unlikely to choose a course leading to national suicide, and the credibility of their threats and promises of nuclear action declined. Indeed, after the Cuba crisis of 1962, NATO's European members grew less fearful of Soviet threats; and the Soviet occupation of Czechoslovakia in 1968 shook their attitude but did not reverse it. They still relied on United States nuclear protection—but expected it to be based on American self-interest rather than on any abstract commitment to the NATO alliance for its own sake.

Under these conditions, NATO as a primarily military alliance system was likely to decline somewhat in importance, unless it could be broadened in scope to include political and economic matters. In all these respects, moreover, the United States would have to become an ally more nearly equal to the others in letting itself be outvoted on occasion, and in subordinating its national judgment to the collective judgment of the community. In the years 1965–1968, the unilateral United States decision to run the worldwide risks of escalating the war in Vietnam, without the backing of a majority vote either in the United Nations or of its NATO allies, showed how far the United States still was from being fully integrated either in the United Nations or in the Atlantic Alliance.

Regional Organizations as a Path to Integration

The prediction of psychologist Jerome Bruner in 1944 that the American people would not fully join organization which they could not dominate, still remained to be disproved nearly a quarter-century later. They were loyal members of NATO, as it then stood (as they also were loyal members of the United Nations), but they expected their will to predominate. They were more inclined to ask what NATO and the United Nations could do for the United States, than what the United States could do for either of these organizations. Eventually, if NATO was not to decline, something more would be needed from the United States, as well as from the other members; and by 1967 it was not at all clear whether this something more would be forthcoming. But if the United States seemed too large, too self-preoccupied, and too different from its Atlantic partners to merge its identity at any early date in any kind of Atlantic union, were not the countries of Western Europe smaller and in greater need of union? And were they not potentially more like-minded about what kind of integration they wanted, and how it was to be achieved?

Efforts at Unifying Western Europe: The ECC Complex

The years 1946 to 1949 saw the shaping of the basic ideas of unifying Europe which were to influence European politics for the next two decades. In September, 1946, in a famous speech at Zurich, Sir Winston Churchill proposed for the ills of Europe a "remedy" which, as he said:

. . . if it were generally and spontaneously adopted, would, as if by a miracle, transform the whole scene, and would, in a few years, make all Europe, or the greater part of it, as free and happy as Switzerland is today.[1]

To Sir Winston, the nature of "this sovereign remedy" was clear: "We must build a kind of United States of Europe. . . ." He seemed equally clear about the method. "The process," he said, "is simple. All that is needed is the resolve of hundreds of millions of men and women . . ."[2]

Sir Winston's deceptively simple rhetoric was likely to appeal to four groups of experiences and aspirations which were widespread in the Europe of 1946. The first was security. The nations had failed to protect their peoples from the ravages of World War II, and a United Europe, it was hoped, would do better, and would also protect them from the apparent threat of Communist expansion. The second was prosperity. Europe's national economies were damaged and impoverished by the war; and earlier, they had proved extremely vulnerable to the Great Depression of the 1930's. A United Europe, it was thought, would be economically more stable and more prosperous, perhaps soon attaining both the market size and the per capita income level of the United States. The third issue was liberty and mobility. People had chafed for years under wartime rationing of goods and under national restrictions on the movement of persons, goods, and capital, which had been intensified

[1] Sir Winston Churchill, speech at Zurich, September 1946, reprinted in Andrew and Frances Boyd (eds.), *Western Union: A Study of the Trend Toward European Unity* (Washington: Public Affairs Press, 1949), p. 109.

[2] *Ibid.*

Regional Organizations as a Path to Integration

during the depression and the war. Many people now desired "a United Europe, throughout whose area the free movement of persons, ideas and goods is restored."[3] The fourth was power. The nation-states of Western Europe had visibly lost much of their power. Those which had had colonies, had lost some of them, and were likely soon to lose the rest; and no Western European nation in 1946–1948, except England, counted for much in international politics. A United Europe might restore to its peoples jointly much of the power, and perhaps some of the possessions, which they had separately lost.

Although these four considerations—security, prosperity, liberty and mobility, and power—appealed strongly to some, and mildly to many, throughout Western Europe, they never became an urgent concern of the mass of the people, or even of a bare majority, in any country. Against the event of attack, Western European security was protected by national alliances in principle, and by the United States in practice. Prosperity was restored by the economic reconstruction of the nation-states and national economies under the Marshall Plan (1948–1952), again with very substantial aid from the United States. Free mobility of persons and goods was never established, since it would have dismantled effectively the control of the national states over wages and price levels, tax and interest rates, employment levels, living standards, and the rate and direction of economic growth; and no supranational institutions were created to take over these tasks of control, much less to fulfill them in a manner responsive to the varying popular desires in each country. Finally, the Western European countries did not regain their power during the next two decades, either jointly or severally. They lost most of the rest of their colonies, but found themselves more prosperous; and their peoples showed little inclination to make any sustained sacrifices for a new pursuit of empire or power, under either national or European auspices.

Nonetheless, modest advances were made in all four directions; and they were facilitated by the rise of a number of new European institutions which proved viable, even though other projected institutions failed and all European institutions had been conceived originally with more ambitious aims. From the outset, each of these European institutions had been intended to be *transitional*. Though limited to some specific task or function, and often to a particular group of European countries, each new institution was meant to create new needs for further integration and new political attitudes, interests, and habits facilitating further steps toward it. Eventually, so the "Europeans" among the West European statesmen hoped, this integration would be one for general purposes, similar to that of a nation-state, federal or unitary. And it would eventually cover all of non-Communist Europe and even perhaps, so it was hoped, lure in time some of the currently Communist-ruled East European countries away from the Soviet bloc and into Western Europe.

The major efforts toward European integration began with the *Treaty of Dunkirk* (March, 1947) between France and Britain, which was a treaty of alliance and mutual assistance against any possible renewal of German aggression, but which also included a pledge of mutual cooperation in the

---

[3] "Message to Europeans," adopted at the Congress of Europe, The Hague, May 8–10, 1948; cited in A. H. Robertson, *European Institutions* (London: Stevens & Sons, Ltd., 1959), p. 11.

Regional Organizations as a Path to Integration

general interests of the prosperity and economic security of the two countries. This was followed by the first announcement of the Marshall Plan in June, 1947, the formation of the Committee on European Economic Cooperation by Britain, France, and 14 other European countries in July, 1947, and the signing of the *Convention on European Economic Cooperation* in April, 1948.

In the meantime, Western governments had become alarmed by the formation in September, 1947, of an international Communist body, the *Cominform*, by the Communist parties of the Soviet Union and the other Communist-ruled East European countries. This was followed in December, 1947, by the proclamation of a Communist-led "Provisional Democratic Government of Free Greece" (which eventually proved unsuccessful), and in February, 1948, by a Communist coup d'état in Czechoslovakia which established firm Communist control in that country. One Western response to these events was in the form of two military agreements: the *Brussels Treaty*, a military alliance signed in March, 1948, by Britain, France, and the "Benelux" countries (Belgium, Netherlands, and Luxembourg), and initially known as "Western European Union" (WEU); and the *North Atlantic Treaty*, signed in April, 1949, which created the North Atlantic Treaty Organization (NATO).

Steps Toward European Federalism

In May, 1949, the Statute of the *Council of Europe* (CE) was signed, providing for a Consultative Assembly, meeting in public (the so-called "European Parliament" at Strasbourg), and the Committee of Ministers, meeting in private. The Consultative Assembly is composed of representatives elected by the national parliaments, or appointed by the governments of the member states, but voting as individuals—which often means, in practice, along party lines. It was intended to be a sounding-board of European opinion, which it was also expected to help to formulate and lead; but its powers are limited to making recommendations (by majority vote) to the Committee of Ministers. The Committee of Ministers in turn can do no more than make recommendations (but only by unanimous vote of the Ministers or their Deputies, acting in each case as instructed representatives of their governments) to the member governments; and these national governments alone have the power to take any action. "European" opinion thus may at most propose, but each nation-state disposes.

In 1950, a *European Payments Union* (EPU) was established within the framework of OEEC. This was done to facilitate multilateral trade and financial transactions within the trading area of Western Europe and the sterling area, at least until such time as full convertibility of the currencies of a sufficient number of OEEC member nations could be achieved, so as to make EPU unnecessary. The setup worked as planned: EPU did facilitate multilateral European trade in the 1950's, and by the end of the decade had passed out of existence, after the main European currencies had become more or less freely convertible in the international money market. Whether EPU could have been used to prepare the groundwork for a common European

Regional Organizations as a Path to Integration

currency is another question. In any event, all major governments (and, presumably, their peoples) preferred to keep the control over their national currency (and hence much of their national economic life) as much as possible in their own hands; and EPU was dissolved.

In the spring of 1950, there was also launched (by the French Foreign Minister Robert Schuman) the *Schuman Plan* for pooling the control of the entire French and German production of coal and steel in a common market under a joint High Authority with executive powers, based on a deliberate transfer of sovereignty by the participating states; and this new organization was to be open to other European countries. The High Authority was to be responsible to a parliamentary assembly; legal matters were to be decided by a Court of Justice; and the national governments were to be represented by a Council of Ministers. Within its field of competence, the new organization was to be *supranational*—that is (according to our previous definition of the term), it was to supersede or override the decision-making powers of the national governments of the member countries. Its immediate political goal was to keep France safe from any possible revival of German nationalism and militarism in the course of German rearmament, plans for which had been in the making ever since NATO had come into existence, and which soon was to become more salient under the impact of the Korean War. Far beyond this, however, Schuman described his plan in May 1950 as "a first step in the direction of European federation"; and in August he expressed his confidence that "it will rapidly lead us on towards the complete economic and political unification of Europe."[4] By April, 1951, a treaty creating the *European Coal and Steel Community* (ECSC) was signed by "the Six"— France, the German Federal Republic, Italy, and the three Benelux countries—and, duly ratified by all, it entered into force in July, 1952.

Two months earlier, in May, 1952, the foreign ministers of the Six had signed an even more far-reaching treaty (also proposed by France) which was to find them merging their armed forces in a *European Defense Community* (EDC) under a supranational authority similar to that provided by ECSC. This treaty was designed to permit German rearmament, but only within the framework of a European army. At the same time, however, it also would have replaced the French army (or rather the ensemble of French armed forces) by a European one, and thus eliminate France's military arm as a potential force in the national politics of its mother country. Large segments of the French Right and Left united in opposing this prospect. Although the other five member nations of the Six ratified the treaty, it was defeated, and the EDC project buried, in the French parliament in August, 1954.

An even more ambitious draft treaty for a *European Community* (EC), which earlier had been called the *European Political Community, or EPC,* was worked out in 1953 by a European "ad hoc assembly" (composed of the ECSC Assembly with some additional French, German, and Italian delegates); but this draft treaty was never even signed by the governments of the Six, and died stillborn.

[4] Walter Hallstein, *United Europe: Challenge and Opportunity* (Cambridge: Harvard University Press, 1962), pp. 11, 62.

Regional Organizations as a Path to Integration

If European federalism ground to a halt in 1953–1954, at least European functionalism made some progress. A *European Productivity Agency* (EPA), a *Customs Cooperations Council* (CCC), a *European Conference of Ministers of Transport* (ECMT), and a *European Council for Nuclear Research* (CERN) were created in 1953; and a *European Civil Aviation Conference* (ECAC) came into existence in 1955. (A number of European organizations and their varied membership of states are shown in Table 14.)

In an attempt to compensate for the setbacks to European military and political unification, important efforts were launched for promoting European unity in economic matters, at least among the Six. In March, 1957, their foreign ministers signed the *Treaty of Rome*, providing for a *European Economic Community* (EEC) and the gradual establishment of a *European Common Market* with the eventual free movement of goods, persons, services and capital among their countries, to be achieved step-by-step over a period of 12 to 15 years. At the same time, a second treaty was signed, establishing among the Six a *European Atomic Energy Community* (EURATOM), more far-reaching than CERN. Both treaties were quickly ratified, and EEC and EURATOM came into being on January 1, 1958. By 1967, the Common Market was, in legal terms, somewhat ahead of its original schedule: four-fifths of the tariffs among the Six on manufactured goods had been abolished, and agreements on an important range of agricultural products had been reached. Within its limits, functionalism had been successful.

The nature and limits of this success deserve attention. For the first time in history, war within Western Europe is being looked upon by its governments and peoples as illegitimate and improbable, and as not worth preparing for in any major way. In this sense, Western Europe has become a security community. It can still be threatened from without, but its population does not feel threatened from within by any of their Western European neighbors.

At the same time, Western Europe has remained politically pluralistic. Its states have retained almost all their sovereignty in political and military matters, a fact which President de Gaulle demonstrated in 1963 when he vetoed Britain's attempt to enter the European Economic Community; and again, when he refused in 1965 to let France be outvoted on important matters within EEC; and yet again when he moved to delay Britain's renewed effort to enter EEC in 1967. Europe's currencies, its national economies, its labor markets, and its capital markets have not yet become one. To be sure, from 1913 to about 1957 there had been a trend toward the structural integration of the economic and social fabric of Western Europe, as shown by the growing proportions of cross-boundary trade, mail correspondence, travel, and university attendance within the area. Since 1957–1958, however, this trend has halted. The structural unification of Western Europe has reached a plateau on which it may well stay for another decade. Further increases in several major kinds of intra-EEC transactions since 1958 have been no larger than can be accounted for by the effects of prosperity and random probability (or

Regional Organizations as a Path to Integration

Table 14 THE MEMBERSHIP OF EUROPEAN ORGANIZATIONS

Rank of Countries \ Rank of Organizations	ECAC (1)	OEEC (2)	ECMT	CCC (3)	Council of Europe	NATO (4)	CERN	WEU	ECSC	Economic Community	Euratom	Rhine Com'n (5)	Nordic Council	Benelux	Balkan Alliance	Out of 15 Possible Members
1. Belgium																13
2. Netherlands																13
3. France																12
4. Germany																12
5. Italy																11
6. Luxembourg																11
7. United Kingdom																9
8. Denmark																8
9. Greece																8
10. Norway																8
11. Sweden																7
12. Turkey																7
13. Switzerland																6
14. Austria																5
15. Iceland																5
16. Portugal																5
17. Ireland																4
18. Spain																3
19. Yugoslavia																3
20. Finland																1
Out of 20 Possible Members	18	17	17	17	15	13	12	7	6	6	6	6	5	3	3	

NOTES:

1. Yugoslavia is represented by an observer at the ECAC.
2. Canada and the U.S.A. are associate members of OEEC. Spain takes part in some of the work of the organization. Yugoslavia is represented by an observer.
3. The following are also members of the Customs Cooperation Council: Haiti, Indonesia, Israel, Pakistan, and the United Arab Republic.
4. Canada and the U.S.A. are also members of NATO.
5. The U.S.A. is also a member of the Rhine Commission.

ABBREVIATIONS:

BENELUX	Belgium, Netherlands, and Luxembourg	ECSC	European Coal and Steel Community
Council of Europe	Council of Europe	EURATOM	European Atomic Energy Community
CCC	Customs Cooperation Council	NATO	North Atlantic Treaty Organization
CERN	European Council for Nuclear Research	OEEC	Organization for European Economic Cooperation
ECAC	European Civil Aviation Conference	Rhine Com'n	Rhine Commission
ECMT	European Conference of Ministers of Transport	WEU	Western European Union

chance).[5] If greater integration is to occur, a new generation might have to wield political influence, perhaps that generation that was of university age in 1948–1950, a time when the European drive was launched and unity was taken for granted.

Other Efforts at Regional Integration

Supranational integration elsewhere has remained weaker than in Western Europe. The *Organization of American States* (OAS), successor to the Pan-American Union and heir to a tradition of inter-American sympathies (but also of some Latin-American misgivings and resentments of United States economic and political preponderance), is far less integrated than Western Europe in terms of mutual transactions, popular loyalties, and effective institutions.

The *Arab League* has united its member states in terms of a common heritage of language, culture, and (to a large extent) religion; common distrust of outside powers, Western as well as Communist; and a common hostility to the State of Israel. These links have not sufficed, however, to sustain major undertakings in political or economic life, nor to ensure an equitable distribution of oil revenues among the richer and poorer Arab countries, nor to enable the Arab states to prevent major military setbacks in 1948, 1956, and 1967. Here, too, integration is at most at a rather early stage; and many of the positive links among the Arab states still have to be forged in the future.

The integration among the various countries of the *Soviet bloc* has remained no less incomplete. Within the Communist world, warfare would be considered illegitimate, but bitter disputes with vehement mutual abuse have occurred repeatedly, such as between the Soviet Union and Yugoslavia in 1948–1953, between the Soviet Union and Communist China in the 1960's, and between the Soviet Union and Czechoslovakia in 1968, before the occupation of the latter by the troops of Rumania, Poland, Hungary, Bulgaria, and the German Democratic Republic, in the name of the Warsaw Pact.

The Communist Organization for Economic Cooperation, *COMECON*, and for military cooperation, the *Warsaw Pact* (the counterparts of OECD and NATO, respectively), have remained limited to the Soviet Union and its East European allies. For a time they seem to have become looser as the Communist regimes in Yugoslavia, Poland, Czechoslovakia, and Rumania have become somewhat stronger and more confident. Though reliable data are scarce on transactions among Communist countries, comparable to those on Western Europe, they suggest that a pluralism of nation-states has been persisting in the Communist world. With the rise of a new political generation in these countries, liberalism and nationalism may increase below the surface of conformity. Governments will then have to choose between accommodation and repression. Thus when Soviet political controls over Czechoslovakia were loosening, the Soviet Government in August 1968 resorted to military occupation. But the pressures for change are apt to continue in most Soviet-bloc countries and within the Soviet Union itself.

[5] For data see Deutsch, Edinger, Macridis, and Merritt, *op. cit.*, pp. 218–251; and for survey data on the attitudes of the very young, see Ronald Inglehart, "An End to European Integration?", *American Political Science Review* (March, 1967), pp. 91–105.

Regional Organizations as a Path to Integration

Attaining and Maintaining Integration

CHAPTER EIGHTEEN

International organizations have often been seen as the best pathway
for leading mankind out of the era of the nation-state. Beyond the actual
international organizations which now exist, or have existed, there are
the great projects for Atlantic Union or for Federal World Government ???
which still promise much for supranational integration, if they could only
get started. Against these visions of the future, it is worthwhile
to put the experiences of the past. What have been some of the actual
cases of political integration, and what can be learned from them?

There are perhaps four dozen cases of political integration in the world from which something could be learned fairly directly that might help us better to deal with our similar present-day problems. Fourteen of these cases—10 from earlier history and four relatively recent ones—have been studied for the explicit purpose of making such comparisons to our contemporary problems, and some of the findings of these studies are worth summarizing here.[1]

The main *tasks of integration* can be conveniently recalled under four headings: (1) maintaining peace; (2) attaining greater multipurpose capabilities; (3) accomplishing some specific task; and (4) gaining a new self-image and role identity.

All these tasks are operationally testable. Whether stable expectations of *peace* are being maintained within a community can be tested by the absence or paucity of specific preparation for war among the political units, regions, and populations within it. Evidence can be found in data on the deployment of troops, weapons, and military installations; in diplomatic records and in budgetary data; and in opinion data on the elite and mass levels. Whether a community has achieved greater *multipurpose capabilities* would be indicated at least roughly by its total gross national product, its per capita GNP, and the scope and diversity of its current undertakings. Whether the community was fulfilling *specific tasks* would be indicated by the existence, and perhaps by the growth, of appropriate joint functions, joint institutions, and joint resources and sacrifices devoted to these specific ends. Finally, whether the members of the community had attained a new *role identity*, or were in the process of attaining it, would be shown by the frequency of use of common symbols, and by the creation and wide adoption of new ones; by data on relevant elite and mass attitudes; and by relevant aggregate data on the actual behavior of the population, including popular acceptance of unrequited transfers of wealth or other benefits within the community, and of some degree of sharing benefits and burdens within it.

Whether the tasks envisaged for integration can in fact be fulfilled, and whether integration will succeed or fail, depends in part on the *background conditions* prevailing within and among the political units to be integrated. The conditions of integration can again be stated under four headings: (1) mutual relevance of the units to one another; (2) compatibility of values and some actual joint rewards; (3) mutual responsiveness; and (4) some degree of generalized common identity or loyalty. These four conditions interact and may strengthen one another, but in principle each can be verified separately.

Mutual relevance among the units is indicated by the relative volume and weight of transactions among them, such as trade, travel, and mail and other communications; by the extent to which such transactions exceed the levels which could be expected from mere chance and the size of the partici-

[1] The historical studies dealt with the cases of successful integration of England; England and Wales; England and Scotland; the United States; Germany; Italy; and Switzerland; and with the failures of integration of Norway and Sweden; England and Ireland; and the Austro-Hungarian monarchy. The recent cases studied included the successes of the Nordic Council and of the European Economic Community, and the failures of the Federation of the West Indies and of the United Arab Republic. For details see K. W. Deutsch, *et al.*, *Political Community and the North Atlantic Area* (Princeton: Princeton University Press, 1968), and Amitai Etzioni, *Political Unification* (New York: Holt, Rinehart & Winston, 1965).

Attaining and Maintaining Integration

pating units; and by the extent of covariance between their effects on any two different participating political units.

The existence and extent of *joint rewards* for the partners in the prospective larger community can be attested to by the extent of the *positive* covariance of rewards for two or more of them, so that a reward for one is associated with the significant probability of a reward for the other.

The conditions for *mutual responsiveness* include the presence of significant capabilities and resources for communication, perception, and self-steering. A separate source of evidence consists in the actual performance in terms of speed, adequacy, and probability of responsive behavior.

Finally, *common generalized loyalty* can be indicated by the frequency and saliency of perceptions of joint interests, both in terms of distributions of attention and of parallel expectations of reward, as shown by survey data and by the content analysis of mass media and government communications. Another indication would be the objective compatibility or consonance of the major values of the participating populations, permitting cooperation among them to be perceived as legitimate. This could be supplemented by indications of common subjective feelings of the legitimacy of the integrated community, making loyalty to it also a matter of internalized psychic compulsion.

The goals and conditions of integration go far to determine the *processes and instruments* by which integration is approached. Once more, we can organize these instruments under four headings, as processes and techniques of: (1) value production; (2) value allocation; (3) coercion; and (4) identification. *Value production* and *value allocation* refer, respectively, to the production (or acquisition) and the allocation of goods, services, or relationships valued by the populations concerned. *Coercion* means primarily military or other enforcement; and *identification* means the deliberate promotion of processes and sentiments of mutual identification, loyalties, and "we"-feelings.

Types of Communities: Amalgamation vs. Pluralism

THE PROCESS OF ESTABLISHING AN AMALGAMATED SECURITY COMMUNITY

If the main goal of integration is not only the preservation of peace among the integrated political units, but also the acquisition of greater power for general specific purposes, or the acquisition of a common role identity, or some combination of all these, then a so-called *amalgamated political community* with a common government is likely to be preferred. If the main aim is peace, then a *pluralistic security community* may suffice, and in fact may be easier to attain.

An amalgamated community may also be an *amalgamated security community,* within which dependable expectations of peaceful change prevail, as attested by the absence of substantial specific preparations for large-scale warfare within it. Any well-integrated nation-state such as were Britain and the United States in 1968, is such an amalgamated security community. (Even though local violence among racial groups in American cities has been increasing in the 1960's, and some preparations were made for the expected recurrence of such violence in the future, these developments thus far have remained far short of civil war.) But neither a common government nor

193

Attaining and Maintaining Integration

common laws and institutions can ensure such internal peace and security to a country on the verge of civil war, such as was the United States in 1860–1861, India-Pakistan in 1946–1947, and Nigeria in 1967. Indeed, the very effort to maintain the amalgamated community or political union by force may bring on exactly that large-scale warfare which a security community was intended to prevent. The possible relationships between amalgamated communities and security communities are shown in Table 15.

The significance of these relationships is changing. Whereas large-scale civil wars and bloodshed could in the past be survived by the bulk of the warring population because they were waged with weapons of rather limited destructive potential, today the masses of those involved (and perhaps all mankind) could be wiped out in a nuclear civil war fought on a fairly small scale. Accordingly, as the power of weapons has increased, the preserving of peace, and peaceful change and adjustment of conflicts, have become more important; unification for general-purpose power, or for a sense of greater group prestige and identity, has become less important; the legal distinction between international war and civil war has become less relevant; and amalgamated but not integrated political communities have become more dangerous.

Though now more dangerous in case of failure, an amalgamated security community still will continue to look more desirable than its alternates, for if

Table 15 **POLITICAL AMALGAMATION, PLURALISM AND SECURITY: FOR POSSIBLE PATTERNS OF POLITICAL COMMUNITY**

	NON-AMALGAMATION	AMALGAMATION
INTEGRATION	Pluralistic Security-Community *Example* (Norway-Sweden today)	Amalgamated Security-Community *Example* (U.S.A. today)
	— INTEGRATION THRESHOLD —	
NON-INTEGRATION	Not Amalgamated Not Security-Community *Example* (U.S.A.-U.S.S.R., today)	Amalgamated but not Security-Community *Example* (Habsburg Empire, 1914)

(AMALGAMATION THRESHOLD runs vertically through the center of the table)

Note: All four cases involve a high degree of mutual relevance and, therefore, some degree of political unity. In each case, the countries, peoples, and governments concerned must take into account each other's behavior in making their own political decisions.

Source: Karl W. Deutsch, Sidney A. Burrell, *et al, Political Community and the North Atlantic Area: International Organization in the Light of Historical Experience* (Princeton: Princeton University Press, 1957).

Attaining and Maintaining Integration

it succeeds, it will not only preserve peace but will provide greater strength for accomplishing both general and specific governmental services and purposes, and possibly a larger sense of identity and psychic reassurance for the elites and masses of its population. But though more desirable, like all better things it will be harder to attain and keep.

Essential background conditions. One study lists 12 social and economic background conditions, within and among the participating units, which seem to be necessary (though perhaps not sufficient) if an amalgamated security community is to succeed:

1. Mutual compatibility of the main values relevant for political behavior
2. A distinctive and attractive way of life
3. Expectations of stronger and rewarding economic ties or joint rewards
4. A marked increase in the political and administrative capabilities of at least some of the participating units
5. Superior economic growth of at least some participating units (as compared to neighboring territories outside the area of prospective integration)
6. Some substantial unbroken links of social communication across the mutual boundaries of the territories to be integrated, and across the barriers of some of the major social strata within them
7. A broadening of the political elite within at least some political units, and for the emerging larger community as a whole
8. Relatively high geographic and social mobility of persons, at least among the politically relevant strata
9. Multiplicity of the scope of the flow of mutual communications and transactions
10. Some overall compensation of rewards in the flows of communications and transactions among the units to be integrated
11. A significant frequency of some interchange in group roles (such as being in a majority or a minority) among the political units
12. Considerable mutual predictability of behavior

Together, these background conditions provide much of the indispensable social, economic, and psychological environment for the more well-known political conditions for an amalgamated security community, which consist mainly in the willingness and ability of the preponderance of the politically relevant strata in all participating political units to:

1. Accept and support common governmental institutions
2. Extend generalized political loyalty to them and to the preservation of the amalgamated community
3. Operate these common institutions with adequate mutual attention and responsiveness to the messages and needs of all participating units

Even if it has been established, an amalgamated security community, such as a federation or an empire, often is highly vulnerable to civil conflict or secession. Any one of half-a-dozen conditions is likely to make for its disintegration:

1. Any steep increase in economic, military, or political burdens on the community or on any participating unit (particularly if this increase in burdens comes at an early stage, before integration has become consolidated by the learning of deep political loyalties and habits)

195

Attaining and Maintaining Integration

2. A rapid increase in social mobilization and political participation, faster than the process of civic assimilation to the common political culture of the community

3. A rapid increase in regional, economic, cultural, social, linguistic, or ethnic differentiation, faster and stronger than any compensating integrative process

4. A serious decline in the political or administrative capabilities of the government and the political elite, relative to the current tasks and burdens with which they have to cope

5. A relative closure of the political elite, slowing drastically the entry of new members and ideas, and giving rise to hostile counter-elites of frustrated potential elite members

6. A failure of the government and the elite to carry out in time needed reforms and adjustments wanted or expected by the population (and perhaps already demonstrated in some salient areas abroad); or failure to adjust in time to the imminent decline or loss of some privileged or dominant minority position (such as the position of the white minority in the former Federation of Rhodesia and Nyasaland)

Pluralistic security communities are easier to establish and to maintain, and hence often are a more effective means to keep the peace among their members. They seem to require only three major conditions for their existence:

1. Compatibility of major political values
2. Capacity of the governments and politically relevant strata of the participating countries to respond to one another's messages, needs, and actions quickly, adequately, and without resort to violence
3. Mutual predictability of the relevant aspects of one another's political, economic, and social behavior (but these relevant aspects are far fewer in the case of a pluralistic security community than they would be in its much more tightly-knit amalgamated counterpart)

The process of integration. Amalgamated security communities, such as nation-states or federations, are not like organisms. They do not come into existence by a process of growth through a fixed sequence of stages, similar to the way in which a tadpole develops into a frog, or a kitten grows to be a cat. Rather, integration resembles an *assembly-line process*. Integrated communities are assembled in all their essential elements and aspects in the course of history, somewhat as an automobile is put together. It matters little for the performance of the finished car in what sequence each part is added, so long as all its necessary elements eventually are incorporated. Certain characteristics of the process of integration, however, have been observed in many past cases; and they will be worth watching for in present and future ones.

The process of integration often begins around a *core area* consisting of one or a few political units which are stronger, more highly developed, and in some significant respects more advanced and attractive than the rest. The governments and political elites of such potential core areas of a prospective political system. England played this role in the British Isles; Piedmont did so active leader, unifier, or (in Etzioni's term) "elite" for the emerging integrated political system. England played this role in the British Isles; Piedmont did so in the unification of Italy, and Prussia in that of Germany; and Massachu-

Attaining and Maintaining Integration

setts, Virginia, Pennsylvania, and New York did so jointly in the integration of the 13 American colonies into the United States.

Early in the course of the integrative process, a psychological "no-war" community often also develops. War among the prospective partners comes to be considered as illegitimate; serious preparations for it no longer command popular support; and even if some of the prospective partner countries find themselves on opposite sides in some larger international conflict, they conduct themselves so as to keep actual mutual hostilities and damage to a minimum—or else refuse to fight each other altogether. A virtual "no-serious-war" community of this kind emerged among the Swiss Cantons in the sixteenth century; among the Italian states since the mid-eighteenth century; among the American States since 1775; and among the German states since the mid-nineteenth century; and it may have emerged since 1950 among the EEC countries, despite many memories of past wars among them.

Often also the most salient political divisions within the emerging amalgamated security community become weaker, and—still more important—they shift away from the boundaries of the participating units. Political life then becomes dominated by divisions cutting across the original political units and regions. The more varied and salient these mutually *cross-cutting divisions* are, the better for the acceptability of the emerging union. The history of such cross-cutting alignments of political parties, religions, and economic interests (all supplementing, modifying, and partly overriding the old ties to the original units and regions) can be traced in the history of the unification of Britain, Switzerland, Italy, Germany, and the United States.

Conversely, where cleavages among regions and political units are paralleled and reinforced by old or new cleavages of language, religion, ideology, economic interest, and social class, there integration is likely to be halted or reversed. This happened between Britain and most of Ireland; among the various parts of the Austro-Hungarian monarchy; and temporarily between the North and South in the United States. In each case, the amalgamated security community collapsed—only temporarily in the United States, but (so far) permanently in the other cases.

Finally, in the successful cases of integration by political amalgamation, the main cross-regional political factions or parties stood for something new. They were identified with one or several *major cross-regional innovations* which were both important and attractive at that place and time. The Reformation and the reforms of the Tudor kings both played a major part in the integration of England and Wales, and so did the reforms of the Whigs (and their substantial acceptance by the Tories) in the unification of England and Scotland. Liberals and Liberalism played a similar part in the unifications of Switzerland, Italy, and Germany in the nineteenth century, often aided by the acceptance and sponsorship of important reforms and innovations by enlightened conservatives such as Cavour and Bismarck. The United States were unified with the aid of the American Revolution, and both Hamilton's Federalists and Jefferson's Democratic Republicans stood for major (and in part unprecedented) innovations. By contrast, this element of major cross-regional innovation was weaker in the English-Irish Union of 1801; in the Habsburg monarchy after 1810; and in the Norwegian-Swedish Union after 1814; and all these unions eventually were dissolved.

Attaining and Maintaining Integration

The issue of functionalism as a path to integration. In contrast to these major aspects of the process, the much-debated issue of *functionalism* (see pages 166–168) turns out to be much less important. Functionalism, we recall, means partial amalgamation. It works in this way: some specific tasks are handed over by the participating governments to some common agency. But these tasks are not very important, and so usually do not transfer enough general-purpose power to the new agency to allow it to be, even "in effect," capable of any act requiring overall amalgamation. Thus, most of the time, it must settle for partial, or functional amalgamation. Such functional amalgamation sometimes *has* led step-by-step to overall amalgamation. This happened, for instance, in such cases as those of the German Customs Union in the nineteenth century, the common administration of the Western lands by the United States under the Articles of Confederation (1781–1791), and the Swiss Cantons since the late fourteenth and early fifteenth centuries; and between England and Wales and England and Scotland preceding full amalgamation in each case.

On the other hand, Italy was unified without any significant preceding functional amalgamation; and the presence of functional amalgamation did not keep the Norwegian-Swedish Union from dissolving. Moreover, although a period of functional amalgamation preceded full amalgamation in the cases of England and Ireland, and of Austria, Bohemia, and Hungary, these amalgamated communities ultimately failed.

Functionalism and functional arrangements, we may conclude, have little effect by themselves upon the eventual success or failure of efforts to establish amalgamated security communities. The outcome in each case is most likely to depend on other conditions and processes, particularly on how rewarding or unrewarding were the experiences associated with functional arrangements. The most that can be said for functionalism is that it avoids the perils of premature overall amalgamation, and that it gives the participating governments, elites, and peoples more time gradually to learn the habits and skills of more far-reaching, stable, and rewarding integration.

The politics of integration: Leaders and issues. As a political process, integration has a *takeoff point* in time, when it is no longer a matter of a few prophets or scattered and powerless supporters, but turns into a larger and more coordinated movement with some significant power behind it. Before takeoff a proposal for integration is a theory; after takeoff it is a force.

Such larger unification movements may aim mainly at peace, and hence at integration based upon consent to peaceful change and conflict management; or they may aim mainly at power for specific ends, or for general purposes, and hence at amalgamation which may also be accomplished by conquest or coercion. Often, indeed, political unification movements have been broad coalitions, some of whose supporters have chiefly cared for internal peace while others have wanted most of all collective power through this larger union; and still others have wanted both.

To become acute, the basic issue of integration must become salient to substantial interest-groups and to large numbers of people. In the historic cases studied, this happened usually in the course of a threefold process of habit-breaking. First and most important, a new and attractive way of life had to emerge, with common expectations for more good things to come and with

198

enough experiences of recent improvements over the past, or over the standards of neighboring areas, so as to make these common expectations credible and to give the populations and political elites concerned at least some latent sense of unity of outlook and interests. Second, this latent sense of unity had to be aroused by some external challenge which clearly required some new and joint response. And third, a new generation had to arrive on the political scene, taking the earlier degree of common interest and outlook for granted, and ready to treat it as the starting point for new political actions. The third of these events, the arrival of a new generation in politics, is highly probable, since it occurs roughly every 15 years. The second, the impact of some external challenge, is also rather probable, since fairly substantial political and economic challenges are likely to occur in a fast-changing world at least every 20 to 25 years, if not more often. Only the first process is improbable. It is the emergence of a rewarding new way of life, and with it, of a latent sense of unity and common interest in defending or extending it; and in most parts of the world this happens at most once in several generations.

Once this improbable combination of events occurs, political leadership toward unification usually is provided not by a single social class but by a cross-class coalition. Typically, such a coalition in our historical cases linked some marginal or partly alienated members and groups among the elite ("the most outside of the insiders") to some of the strongest and most vigorous groups among the non-elite ("the most inside of the outsiders") who were beginning to press for a larger share of political power.

From the outset, major *political compromises* will be needed to hold together these integrated movements and broad cross-class coalitions whose members are apt to be quite diverse in background, interests, and outlook. But they are likely to be special kinds of compromises. They will be designed not to frustrate all parties by giving each much less than what it wants most, but on the contrary to reward each by conceding it much or all of that demand which is most salient to it, in return for its concessions on other matters which are less urgent to it but more salient to other partners in the coalition. Such compromises imply political "log-rolling" instead of mutual obstruction; instead of frustrating one another, the partners must discover a way to exchange political favors and to dovetail genuine and substantial concessions to one another's vital interests.

This work of discovering and establishing viable patterns of mutual political accommodation often will take considerable time. Accordingly, many integration movements show a succession of three stages. At first, there is a stage of *leadership by intellectuals,* during which the movement is mainly supported by intellectuals (and not necessarily by a majority of these) and by relatively few and limited groups from other strata. Later on, there comes the stage of the *great politicians,* when broader interest-groups begin to swing behind the integration movement, and mutually rewarding political compromises are worked out. Finally, this stage shades over into the stage of *mass movements* and/or *large-scale elite politics,* when the issue of political unification becomes intensely practical. Even so, the movement is likely to have setbacks and failures. As Richard Merritt's study of the unification of the American colonies suggests, integrative activities and popular support for them are likely to rise and then decline again in a manner somewhat resem-

Attaining and Maintaining Integration

bling a learning curve. If the social learning process is successful, however, each peak and each trough on this curve will be higher than its corresponding predecessor, until the process crosses some critical threshold and some major step toward an amalgamated security community has been accomplished.

Appeals and methods. In the course of this social learning process, the relevant elites and populations have to learn to connect all or most of their important political concerns and issues with the issue of unification; and they must come to perceive this issue clearly as a single and relatively simple decision, uncluttered by too many competing alternative proposals. Most effective among the political appeals and interests to be harnessed to the cause of integration are appeals for new or greater rights and liberties for individuals or groups. Next in effectiveness to the appeals for greater liberty rank the appeals for more equality—political, social, and/or economic. Close to these two, there ranks the appeal of a rewarding way of life, often including some experience and/or promise of prosperity and material well-being. In contrast to these three effective appeals, the appeals of seeking greater collective power for its own sake, or of defending and preserving some special minority privileges of group or class, seem to have had little or no effect in deciding the outcome of an integrative process: in one historical study, these last two types of appeal occurred about as often in cases of failure of integration as in cases of success.

To promote political amalgamation, all the usual political methods have been used, but not all have been equally effective. By far the most effective method, in terms of the relative frequency with which it was followed by success, was the enlistment of broad popular participation and support. Among the cases studied, every amalgamation movement that won such popular participation was eventually successful. The second most effective method was the acceptance of pluralism, and hence of the autonomy and sovereignty of the participating political units for substantial transition periods. Next in terms of effectiveness ranked the large-scale use of propaganda; the promise to abolish specific items of unpopular legislation; and the promotion of political or administrative autonomy for the participating units.

By contrast, some methods had little or no effect in making amalgamation come about: they occurred about as often in cases of success as they did in cases of failure. Such relatively ineffective methods included the promotion of specific political institutions, the use of symbols, and the use of patronage for the appointment of purposefully selected individuals to political or administrative office. All these methods may have been necessary, but by themselves they seem to have contributed little or nothing to make success more likely.

Three methods turned out to be counterproductive—that is, they were significantly more often associated with the failure of amalgamation than with its success. These counterproductive methods were early insistence on overall amalgamation, early efforts to establish a monopoly of violence, and outright military conquest.

Opposition to amalgamation most often came from peasants, farmers, and other rural groups; and in the second place, from privileged groups or regions which feared to lose something from amalgamation. Peasant opposition seems to have made no significant difference to the success or failure of amalgamation movements, but active peasant support, though rare, was invariably

200

Attaining and Maintaining Integration

associated with success. Privileged groups seem to have made no difference to the eventual success or failure of integration, neither by their opposition nor by their support, but they almost always gained some substantial concessions to their interest; and as far as the amalgamation movement in each case was concerned, the making of such concessions to the privileged groups seems to have had a low but distinct effect in favor of success.

In the end, amalgamation movements often succeeded through a combination of closure and creativity. They usually succeeded by closing out all competing proposals and alternatives, so as to eventually channel all political attention and action toward the single paramount issue and policy of amalgamation. But they often succeeded in doing so, and in maintaining and broadening their political coalition, only by means of the originality and resourcefulness with which the proponents of amalgamations invented and formulated specific plans for union and specific institutions to make it work. Often this element of political invention and innovation seems to have been critical. Many of the central institutions of successfully amalgamated security communities were original and relatively improbable at the time and place at which they were adopted. Conversely, several amalgamated security communities were wrecked by routine policies and views, and by obvious decisions, all of which were highly probable but inadequate at the time and place they occurred. In the politics of amalgamation, too, genius often consisted in discovering an improbable but highly relevant solution, or a sequence of solutions of this kind, and in turning them into reality.

The process of establishing a pluralistic security community. Just as a pluralistic security community requires fewer favorable background conditions for its success, so it requires simpler, though perhaps subtler, processes in order to come into existence.

The main process required seems to be an increasing unattractiveness and improbability of war among the political units of the emerging pluralistic security community, as perceived by their governments, elites, and (eventually) populations. A second process, similar to that favoring the rise of amalgamated security communities, is the spread of intellectual movements and traditions favoring integration, and preparing the political climate for it. A third process, perhaps, is the development and practice of habits and skills of mutual attention, communication, and responsiveness, so as to make possible the preservation of the autonomy and substantial sovereignty of the participating units, and the preservation of stable expectations of peace and peaceful change among them. The difficulties in the way of these three processes are by no means trivial; but they are less than the difficulties in the path of outright amalgamation among almost any group of sovereign nation-states in today's world.

Some Emerging Issues of Integration and World Politics

Three broad philosophic issues emerge from our survey of the conditions and processes and integration. The first is the issue of the primary goal to be adopted. Is it to be *peace* within the integrated area, *or* is it to be some form of corporate *power,* perhaps for its defense against outsiders, or for some variety

Attaining and Maintaining Integration

of other purposes? Or if both peace and power are emphasized as long-run goals, which is to be sought first, and what time-path toward the ultimate attainment of both goals is to be envisaged?

The second issue is that of the possible *hegemony* of one political unit (such as the most powerful nation-state) within the emerging security community, as against the substantial equality or near-equality of its more-or-less sovereign members. Related to this question is that of majority voting, as against negotiations and special concessions. Though majority voting looks like—and sometimes is—an equalitarian device, it also can be used to establish the hegemony of one great power, or of a few of them, with the help of the easily influenced or controlled votes of some lesser powers.

The result could be a pattern resembling a pyramid of holding companies. A power with great but limited resources could secure for itself a practically paramount role in the decisions of a small group of countries. This group—let us call it alliance *A*—could jointly command paramount influence within some larger alliance *B*. Alliance *B*, in turn, could be used to control alliance *C*; and so forth, until some alliance finally would lead to formal majority control of the United Nations, and to substantive control of much (and ideally all) of the world. Nothing quite like this has ever happened, but the possibility is there; and the almost instinctive resistance of many countries to far-reaching majority voting in international or supranational bodies, and their preference for mutual negotiations and responsiveness among sovereign units, may be related to these considerations.

The third issue is related to the second. It is this: can larger organizations be built up best by downgrading their components, so as to make them easier to control and cheaper to replace? Specifically, are federations to be built up by weakening their member states, and international organizations by weakening the nations of which they are composed?

For the near future, some tentative answers can be indicated. Keeping an uneasy but tolerable peace is likely to appear more urgent to most governments than creating large supranational organizations with vast powers for more or less general purposes. Sovereignty with only a few limitations will seem more attractive to most governments than submission to the hegemony of any great power or partial coalition of great powers. And the upgrading, rather than the downgrading, of the capabilities and the prestige of nation-states will look both more practical and more desirable to most of their governments and peoples.

An era of pluralism and, at best, of pluralistic security communities, may well characterize the near future. In the long term, however, the search for integrated political communities that command both peace and power, and that entail a good deal of amalgamation, is likely to continue until it succeeds. For such success, not only good will and sustained effort, but political creativity and inventiveness will be needed, together with a political culture of greater international openness, understanding, and compassion.

Without such a new political climate and new political efforts, mankind is unlikely to survive for long. But the fact that so many people in so many countries are becoming aware of the problem, and of the need for increasing efforts to deal with it, makes it likely that it will be solved.

Attaining and Maintaining Integration

Appendix: The Flow of Policy Making in the Department of State[*]

NOTE: *Time has left its mark on Mr. Ogburn's essay as on all else. Consulate General Brazzaville is now American Embassy Brazzaville; the fifth floor location of the Secretary of State and his top aides in New State has become the seventh floor in new New State; Dependent Area Affairs are no longer dealt with by a separate office in the Bureau of International Organization Affairs; but Africa does have a separate office to analyze its problems in the Bureau of Intelligence and Research. These are minor changes. Mr. Ogburn's essay still captures brilliantly some of the typical decision-making patterns and activities of the Department of State.*

The Department of State is an organism that is constantly responding to a vast assortment of stimuli. A new Soviet threat to Berlin, a forthcoming conference of Foreign Ministers of the Organization of American States, a request from Poland for credit, a solicitation for support of a candidacy for the Presidency of the United Nations General Assembly, a plea from an ambassador that the head of the government to which he is accredited be invited to visit the United States officially, a refusal by another government to permit the duty-free importation of some official supplies for a U.S. consulate, a request from the White House for comment on the foreign affairs section of a major presidential address, an earthquake in the Aegean creating hardships which it appears the U.S. Navy might be able to alleviate, a request for a speaker from a foreign policy association in California, a transmittal slip from a Member of Congress asking for information with which to reply to a letter from a constituent protesting discriminatory actions against his business by a foreign government, letters from citizens both supporting and deploring the policy of nonrecognition of Communist China, a continuing inquiry by a press correspondent who has got wind of a top secret telegram from Embassy Bonn on the subject of German rearmament and is determined to find out what is in it, a demand by a Protestant church group that the Department take steps to prevent harassment of their coreligionists in a foreign country, a request by a delegation of a federation of women's clubs for a briefing on southeast Asia and suggestions as to how its members might be useful in their planned tour of the area, a request from Consulate General Brazzaville for a revision of cost-of-living allowances, a visit by a commission of inquiry into the operations of U.S. foreign aid programs, a notification from the staff of the National Security Council that a revision of the National Security Council paper on dependent areas is due, a telegram from a U.S. embassy in the Near East declaring that last night's flareups make a visit by the Assistant Secretary for Near Eastern and South Asian Affairs, now in mid-Atlantic, inopportune at the moment, a warning by a European Foreign Minister of the consequences should the United States fail to support his

* By Charlton Ogburn, Jr., in H. Field Haviland, Jr. and Associates, *The Formulation and Administration of United States Foreign Policy*, a Report for the Committee on Foreign Relations of the United States Senate (Brookings Institution, 1960), pp. 172–77.

nation's position in the Security Council, and a counterwarning by an African representative at the United Nations of the consequences should the United States do so--this is a sample of the requirements made of the Department of State in a typical day. Of course it does not include the oceans of informational reports that come into the Department by telegram and air pouch or the countless periodicals from all parts of the world that arrive by sea.

What is required to begin with is that the flow be routed into the right channels. This does not apply to press correspondents and foreign embassy officials; they usually know where to go without being directed. For the rest, almost every piece of business—every requirement or opportunity for action—comes within the Department's ken first as a piece of paper. These pieces of paper—telegrams, dispatches (or "despatches," as the Department prefers to call them), letters—must be gotten as speedily as possible into the hands of the officers who will have to do something about them or whose jobs require that they know about them.

The telegram and mail branches of the Division of Communication Services, a part of the Bureau of Administration, receive the incoming material and, after decoding and reproducing the telegrams, indicate on each communication the distribution it should receive among the bureaus or equivalent components of the Department. If, in the case of a letter or a dispatch, there are not enough copies to go around, the recipients are listed one after another and receive it consecutively, the original going first to the bureau responsible for taking whatever action the document requires. With telegrams, the deliveries are simultaneous. Several score copies of a telegram may be run off. A yellow copy, called the action copy, like the original of a dispatch or letter, goes to the bureau responsible for taking any necessary action; white copies go to all others interested.

A telegram (No. 1029, let us say) from a major U.S. embassy in Western Europe reports the warning of the Foreign Minister of X country that a grave strain would be imposed on relations between X and the United States should the latter fail to vote with X on a sensitive colonial issue in the United Nations General Assembly. Such a telegram would have a wide distribution. The action copy would go to the Bureau of European Affairs. The action copy of a telegram to the same purpose from the U.S. delegation to the United Nations in New York, quoting the X delegation, would go to the Bureau of International Organization Affairs. This is a matter of convention.

Information copies of a telegram of such importance would go to all officers in the higher echelons—the Secretary of State (via the executive secretariat), the Under Secretaries, the Deputy Under Secretaries, the counselor. They would also go the Policy Planning Staff, to the Bureau of African Affairs because of the involvement of certain territories within its jurisdiction, to the Bureau of Far Eastern Affairs and the Bureau of Near Eastern and South Asian Affairs because the telegram concerns the incendiary question of European peoples' ruling non-European peoples, and of course to the Bureau of Intelligence and Research. Other copies would go to the Department of Defense and the Central Intelligence Agency. The executive secretariat would doubtless make certain that the Secretary would see the telegram. In addition, its staff would include a condensation in the secret daily summary, a compendium distributed in the Department on a need-to-know basis. If classified top secret, it would be included in the top secret daily staff summary, or black book, which goes only to Assistant Secretary-level officials and higher.

In the bureaus, incoming material is received by the message centers. There a further and more refined distribution would be made of telegram 1029. Copies would go to the Office of the Assistant Secretary (the so-called front office), to the United Nations adviser, to the public affairs adviser (since the United States is going to be in for trouble with public opinion in either one part of the world or

Appendix

the other), and to whatever geographic office or offices may seem to have the major interest. In the Bureau of International Organization Affairs, this would be the Office of United Nations Political and Security Affairs. Another copy, however, might go to the Office of Dependent Area Affairs.

In the Bureau of European Affairs, the yellow action copy of the telegram goes to the Office of Western European Affairs and thence to the X country desk, where it is the first thing to greet the desk officer's eye in the morning. As it happens, the desk officer was out the evening before at an official function where he discussed at length with the first secretary of the X embassy the desirability of avoiding any extremes of action in the United Nations over the territory in question. In the front office of the Bureau, the staff assistant has entered in his records the salient details of the problem the Bureau is charged with and has passed the telegram on to the Assistant Secretary.

The following scenes are now enacted:

The X country desk officer crosses the hall to the office of his superior, the officer-in-charge, and the two together repair to the office of the Director of the Office of Western European Affairs. The three officers put in a call to the Assistant Secretary for European Affairs and tell his secretary that they would like as early an appointment as possible.

The Director of the Office of United Nations Political and Security Affairs (UNP) telephones the Director of the Office of Western European Affairs (WE). He says he assumes WE will be drafting an instruction to the U.S. embassy in X to try to dissuade the Foreign Office from its course, and that UN would like to be in on it. He adds that they had thought of getting the U.S. delegation to the United Nations (US Del) to present this view to the X mission in New York but that there seemed to be no point in doing so since the latter would already be advising its government to take account of world opinion.

After the Secretary's morning staff conference, where the matter is discussed briefly, a conference is held in the Office of the Assistant Secretary for European Affairs to decide on a line to take with the X government. The desk officer is designated to prepare the first draft of a telegram embodying it. The draft is reviewed and modified by his officer-in-charge and the Office Director for Western European Affairs.

The telegram instructs the U.S. embassy in X to make clear to the X government our fear that its projected course of action "will only play into hands of extremists and dishearten and undermine position elements friendly to West" and suggests that the X government emphasize its policy to take account of the legitimate aspirations of the indigenous population of the territory in order to improve the atmosphere for consideration of the problem by the General Assembly. The Assistant Secretary, after scrutinizing and approving the telegram, finds it necessary only to add the Bureau of Near Eastern and South Asian Affairs to the clearances. Those already listed for clearance are the Deputy Under Secretary for Political Affairs, the Bureau of International Organization Affairs, and the Bureau of African Affairs. He says it can be left to the Deputy Under Secretary for Political Affairs to sign the telegram; he does not see that the telegram need go higher.

It remains for the drafting officer to circulate the telegram for approval by those marked for clearance. In the Bureau of African Affairs the telegram is termed extremely gentle to the X government but is initialed as it stands. The Office of United Nations Political and Security Affairs (UNP) wishes to remind X that the United States, setting an example of its adherence to the principle of affording the widest latitude to the General Assembly, had even accepted on occasion the inscription of an item on the agenda accusing the United States of aggression. The X desk officer states, however, that WE would not favor such an addition, which might only further antagonize the X government. Thereupon, UNP, yielding on

Appendix

this point, requests deletion of a phrase in the telegram seeming to place the United States behind the X contention that the question is not appropriate for discussion in the United Nations. The drafter of the telegram telephones the Director of the Office of Western European Affairs who authorizes the deletion, having decided that he can do so on his own without referring the question to his superior, the Assistant Secretary.

With that, the Director of the Office of United Nations Political and Security Affairs initials the telegram for his Bureau, and the X desk officer "hand carries" the telegram (in the departmental phrase), with telegram 1029 attached, to the Office of the Deputy Under Secretary for Political Affairs and leaves it with his secretary. At 6 o'clock he is informed by telephone that the Deputy Under Secretary has signed the telegram (that is, signed the Secretary's name with his own initials beneath) without comment. The desk officer goes to the fifth floor, retrieves it, and takes it to the correspondence review staff of the executive secretariat, where the telegram is examined for intelligibility, completion of clearances, conformity with departmental practices, etc., before being sped to the Telegram Branch of enciphering and transmission.

The next morning, all officers of the Department participating in the framing of the telegram receive copies of it hectographed on pink outgoing telegram forms. The telegram, bearing the transmission time of 8:16 p.m., has entered history as the Department's No. 736 to the embassy in X. The X desk officer writes "telegram sent," with the date, in the space indicated by a rubber stamp on the yellow copy of the original telegram 1029, and the staff assistant in the front office makes an equivalent notation in his records. The yellow copy is then sent on to the central files, whence in time it will probably be consigned to the National Archives. Only the white copies may be kept in the Bureau's files.

In this case, however, no one is under any illusion that the matter has been disposed of. Scarcely 24 hours later comes a new telegram 1035 from the embassy in X reporting that, while the X government may possibly make some concessions, it will certainly wage an all-out fight against inscription of the item and will expect the United States to exert itself to marshal all the negative votes possible. The question is, what position will the United States in fact take and how much effort will it make to win adherents for its position? No one supposes for a moment that this explosive question can be decided on the bureau level. Only the Secretary can do so—as the Secretary himself unhappily realizes.

At the end of a staff meeting on Berlin, the Secretary turns to the Assistant Secretary for Policy Planning and asks him to give some thought within the next few days to the alternatives open on the question. The official addressed sets the wheels in motion at once. A meeting is called for the next morning. Attending are: the Assistant Secretary for Policy Planning himself and several members of his staff (including the European and African specialists), the Director of the Office of United Nations Political and Security Affairs, the Western European officer-in-charge, the X desk officer, a member of the policy guidance and coordination staff of the Bureau of Public Affairs, and two intelligence specialists, namely, the Director of the Office of Research and Analysis for Western Europe and the Director of the Office of Research and Analysis for the Near East, South Asia, and Africa.

The discussion explores all ramifications of the issues involved and is generally detached and dispassionate. The object of the meeting is to help clarify the issues so that the Policy Planning Staff may be sure all relevant considerations are taken into account in the staff paper it will prepare for the Secretary.

The Secretary is in a difficult position. The President's views on what course of action to take are somewhat different from his. The Congress is also of divided view, with some Members impressed by the irresistible force of nationalism among dependent peoples, others by the essential role of X in NATO and European defense. The ambassadors of some countries pull him one way, others another. One of the Nation's leading newspapers editorially counsels "restraint, understanding and vision." At the staff meeting he calls to arrive at a decision, the Secretary perceives that his subordinates are as deeply divided as he feared. He takes counsel with each—the Assistant Secretaries for Policy Planning, European Affairs, African Affairs, and Near Eastern and South Asian Affairs. At the end he sums up and announces his decision. Thereupon the following things happen:

The Assistant Secretaries take the news back to their bureaus.

An urgent telegram is sent to the U.S. Embassy in X reporting the decision.

Telegrams are sent to embassies in important capitals around the world instructing the ambassador to go to the Foreign Office and present the U.S. case in persuasive terms.

A similar telegram is sent to the U.S. delegation in New York for its use in talks with the delegations of other United Nations members.

Conferences attended by representatives of the geographic bureaus concerned, of the Bureau of Public Affairs, and of the U.S. Information Agency, are held. Afterward, the representatives of the U.S. Information Agency return to their headquarters to draft guidances to the U.S. Information Service establishments all over the world. Such guidances tell how news of the U.S. decision is to be played when it breaks.

The more important the problem, the more the upper levels of the Department become involved. In a crisis—one brought about, say, by the overthrow of A, a Western-oriented government in the Middle East—the Secretary himself will take over. However, the bulk of the Department's business is carried on, of necessity, by the lower ranking officers. Even when a crisis receives the Secretary's personal, day-to-day direction, the desk officer and the officer-in-charge are always at hand to provide the detailed information only specialists possess, while in the intelligence bureau, country analysts and branch chiefs will be putting in 10-hour days and 6- or 7-days weeks. Generally, moreover, the crisis will have been preceded by a good deal of work on the part of lower level officials.

In the case suggested, it was apparent for some time that all was not well in A. The U.S. Embassy in A was aware of growing discontent with the regime through its indirect contacts with opposition political elements, from information from Cairo, from evidences of tension, from clandestine publications. Additional straws in the wind were supplied by the public affairs officer in A both to the embassy and to the U.S. Information Agency because of his special contacts among professional groups. On the strength of these reports and of dispatches from American foreign correspondents in the area, and equipped with analyses from the Bureau of Intelligence and Research, all pointing in the same direction, the desk officer at a staff meeting of the Office of Near Eastern Affairs imparts his disquiet. He is directed to prepare a memorandum which, if convincing in its presentation, the Office Director undertakes to put before the Assistant Secretary.

What the desk officer has in mind will require national action, so what he drafts takes the form of a memorandum to the Secretary. It embodies a statement of the problem, the actions recommended, a review of the facts bearing upon the problem, and a conclusion. At the end are listed the symbols of the offices of the Department from which concurrences must be sought. Backing up the memorandum will be supporting documents, especially telegrams from the embassy, each identified by a tab. The mass fills a third of an in-box.

The problem is defined as that of strengthening the present pro-Western regime of A. By way of recommendation, the desk officer is especially sensitive

207

Appendix

to the problems and needs of the country for which he is responsible. He calls for more detachment of the United States from A's rival, B, expediting U.S. arms deliveries to A and the supply of certain recoilless rifles and jet fighter planes the A government has been requesting, support for A's membership in various United Nations agencies, a Presidential invitation to the Prime Minister of A to visit the United States. Much of what the memorandum recommends has to be fought out in the Bureau and even in the Office since it conflicts with the claims of countries (and the desk officers responsible for them) in the same jurisdiction. While neither the Office Director nor the Assistant Secretary doubts that support of B is a handicap in the region, they consider that a proposal for a radical departure would simply doom the memorandum by preventing anyone from taking it seriously.

As it finally leaves the Bureau with the Assistant Secretary's signature, the memorandum is considerably revised, and further change awaits it. The Department of Defense cannot provide the desired recoilless rifles and jet fighters. The Bureau of International Organization Affairs cannot offer any undertakings at this stage with respect to the question of membership in United Nations agencies. The Deputy Under Secretary for Political Affairs rules out a request of the President to invite the A Prime Minister for an official visit because the number of those invited is already too large.

Among recommendations in memorandums to the Secretary, as among salmon battling their way upstream to the spawning grounds, mortality is heavy. Almost everywhere in the world, things are far from satisfactory, but the United States cannot be doing everything everywhere at the same time. And A, far from seeming to cry out for attention, looks like the one Middle Eastern country about which it is not necessary to worry.

Then the uprising occurs in A. Early in the morning, the officer-in-charge of A and one other country is awakened by the ringing of the telephone. In a flash, before his feet have touched the floor, he has visualized every conceivable disaster that could have befallen his area and has picked the overthrow of the monarchy in C as the most likely. Or did the security people find a top secret document under his desk?

On the telephone, the watch officer at the Department tells him that a "Niact" (a night action telegram, which means "Get this one read immediately even if you have to rout someone out of bed") is coming off the machine and it looks serious—he had better come down. En route, the officer-in-charge turns on his car radio and picks up a news broadcast, but nothing is said about A. Uncle Sam has beaten the press agencies.

At the Department, he finds the telegram wholly decoded and reads the hectograph master. There is revolution in A. The top leadership has been either murdered or banished. The officer in charge could legitimately awaken the Assistant Secretary, but for the moment it seems there is nothing that can be done, so he decides to hold off until 6 a.m. and then call the Office Director and put it up to him. He does, however, call the A desk officer and tell him to get on his way. To share his vigil beside the watch officers window there is a representative of the executive secretariat, who will have the telegram ready for the Secretary to read immediately on his arrival. In the Bureau of Intelligence and Research—it being now after 4 o'clock—the morning briefers have arrived to go over the night's take and write up items of importance, with analyses, for the Director's use in briefing the Secretary's morning staff conference. The briefer for the Office of Research and Analysis for the Near East, South Asia and Africa—a GS-11 specialist on India—takes one look at the Niact on A and gets on the telephone to the A analyst.

By the time the Secretary has stepped from his black limousine and headed for the private elevator a good deal has happened. In the Bureau of Near Eastern and South Asian Affairs, everyone concerned with A from the Assistant Secretary down, and including the officer-in-charge of Baghdad Pact and Southeast Asia Treaty Organization affairs and the special assistant who serves as a policy and planning adviser, has been in conference for an hour laying out the tasks requiring immediate attention. Two more Niacts have come in from A, one reporting that so far no Americans are known to have been injured but offering little assurance with respect to the future. The Assistant Secretary has already put in a call to the Director of Intelligence Research to ask that all possible information on the new leader of A and his connections be marshaled and that the Central Intelligence Agency be informed of the need. For the rest, the following represent the Assistant Secretary's conception of what should be done first:

1. The Department of Defense must be apprised of the Department of State's anxiety and be requested to have transport planes in readiness at nearby fields for the evacuation of Americans if necessary in accordance with prearranged plans. There must be consultation on what instruments are available if American lives have to be protected by force.

2. The U.S. embassy in C, a friendly neighbor of A's to which the Niacts have been repeated, will be heard from at any moment, and the Special Assistant for Mutual Security Coordination in the Office of the Under Secretary for Economic Affairs and, also, the Office of International Security Affairs in the Department of Defense will have to be alerted to the possibility of emergency military assistance for C.

3. Anything in the pipeline for A should be held up. The Special Assistant for Mutual Security Coordination must be advised of this.

4. The possibility of a demonstration by the U.S. 6th Fleet in support of C's independence and integrity will have to be discussed with the Department of Defense.

5. A crash national intelligence estimate will be requested of the Central Intelligence Agency, provided the Agency does not consider the situation too fluid for a formal estimate to be useful.

6. The public affairs adviser will get in touch with the Bureau of Public Affairs, the departmental spokesman and the U.S. Information Agency to agree on the kind of face the United States will put on the affair.

7. The B Ambassador will probably have to be called in and apprised of the critical need for his government's acquiescence in overflights of B for the purpose of getting supplies to C. The B and C desk officers had better get busy immediately on a draft telegram to embassy B (repeat to C) setting forth the case the ambassador should make urgently to the B Foreign Office.

At 9:12, anticipating that he will be called to accompany the Secretary to the White House, the Assistant Secretary instructs his secretary to cancel all his appointments for the day, including one with the dentist but excepting his appointment with the C ambassador. ("Mr. Ambassador, you may assure His Majesty that my Government remains fully determined to support the sovereignty and territorial integrity of his nation.")

At 9:14, 1 minute before the scheduled commencement of the staff meeting, the Assistant Secretary joins his colleagues in the Secretary's anteroom, prepared to hear the estimate of the Director of Intelligence and Research and to give his own appraisal and submit his plan of action.

Appendix

To Explore Further

GOOD GENERAL SURVEYS: K. J. Holsti, *International Politics* (Prentice-Hall, 1967); H. J. Morgenthau, *Politics among Nations* (Knopf, 1967); A. F. K. Organski, *World Politics* (Knopf, 1958); N. Padelford and G. Lincoln, *The Dynamics of International Politics*, 2nd ed. (Macmillan, 1967); F. Schumann, *International Politics*, 5th ed. (McGraw-Hill, 1953); J. G. Stoessinger, *The Might of Nations*, 2nd ed. (Random House, 1965); J. K. Zawodny, *Guide to the Study of International Relations* (Chandler, 1966); *International Affairs*, Vol. I, prepared by A. DeGrazia (Universal Reference System, 1965).

BASIC QUANTITATIVE DATA: A. S. Banks and R. B. Textor, *A Cross-Polity Survey* (M.I.T. Press, 1963); R. L. Merritt and S. Rokkan, eds., *Comparing Nations* (Yale Univ. Press, 1964); B. M. Russett, *et al.*, *World Handbook of Political and Social Indicators* (Yale Univ. Press, 1964).

BASIC THEORY: J. W. Burton, *International Relations* (Cambridge Univ. Press, 1967); W. T. R. Fox, *Theoretical Aspects of International Relations* (Univ. of Notre Dame Press, 1959); S. Hoffman, *Contemporary Theory in International Relations* (Prentice-Hall, 1960) and *The State of War* (Praeger, 1954); K. Knorr, *The War Potential of Nations* (Princeton Univ. Press, 1956); C. A. McClelland, *Theory and the International System* (Macmillan, 1966); B. M. Russett, *Trends in World Politics* Macmillan, 1965); K. and S. Verba, eds., *The International System* (Princeton Univ. Press, 1961).

CONTRIBUTIONS FROM PSYCHOLOGY AND THE BEHAVIORAL SCIENCES: H. C. Kelman, *International Behavior* (Holt, Rinehart & Winston, 1965); J. N. Rosenau, ed., *International Politics and Foreign Policy* (Free Press of Glencoe, 1961); J. D. Singer, ed., *Human Behavior and International Politics* (Rand McNally, 1965) and *Quantitative International Politics* (Free Press, 1968); J. K. Zawodny, *Man and International Relations*, 2 vols. (Chandler, 1966).

BASIC THEORETICAL CONCEPTS: I. Claude, *Power and International Relations* (Random House, 1962); R. Dahl, *Modern Political Analysis* (Prentice-Hall, 1963); D. Easton, *A Framework for Political Analysis* (Prentice-Hall, 1965) and *A Systems Analysis of Political Life* (Wiley, 1965); H. Lasswell, *Politics: Who Gets What, When, and How* (World, 1966) and *World Politics and Personal Insecurity* (Free Press, 1965); R. Rosecrance, *Action and Reaction in World Politics* (Little, Brown, 1963); O. R. Young, *Systems of Political Science* (Prentice-Hall, 1968).

SPECIALIZED STUDIES ON INTEREST GROUPS, CLASSES, AND LEADERS: R. A. Bauer, *et al.*, *American Business and Public Policy* (Atherton, 1963); T. B. Bottomore, *Classes in Modern Society* (Pantheon, 1966); R. Dahrendorf, *Class and Class Conflict in Industrial Society* (Stanford Univ. Press, 1961); L. J. Edinger, ed., *Political Leadership in Industrialized Societies* (Wiley, 1967); H. Lasswell and D. Lerner, *World Revolutionary Elites* (M.I.T. Press, 1966); T. H. Marshall, *Class, Citizenship, and Social Development* (Doubleday, 1964); S. Ossowski, *Class Structure in the Social Consciousness* (Free Press of Glencoe, 1963).

NATIONALISM AND MODERN NATIONS AND EMPIRES: C. E. Black, *The Dynamics of Modernization* (Harper and Row, 1966); I. Claude, *National Minorities* (Harvard Univ. Press, 1955); H. B. Davis, *Nationalism and Socialism* (Monthly Review Press, 1967); K. W. Deutsch, *Nationalism and Social Communication* (M.I.T. Press, 1966); K. W. Deutsch and W. J. Foltz, eds., *Nation Building* (Atherton, 1963); L. W. Doob, *Patriotism and Nationalism* (Yale University Press, 1964); S. N. Eisenstadt, *The Political Systems of Empires* (Free Press of Glencoe, 1963); R. Emerson, *From Empire to Nation* (Beacon, 1960); F. Fanon, *The Wretched of the Earth* (Grove, 1963); H. Kohn, *Nationalism: Its Meaning and History* (Van Nostrand, 1955); V. I. Lenin, *Imperialism* (Vanguard, 1926); A. Lijphart, *The Trauma of Decolonization* (Yale Univ. Press, 1966); S. M. Lipset, *The First New Nation* (Basic Books, 1963); M. Perham, *The Colonial Reckoning* (London: Collins, 1961); L. W. Pye, ed., *Communication and Political Development* (Princeton Univ. Press, 1963); L. W. Pye and S. Verba, eds., *Political Culture and Political Development* (Princeton Univ. Press, 1965); J. Schumpeter, *Imperialism and Social Classes* (Meridian, 1955) and *The Dynamics of Nationalism* (Van Nostrand, 1964).

NATIONAL CHARACTER: A. Inkles and D. J. Levinson, "National Character; The Study of Modal Personality and Sociocultural Systems," in G. E. Lindzey, *Handbook of Social Psychology*, Vol. 2 (Addison-Wesley, 1959); D. Potter, *People of Plenty* (Univ. of Chicago Press, 1954).

COMMUNICATION AND DECISION-MAKING: R. J. C. Butow, *Japan's Decision to Surrender* (Stanford Univ. Press, 1965); K. W. Deutsch, *The Nerves of Government* (Free Press, 1965); P. Kecskemeti, *Strategic Surrender* (Stanford Univ. Press, 1958); G. D. Paige,

The Korean Decision (Free Press, 1968); R. C. Synder, *et al.*, *Foreign Policy Decision-Making* (Free Press of Glencoe, 1962); R. Wohlstetter, *Pearl Harbor: Warning and Decision* (Stanford Univ. Press, 1962).

COMPARATIVE FOREIGN POLICY: J. E. Black and K. W. Thompson, *Foreign Policies in a World of Change* (Harper and Row, 1963); R. C. Macridis, ed., *Foreign Policy in World Politics* (Prentice-Hall, 1967); K. N. Waltz, *Foreign Policy and Democratic Politics* (Little, Brown, 1967).

UNITED STATES FOREIGN POLICY: G. A. Almond, *The American People and Foreign Policy* (Praeger, 1962); G. W. Ball, *The Discipline of Power* (Little, Brown, 1968); S. Brown, *The Faces of Power* (Columbia Univ. Press, 1968); T. Draper, *Abuse of Power* (Viking Press, 1967); J. William Fulbright, *The Arrogance of Power* (Random House, 1967); R. Hilsman, *To Move a Nation* (Doubleday, 1967); S. Hoffman, *Gulliver's Troubles* (McGraw-Hill, 1968); H. A. Kissinger, *The Necessity for Choice* (Harper, 1961) and *The Troubled Partnership* (McGraw-Hill, 1965); W. W. Rostow, *View from the Seventh Floor* (Harper and Row, 1964); B. Sapin, *The Making of United States Foreign Policy* (Brookings Institution, 1966); C. Yost, *The Insecurity of Nations* (Praeger, 1968); R. S. McNamera, *The Essence of Security* (Harper & Row, 1968); D. Wise and T. B. Ross, *The Invisible Government* (Bantam, 1965); F. Schurman, *et al.*, *The American Policy of Escalation in Vietnam* (Fawcett, 1966).

THEORY OF GAMES AND ANALYSIS OF CONFLICTS: K. E. Boulding, *Conflict and Defense: A General Theory* (Harper and Row, 1963); H. Kelman, ed., *International Behavior* (Holt, Rinehart, & Winston, 1965); A. Rapoport, *Fights, Games, and Debates* (Univ. of Michigan Press, 1960) and *Strategy and Conscience* (Harper and Row, 1964); W. H. Riker, *The Theory of Political Coalition* (Yale Univ. Press, 1962); T. C. Schelling, *The Strategy of Conflict* (Harvard Univ. Press, 1960) and *Arms and Influence* (Yale Univ. Press, 1966); P. Seabury, ed., *Balance of Power* (Chandler, 1965); A. Rapoport and A. Chammah, *The Prisoners' Dilemma* (Univ. of Michigan Press, 1966); D. Luce and H. Raiffa, *Games and Decisions* (Wiley, 1957); J. von Neumann and O. Morgenstern, *Theory of Games and Economic Behavior,* (Princeton Univ. Press, 1964).

WAR AND ITS ASPECTS: H. Eckstein, ed., *Internal War* (Free Press of Glencoe, 1964); M. H. Halperin, *Limited War in the Nuclear Age* (Wiley, 1963); H. Kahn, *On Escalation* (Praeger, 1965); J. N. Rosenau, *International Aspects of Civil Strife* (Princeton Univ. Press, 1964); J. D. Singer, *Deterrence, Arms Control, and Disarmament* (Ohio State Univ. Press, 1962); Q. Wright, *A Study of War*, 2nd ed. (Univ. of Chicago Press, 1965).

DIPLOMACY: G. A. Craig and F. Gilbert, eds., *The Diplomats 1919–1939* (Princeton Univ. Press, 1953); E. A. J. Johnson, *The Dimensions of Diplomacy* (Johns Hopkins Press, 1964); G. F. Kennan, *American Diplomacy, 1900–1950* (Univ. of Chicago Press, 1951) and *Memoirs 1925–1950* (Little, Brown, 1967); H. Nicolson, *Diplomacy*, 3rd ed. (London: Oxford Univ. Press, 1963); E. Satow, *A Guide to Diplomatic Practice* (London: Longmans, Green, 1952).

INTERNATIONAL LAW: J. L. Brierly, *The Law of Nations*, 6th ed. (Oxford Univ. Press, 1963); P. E. Corbett, *Law in Diplomacy* (P. Smith, 1967); K. W. Deutsch and S. Hoffmann, eds., *The Relevance of International Law* (Schenkman, 1968); R. A. Falk, ed., *The Vietnam War and International Law* (Princeton University Press, 1968); R. A. Falk and S. Mendlovitz, eds., *International Law*, 4 vols. (World Law Fund, 1966); R. E. Osgood and R. Tucker, *Force, Order, and Justice* (Johns Hopkins Press, 1967).

INTERNATIONAL ORGANIZATIONS: I. Claude, *Swords into Plowshares* (Council on International Relations, 1956); J. P. Sewell, *Functionalism in World Politics* (Princeton Univ. Press, 1966).

POLITICAL INTEGRATION: M. Camps, *European Unification in the Sixties* (London: Oxford Univ. Press, 1967); K. W. Deutsch, S. A. Burrell, *et al.*, *Political Community in the North Atlantic Area* (Princeton Univ. Press, 1968); E. Haas, *Beyond the Nation-State* and *The Uniting of Europe* (Stanford Univ. Press, 1968); W. Hallstein, *United Europe* (Harvard Univ. Press, 1962); P. E. Jacob and J. V. Toscano, eds., *The Integration of Political Communities* (Lippincott, 1964); U. W. Kitzinger, *The Politics and Economics of European Integration* (Praeger, 1963); J. S. Nye, *International Regionalism* (Little, Brown, 1968); B. M. Russett, *International Regions and the International System* (Rand McNally, 1968).

CASES OF INTERNATIONAL INTEGRATION: K. W. Deutsch, *et al.*, *France, Germany, and the Western Alliance* (Scribner's, 1967); W. J. Foltz, *From French West Africa to the Mali Federation* (Yale University Press, 1965); L. M. Lindberg, *The Political Dynamics of European Economic Integration* (Stanford Univ. Press, 1963); R. L. Merritt, *Symbols of American Community* (Yale Univ. Press, 1966); R. L. Merritt and D. J. Puchala, eds., *Western European Perspectives on International Affairs: Public Opinion Studies and Evaluations* (Praeger, 1968); R. E. Osgood, *NATO: The Entangling Alliance* (Univ. of Chicago Press, 1962); B. M. Russett, *Community and Contention: Britain in the 20th Century* (M.I.T. Press, 1963).

Index